SONORAN
STRONGMAN

Ignacio Pesqueira

SONORAN STRONGMAN

Ignacio Pesqueira and His Times

RODOLFO F. ACUÑA

THE UNIVERSITY OF ARIZONA PRESS
Tucson, Arizona

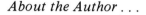

About the Author . . .

RODOLFO ACUÑA, descendent of one of Sonora's most active families —
the Elíases — has been interested from childhood in fables, myths, and
histories about Sonora told to him by his maternal grandfather, Don Miguel
Elías. In 1964 Acuña wrote a doctoral seminar paper about Sonora in which
Ignacio Pesqueira's shadow loomed prominently; in 1968 he received his
Ph.D. in Latin American studies, writing his dissertation on the times of
Ignacio Pesqueira. In 1969 Acuña became the first chairman of the Chicano
Studies Department at California State University at Northridge, one of the
largest such programs in the United States. In addition to numerous book
reviews and articles, while at CSUN he has authored *The Story of the Mexican
American* (1969), *Cultures in Conflict* (1970), *A Mexican American Chronicle*
(1970), and *Occupied America: The Chicano's Struggle for Liberation* (1972).

THE UNIVERSITY OF ARIZONA PRESS

I. S. B. N.-0-8165-0370-2 cloth
I. S. B. N.-0-8165-0462-8 paper
L. C. No. 72-92105

Contents

ILLUSTRATIONS

Preface

Geographically northern Mexico is closest to the United States, but also it is the region of Mexico least known to U.S. historians. The vast borderlands on the United States and Mexican side have a common history, both originally belonging to Mexico's northwest. On both sides of the border, a mode of life developed which included the vaquero, the mustang, and the longhorn. Ranching dominated the economy of both regions; a hardy breed of men inhabited this area — men who reminded many observers of the invading Tartars of yesteryear. In Mexican history they became known as *los hombres del norte* (men of the north), horsemen who invaded Mexico's interior during the 1910 Mexican Revolution and dominated the nation's political destiny during that time. The revolutionary armies of Carranza, Villa, and Obregón swept into the central mesa, seizing control of the nation.

Historians, however, have neglected the historical roots of these *norteños*, ignoring an exciting history essential to an understanding of U.S.-Mexican relations and the history of Mexico. This book follows the rise and decline of the career of the caudillo Ignacio Pesqueira, one of the most important of the powerful *norteños*. Pesqueira, along with men such as Santiago Vidaurri — who ruled the states of Nuevo León and Coahuila — and Luis Terrazas — cattle baron of Chihuahua who frequently functioned as chief executive of that state — often ruled his state independently of the Mexican capital. Pesqueira was probably the least known of the three *norteños*, although his dominion in many ways was the most complete.

The narrative is intended to encourage an interest in northern Mexico in addition to an appreciation of the suffering of her people and the work of her leaders, who withstood Anglo-American enchroachment. Although Pesqueira, as most of the era's leaders, was ruthless and arbitrary, he fought tremendous odds, living during a period when middle-class merchants — nineteenth-century liberals — were attempting to drag the nation out of feudalism and end the control of the church, the large landowners, and the military. Pesqueira, a product of this change, was catapulted to power by the merchants of his state who supported him against the large ranchero class led by Manuel María Gándara.

Although Ignacio Pesqueira was a liberal — a federalist, a mason, and an anticleric who supported the Constitution of 1857 — he was never a champion of the masses. During Pesqueira's time, the mestizo and the Indian, who together comprised the majority of the citizens within the state and the nation, were without voice and alienated from the political mainstream. Pesqueira, significantly, did not accept Indian participation in government. When he did respond to public pressure, it was to that of miners, merchants, ranchers, hacienda owners, and occasionally foreign businessmen. As soon as he failed to meet the needs of these special interests, Pesqueira was overthrown.

This record of the Sonora caudillo's rise and fall was made possible by the encouragement and assistance of many people. Scholarly guidance and suggestions were extended by Manual Servín, chairman of my dissertation committee; Joseph Park, curator of the Western Collection at the University of Arizona Library; Fernando Pesqueira, former director of the Biblioteca y Museo de Sonora; and Alberto Pradeau, whom I consider the dean of Sonora historians. Research opportunities were provided by the Bancroft Library of the University of California, the Archives of the State of Sonora, and the libraries of the University of Arizona and the Arizona Historical Society, Tucson. Valuable clerical assistance was contributed by Avelina Hernández.

Permissions are gratefully acknowledged from Wallace Hebberd, Publisher, Santa Barbara, California, for *Reminiscences of a Ranger* by Horace Bell, copyright 1927, and from Prentice Hall, Inc., Englewood Cliffs, New Jersey, for *California* by John Walton Caughey, copyright 1953.

In addition, I wish to thank the University of Arizona Press for effecting publication.

Finally, I wish to thank my father, Frank Acuña, who has always been a perfect example to emulate, and my mother, Alicia, who encouraged my education. I am indebted to my wife, Irmgard, for her patience and sacrifice, without which it would not have been possible to complete this book, and to my sons, Frank and Walter, for sharing their father.

SONORAN
STRONGMAN

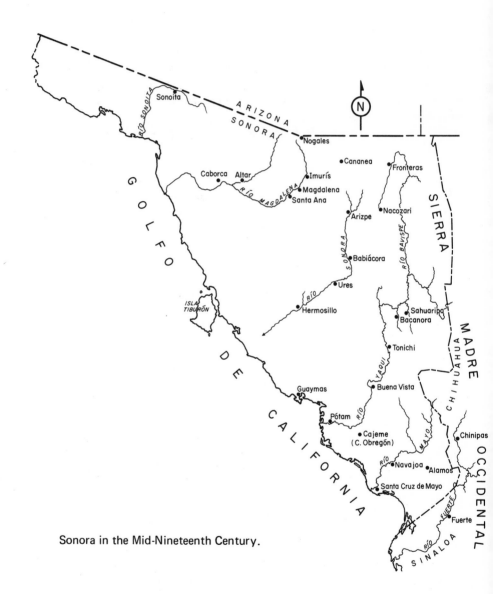

Sonora in the Mid-Nineteenth Century.

CHAPTER 1

Ignacio Pesqueira's Sonora

On August 28, 1857, the deputies of the Mexican state of Sonora assembled for the inaugural address of their newly elected governor, Ignacio Pesqueira. This day climaxed a year of civil turmoil during which Pesqueira had gained power. Pesqueira had been instrumental in quelling the rebellion after Manuel María Gándara's seizure of power on July 15, 1856, as well as in suppressing Henry A. Crabb's invasion of Sonora in the spring of 1857.

In April 1857, Crabb had led an expedition to Sonora which the Sonorans finally stopped by killing almost every member of the party. The Anglo-American press claimed that Crabb had been betrayed; Sonorans called him a *filibustero* (see Chapter 3). Gándara, Pesqueira's chief rival, dominated Sonora politics from 1838 to 1856, leading the centralist forces. Gándara's political activities paralleled those of Antonío López Santa Anna; both leaders frequently switched political views to fit their personal ambitions.

At the time of Pesqueira's inauguration, conditions in Sonora remained relatively calm, although certain precarious situations threatened to explode. The deputies who assembled to listen to the governor must have speculated as to how long peace would last, for everyone knew that Manuel María Gándara's power still remained intact. The deputies were aware of the older caudillo's ability to rally his followers and threaten the present administration. Gándara had controlled Sonora for the past eighteen years and his memory still shadowed the assembly. Ships arriving at the port of Guaymas from the interior of Mexico heightened the tension, bringing rumors of Gándara's return: they reported that any day he would ride into the Yaqui River Valley and incite the Indians to rebel.[1]

The Constitution of 1857 had created a political schism and included many reforms which the Roman Catholic hierarchy, the military, and the large landowners considered an attack. In Sonora, the church had many followers who would threaten Pesqueira with revolt if he implemented the reforms of the 1857 constitution.

Sonorans nevertheless hoped that Pesqueira would be strong enough to secure peace for the state. Pesqueira — as his great-grandfather, grandfather, and father — had been raised on the northern frontier. In order to survive, his family had devoted much of their lives to fighting the Apache. Following his relatives, Ignacio Pesqueira joined the militia and achieved statewide recognition.

Pesqueira brought a frontier spirit to the governorship.[2] His appearance reflected the ruggedness of a borderland vaquero; measuring five feet nine

1

inches tall and weighing approximately 165 pounds, he had dark brown hair and eyes and prominent pockmarks on his ruddy complexion. Although Ignacio could not be described as a handsome man, he possessed the charismatic personality which was essential to the era's Mexican caudillo.*

His rhetoric resembled that of most caudillos: he swore before God and man to respect constitutional government and to implement the reforms of the 1857 constitution. Pesqueira assured the deputies of an ambiance that would promote political stability and economic progress.[3] In spite of Pesqueira's optimism, most Sonorans questioned the state's future, for it faced seemingly insurmountable problems. Pesqueira, as incoming governor, was confronted by the bankruptcy of Sonora, caused by thirty years of incessant strife and other internal and external problems.

THE LAND

In 1857, the land was both the greatest asset and the foremost liability of Sonora. It stood isolated from the rest of the nation in the northwest corner of the Mexican trunk, limited on the east by the Sierra Madre Occidental Mountains, the west by the Gulf of California, the north by the United States, and the south by the state of Sinaloa.

The Sierra Madre Occidental Mountains separate Sonora from Chihuahua, rising seven to ten thousand feet. They cut diagonally from the northeast, forming a bottleneck in the southwest, and allow Sonora only limited contact with Sinaloa. The narrowness of this exit became critical when the Mayo and the Yaqui went on the warpath, cutting Sonora's communication with the rest of the nation.

On the west, Sonora is bounded by nine hundred miles of coastline. Even with access to the sea and an abundance of good harbors, which normally work to the advantage of land, Sonora is handicapped. Guaymas is one of the best ports on the Pacific side of the Americas, but the peninsula of Baja California obstructs direct entrance, thus neutralizing the value of the entry. To the north, the states of Arizona and New Mexico bound Sonora. An Apache Indian — rather than physical — barrier separated the U.S. and Sonora. During the colonial period, the Apache had checked the northward movement of the Spanish missionaries, driving newcomers out of the Mesilla Valley and Sonora's northern frontier. By 1857, Mexican settlers had abandoned most of the land along the border: valuable mines lay unworked, the once rich grazing lands lay abandoned, and farm lands lay fallow.

Sonora's isolation made it imperative that the land be tilled and the state become self-sufficient, but again land conditions limited development. Sonora is a region of contrasts, with vast stretches of deserts, mountains, and

---

*Statement made by Fernando Pesqueira, a grand-nephew of Don Ignacio, at the former's office in the Library and Museum of the University of Sonora, Hermosillo, Sonora, Mexico, August 22, 1966. The *Yuma Sentinel*, March 2, 1879, described Ignacio Pesqueira as about five feet ten inches in height and weighing about 180 pounds.

valleys, and hundreds of miles of rugged coastline. The weather ranges from freezing in the winter to extreme heat in the summer, and the land is arid. The most important towns — Hermosillo, Ures, and Arizpe — were settled along the Sonora River.

It is not surprising that the water-starved Sonorans should turn to the potentially rich lands along the Yaqui and Mayo rivers. During the colonial period, these valleys had been the most productive in the state, supporting abundant agricultural activities and serving as the food basket for the California missions. Spanish settlers coveted this land, but the Jesuit padres barred their entrance. After independence, however, the Indians of the river valleys technically became Mexican citizens and their lands were subject to colonization. Encroachments stiffened the determination of the Yaqui and Mayo Indians to keep out the hated *yoris* (anyone other than a Yaqui), and bloody wars ensued. At the time Pesqueira took office, these rich lands remained under Indian control, but the covetousness of the government officials was destined to cause much bloodshed.[4]

The Yaqui and Mayo wars separated Sonora's interior from its southern districts. The wars cut communication with the city of Alamos and access to Sinaloa, and contact with the rest of the nation grew more difficult. In order to unite Sonora and exploit its land, Pesqueira had to control the Yaqui and the Mayo Indians.

In addition to agricultural possibilities in the Yaqui and Mayo valleys, the state's topography attracted settlers to Sonora for it indicated wealth in minerals. Sonora is mountainous, and the presence of mountains is indicative of mineral deposits; moreover, other clues, such as certain soil formations, existed.

By the time of Pesqueira, Sonora mines had "a peculiar reputation, sometimes bordering on the mysterious."[5] The silver mines of Alamos in southern Sonora had been worked for many years, producing large amounts of ore. Other mines had been found, producing silver, copper, lead, and iron.[6] Many mines which had been operating at the end of the colonial period were forced to close because of the lack of water and the mounting Apache raids. The mineral potential in Sonora attracted foreign powers such as the U.S. and France, who wanted to exploit Sonora's legendary mines.

Pesqueira had to solve the land problems before he could revive his ailing Sonora. These problems were to influence the course of his actions.*

THE PEOPLE

No accurate record exists of the number of people living in Sonora when Pesqueira took the oath of office; most census reports represent no

---

*Robert Conway Stevens, "Mexico's Forgotten Frontier," p. 27. During the eighteenth century, Sonora went through its golden years in agriculture and ranching, but the nineteenth century showed a retardation. There was always a hope that the success of the earlier years could be recaptured.

more than guesses. The following table, adapted from Robert Stevens's work on Sonora, illustrates the inconsistency of census estimates:[7]

1828	Censo general	80,000 (estimate)
1831	Censo general	93,847 (estimate)
1841	Federal Congress (of Mexico)	124,000
1845	Velasco	85,564
1864	Malte Brun	147,133

José Franciso Velasco, one of the above statisticians, clearly illustrates the difficulty in obtaining even these figures:

It is necessary to say, without equivocating, that if there is any state among those which compose the Republic of Mexico of which it is difficult to present exact statistics, that state is undoubtedly Sonora. Populated by an indigenous people, disseminated over the whole state, without laws or politics, and mingled with the nation of which it forms a part, it is very difficult to ascertain its numbers from its leaders. It is for this reason that I have only been able to give the approximate number of inhabitants. I have only undertaken as work that at least approximate toward the truth, limiting myself to certain notices which may give light to other writers on the subject (of Sonora population).[8]

Sonora's declining population compounded the difficulty of calculating census estimates. Many people left Sonora during the California Gold Rush; some of them returned, but most remained in the U.S. Others, because of insecurity within the state, emigrated to Arizona. The population drain had dire consequences, especially on the frontier, where the sparse Mexican settlements made existence precarious.[9] Without a population buffer, the interior became more vulnerable to attack from the Apache. These attacks in turn caused economic decline, thus accelerating the exodus.

Racially, Sonorans were heterogeneous, as was the rest of Mexico. The Indians outnumbered the so-called whites, but had relatively little power. The mestizo population was increasing, however; it mixed with the Indians instead of the Hispanic settlers. The *criollo* (Mexican-born Spanish) minority in turn dominated the politics and economy of Sonora.[10]

Mestization in Sonora nevertheless remained slower than in the rest of Mexico, largely because the Indians of Sonora's northern frontier displayed more independence and less willingness to assimilate with the incoming peoples.* Moreover, the older Spanish and *criollo* families, proud of the purity of their blood, discouraged miscegenation.[11]

---

*John Ross Browne, *Adventures in Apache Country,* p. 172. To some observers, this *mestizaje* was too fast. Browne criticized the mixing of the races by writing: "For this reason I think Sonora can beat the world in the production of villainous races. Miscegenation has prevailed in this country for three centuries. Every generation that population grows worse; and the Sonorans may now be ranked with their natural compadres — Indians, burros, and coyotes."

Sonora *criollos* developed a basic stock of rugged frontiersmen, who would become prominent leaders of the Mexican Revolution of 1910. Adolfo de la Huerta, Alvaro Obregón, Plutarco Elías Calles, and Abelardo Rodríguez, all of whom were revolutionary presidents, are known as *los hombres del norte.* During the Pesqueira years, the *criollo* stood out as the ruling Sonoran. The invisible Sonoran — the Indian — exercised little influence or power; although he formed the bulk of the state's work force, the Indian did not participate in its government.

Most Sonora Indians lived on *rancherías* — villages of about three hundred inhabitants. They led sedentary lives, farming land and raising corn, squash, and beans. They built their homes from brush or thatched grass, and each tribe lived in a fixed area within the state. Most of the *ranchería* Indians had been missionized, and by Pesqueira's time a large number had learned the white man's ways. Many were in the process of being absorbed into the state's mainstream; however, there were others who bitterly resisted the *criollo's* attempts to control them. The principal *ranchería* tribes were the Cahita, the Lower and Upper Pima, and the Opata.

The Mayo and the Yaqui comprised the Sonora Cahita.[12] The Mayo settled the lands along the Mayo River in the southernmost part of Sonora; they were cousins of the Yaqui who lived to the north of them along the Yaqui River. Historically, these two tribes were treated as one, for they spoke the same language and shared a common heritage. By the time Pesqueira took power, however, the Mayo and Yaqui had developed distinct differences. The Mayo's location made them more vulnerable to Mexican influences and therefore interbreeding was more prevalent among the Mayo than among the Yaqui. Linguistic and racial differences thus developed between the two tribes. Nevertheless, the Mayo joined the Yaqui in resisting the *yori* during most of the nineteenth century.* These wars, which lasted from 1826 until 1888, were caused by the Sonora government's increasing encroachments on the Cahitan lands.

On the other hand, Yaqui Indians formed a substantial part of Sonora's work force.[13] As a field hand, he knew no equal, for the Yaqui worked under the blistering sun to harvest much of the state's crops. Fortunato Hernández, in *Las razas indígenas*, described the Yaqui laborer in the field:

This race is one of the most vigorous that I know, and is for this reason so very well adapted to the climate of Sonora, that day by day it would be impossible to substitute it. I have seen the indefatigable Yaquis working in the harvesting of wheat during the months of June and July under the rays of a subtropical sun, when the thermometer marked 110 degrees in the shade,

---

*Francisco P. Troncoso, *Las guerras con las tribus Yaqui y Mayo*, p. 236; Fortunato Hernández, *Las razas indígenas*, p. 95. The Yaqui resistance was fanatical; Yaqui mothers frightened their children with stories of the cruelty of the *yori.*

and 140 and 150 in the sun; these men, however, did not give signs of fatigue and worked with their accustomed vigor, without having the horrible temperature lessen the exceptional resistance of their muscular system and the extraordinary energy of their nervous system.[14]

Statistician José Francisco Velasco heaped further accolades on Yaqui labor:

This race of Indian possesses remarkable natural abilities, and with very little application they soon become proficient in all mechanical arts. We find among them masons, blacksmiths, carpenters, coppersmiths, makers of fireworks, and skillful players on the harp and violin — all of which they seem to acquire intuitively.[15]

It was, therefore, evident that the Yaqui and to a lesser extent, the Mayo, were essential to the economy of Sonora.* Therein was the dilemma: Mexicans needed the Cahita as a laborer but coveted his lands, which they could only acquire through incessant wars.

The Pima to the east and north of the Yaqui played a different role in the history of Sonora.[16] By the 1850s, Mexican settlers had brought the Pima under control, and the tribal numbers definitely had declined. Many Pima intermarried with Hispano and mestizo settlers, and, like the Cahita, worked on haciendas and in mines. The government frequently used the Pima as soldiers in fighting the Apache.

The Lower Pima lived next to the Yaqui; the Upper Pima settled in northern Sonora and in present-day southern Arizona. Neither were as effective in resisting incoming settlers as the Yaqui or the Mayo had been, for unlike the Cahita, the Pima were not united. The Pima also settled over a much larger area. While united by their language, they differed in levels of development. When the Spanish settlers poured into central and northern Sonora, they divided and conquered the Pima, and usurped his lands. The Pima, most of whom lived in southern Arizona, presented no real threat to the intruders and, by the 1850s, many had been pushed out of their homes.

The Opata inhabited lands in the midst of the Lower and Upper Pima in contemporary central Sonora.[17] Historians consider the Opata the most assimilated of the Sonora Indian tribes. Like the Pima, they did not have a united tribe, and also proved vulnerable to the Spanish and Mexican settlers. The Mexicans settled Opata's lands more heavily than any other region of the state, and as a consequence, by the 1850s, the number of Opata had drastically declined.

In the central section, the racial strain associated with modern Mexico had already appeared. Intermarriage accelerated the assimilation process, and

---

*John Russell Bartlett, *Personal Narrative*, I, 442. Bartlett likened the role of the Yaqui to that of the Irish in the U.S. He marvelled at the Yaqui's craftsmanship and endurance.

this relationship between the Indian and the intruder was reinforced by the *compadre* (father and Godfather) kinship. By the 1850s, the Opata had lost their identity; they had vanished as an entity, and began to form the Sonoran of the future — the mestizo. During Pesqueira's era, the Opata was almost completely Mexicanized.

The nomadic Indians, however, resisted Hispano-Mexican customs and institutions. These wanderers did little farming and subsisted on the land, hunting and gathering food. The nomads were regarded as a negative influence in the state, and their depredations retarded its economic growth. By the time of Pesqueira's administration, only two nomadic tribes could be considered important — the Seri and the Apache. The Seri lived along the coast and on the state's offshore islands, principally on Tiburón. Many of the Seri fished, but most lived on what they could scratch from the land or steal from passing travelers.[18] During the eighteenth century, the Seri had been a serious threat to the security of the interior, but by the 1850s, authorities had largely brought them under control.

The Spaniards and the Mexicans, however, failed to subjugate the Apache, who remained the most dangerous of the nomadic Indians. The Apache roamed the borderlands of present-day Arizona, New Mexico, western Texas, northern Chihuahua, and northern Sonora. In Arizona, the Apache impeded the northward movement of the Spaniards during the colonial period. Attempts to missionize and subdue the Apache were increasingly unsuccessful, especially after they learned to use the horse in the eighteenth century.*

The Spanish controlled the Apache only for a brief period, from about 1790 to 1810, when the Spanish bribed the Indians to camp close to the presidios. It cost the Spaniards eighteen to thirty thousand dollars per year, which they used to furnish the Apache with supplies in return for not raiding Hispano-Mexican settlements. After the War of Independence, because of its bankrupt state, the newly created Mexican government did not extend the dole. When the Apache learned that the gifts would not continue, they returned to marauding. From about 1831 to 1856, the Apache imposed a reign of terror that almost depopulated Sonora's northern frontier.

By the 1850s, the Apache threatened towns of the state's interior; it was felt Sonora could make no progress as long as they remained at large.†

---

*Of interest we note Ignaz Pfefferkorn, in *Sonora*, p. 32, states: "Even the savage Apaches were attracted to such an extent by the gentle call of Father Kino that, of their own accord, they requested missionaries for instruction in Christianity."

† José Francisco Velasco, *Noticias estadísticas*, p. 239. Velasco calls the Apache the scourge of the frontier, and tells in detail of their negative influence. Stevens, in "The Apache Menace," p. 222, points out that in the 1850s the Apache enmity shifted from the Mexicans to the westward advancing Anglo-Americans. Nevertheless, Sonora was still subject to the onslaught of marauding Apache.

The Apache prevented the Mexicans from developing the mines and lands in the north, causing the loss of much-needed revenue and weakening the state internally, making it vulnerable from the outside.

THE POLITICAL REALITIES

José Francisco Velasco wrote that Sonora was a state "without laws or politics." On July 25, 1850, Sonora governor José de Aguilar sent an urgent letter to the Minister of Internal and External Relations of the United States of Mexico, summarizing the consequences of this chaos. He pleaded:

> For more than twenty years this state, threatened by the incursions of the barbarous Apache, has suffered the insecurity of the property and life of its inhabitants; from year to year and day to day, the enemy has become more aggressive, and our towns have worsened under the destruction that war has always caused, leaving some towns deserted, others weakened, and all uncertain of existence. Throughout the times which we have passed, the clamor of these pueblos has been general, looking for the protection of the supreme government, and at no time has attention been paid to this matter of such grave importance. Previously the frontier had a large population. The inhabitants owned fertile lands and abundant animals of all kinds, and enjoyed a favorable position which lifted their spirits and gave them hope of rapid progress in the state. Today this picture has changed; the frontier is deserted, the prosperity lost, and the lands which had been cultivated reflect only the shadow of what they had been and the graves of many victims sacrificed to the fury of the savages.[19]

Aguilar's letter reflected the frustrations of most Sonorans. The state had once been a land of promise but had become overwhelmed as a result of political and economic abandonment by the national government.[20]

Sonora's problems actually began at the time of Mexico's independence from Spain. Sonora historian Eduardo Villa concluded that "as the state left the Spanish period, its problems multiplied."[21] Mission padres and soldiers helped control the Indians on the frontier and made it possible for Hispano-Mexican settlers to remain. But with independence, the Mexican government abandoned the mission system, expelling needed priests.* Since Mexico was too poor to support large contingents of soldiers on the frontier, the result became incessant war.

Events in México D.F. further aggravated conditions in Sonora. Discord and factionalism split the national government.[22] Historian Wilfred Callcott said of the period between 1821 and 1856:

---

*Rufus Kay Wyllys, *Pioneer Padre*, p. 195, states that the mission system had been on the decline since the time of Kino. He blames the decline on lack of leadership and encroachment of white settlers.

Before 1857 the people of Mexico had experienced the ordeal of the War of Independence, and then some twenty-five years of turmoil, during which they were attempting to adjust themselves to the theory of democracy. The struggle centered largely around a contest between church and state for political power. The clergy, supported by the wealthy landlords and army officials, were opposed by the radicals, the political theorists of the day.*

The national government, in not furnishing leadership to Sonora, forfeited the state to a band of opportunists who used it for selfish aims. A power struggle ripped Sonora apart, diverting attention and protection from the frontier and encouraging the Apache to raid Mexican settlements. In the 1850s, neither the state nor the national government could subdue them. Operators, workers, and their families abandoned mines, haciendas, ranchos, and pueblos on the northern frontier. The state militia attempted to restore order, but to no avail.

Political factionalism frustrated political and economic development. [23] In fact, the state government was bankrupt. The customshouse at Guaymas furnished the main source of income, but, ironically, this mainly benefited the national government.† State taxes − such as excise, property, and forced loans − were administered inequitably. Relatively few taxes were collected and the currency was unstable. Copper coins, up to 50 percent counterfeit, were one of the main problems. [24]

Sonora bled while its leaders fought for control of the government and the right to exploit the resources. To these men, the terms *liberal* and *conservative* meant little but were used to justify their chicanery. Manuel María Gándara, principal Sonora caudillo from 1838 to 1856, epitomized the perfidious politician. Historians state that he was the son of a conservative Spaniard. Like most Sonorans of his day, Gándara is difficult to label: it is known that he had no compunction about switching parties if it served his purposes. In addition, it is said that he was power-hungry.

The exploitation of Sonora by men like Gándara impeded orderly government and made the years 1838 and 1846 especially turbulent. A power struggle between Gándara and General José Cosme Urrea, a native Sonoran and leader of the federalist party, threw the state into civil war. Gándara exploited Sonora Indians for his own purposes, rallying them behind his

---

Liberalism in Mexico, p. vii. A very good account of the period from independence to the time of Ignacio Pesqueira is Wilfred Hardy Callcott, *Church and State in Mexico*.

†Stevens, "Mexico's Forgotten Frontier," p. 48. The port of Guaymas should have improved conditions since Mexican independence had removed the monopoly of Veracruz and Acapulco. Also, Guaymas was a natural water outlet for the American territory of Arizona. But chaotic conditions in the state complicated the enforcement against smuggling.

banner and using them against his foes.* Ultimately, Gándara won the tug-of-war, but not before he bled the state dry.[25] By Pesqueira's day, Sonora was still attempting to cast off Gándara's yoke. Consequently, Pesqueira had to restore order before he could govern Sonora.

THE NORTH AMERICANS

When Ignacio Pesqueira took office, the Mexican nation had suffered twice — in 1848 and 1853 — at the hands of the U.S.† Sonora's weakened condition rendered it easy prey for aggressive North Americans, many of whom still considered Mexico an area for future expansion. Sonorans feared the course of U.S. policy, which was determined chiefly by self-interest. Many U.S. administrators openly admitted they wanted Mexico's northern lands, especially the fabled Sonora mines.[26]

In addition to the friction caused by North American aggression, irritation was intensified between the U.S. and Mexico by Article XI of the Treaty of Guadalupe Hidalgo of 1848. This article obligated the U.S. to control the Indians (among them the Apache) along the border.[27] The U.S., however, attempted to circumvent this obligation, and charged the Mexican government with inability to control the Apache. Through manipulation and coercion, North American delegates forced Mexico to include as one of the provisions of the Gadsden treaty a release from this contractual obligation. [28] This action caused bitterness on the part of Sonorans, who considered it part of a conspiracy to steal their land. Their feelings are summarized in a letter from Joaquín Corella, head of the Arizpe Ayuntamiento, to the governor on January 25, 1856:

The treaty of Mesilla has deprived us of this right and with it all hope given us by the obligation we had with the United States through Article XI of the Treaty of Guadalupe. The Gadsden Treaty, we repeat, has marked again the misfortune of Sonora; through it she had been deprived of her most valuable lands, through it the greatest protection has been given to the Apache who launch hostilities from these lands and to the North Americans themselves who live among them because in less than twenty-four hours they cross the boundary; thus the robbers and assassins remain without punishment, and in our opinion it is necessary and indispensable to garrison because upon this depends the territorial outcome of their operations and defense of the integrity of a state threatened by filibuster.[29]

---

*Nicoli, *El estado de Sonora*, p. 160. While Urrea is characterized as the "good guy" in most works, Nicoli says he was a secessionist; at the same time, the author condemns Gándara for rousing the Indians.

†Actually, while the U.S. government was not a de jure party to the war with Texas in 1836, many Mexicans claim the U.S. was in fact involved in this war. Mexico lost more land to the U.S. in 1848 as a result of the Mexican American War (1846-1848) and in 1853 as a result of the Gadsden Purchase when U.S. minister James Gadsden forced Mexico to sell the Mesilla Valley to the U.S.

After the Gadsden Purchase, conditions along the border continued in a state of flux. Added to the tension caused by the Apache was the uncertainty of the international boundary and general lawlessness along its length. Sonorans complained about the Anglo-American outlaws who roamed southern Arizona, plundering, scalp hunting, and raiding the Mexican side of the border. Reprisals followed, and by 1856, relations between the Sonorans and North Americans had deteriorated to a critical point.[30] Sonora historian Laureano Calvo Berber sums up the bitterness of the Sonorans, who blamed the U.S. for the "impoverished condition of northern Mexico and Alta California," charging that the Yanqui wars upon the Indians had driven the Indians into Mexico. Moreover, Calvo Berber indicts the U.S. government for allowing "unscrupulous traders" to buy goods stolen in Mexico and to sell arms and equipment to the Apache.[31]

The North American press inflamed Mexican distrust by openly expressing U.S. intentions. An article in the *Alta California*, September 1853, read: "They [the Sonorans] cannot protect themselves, and the government cannot protect them; their only hope is a war and occupation of their territory by United States troops." The article further lamented the fate of the poor Sonora peons, concluding that the U.S. should make a humanitarian gesture and liberate the state.[32] In fact, California-based filibustering expeditions presented a threat of intervention during the 1850s.

The rash of Sonora-bound parties began in the spring of 1851, when Joseph C. Morehead formed a filibustering expedition. Morehead planned to annex Sonora to the U.S., however, his project failed, but not before alarming the Sonorans.[33]

William Walker, the most notorious filibuster, intensified the fear of annexation. In 1854 he made his debut by leading an expedition into Baja California to annex Lower California and Sonora. The expedition failed when Mexican officials chased Walker out of Mexican California, almost capturing him.[34]

Sonorans also balked at the prospect of French emigration from California to Sonora. Many disappointed Frenchmen, arrivals in California during the 1849 Gold Rush, wished to migrate to Sonora. In 1851 Charles Pindray led a colonizing expedition into Sonora. He and his French compatriots had been invited by the Mexican government to colonize frontier military communities, but they encountered difficulty from the beginning. Government officials, while at first helping Pindray, soon turned on him. After a series of perplexing events, followers found Pindray in his room mysteriously shot through the head; many thought he had been murdered, but evidence pointed to suicide. Nevertheless, the incident increased Sonorans' suspicion of outsiders.

Soon afterward one of the most colorful of the intruders, the Count Gaston Raousset-Boulbon, arrived. The dashing young French nobleman had come to California for adventure but, like so many other Frenchmen in California, he had become discouraged by California's opportunities. Disliking the discrimination against the French, he looked elsewhere to better his condition. Raousset-Boulbon turned to Mexico, where he entered into an agreement with the French Banking Company of Jecker-Torre Company, forming *La Compañía Restauradora del Mineral de la Sonora* to exploit the mines of northern Sonora. The Mexican government signed the contract, giving a franchise to Raousset-Boulbon's group.

In 1852 Raousset-Boulbon and his men first landed in Sonora. This expedition ended in open warfare between French and Mexican authorities, and in the exile of Raousset-Boulbon. In 1854 he returned as the leader of another colony, an adventure which ended in his execution.[35] Sonorans celebrated their triumph and have continued to commemorate the defeat of Count Raousset-Boulbon.

The last filibusters to invade Sonora were members of the Henry Crabb party. The violent reaction of Sonorans to Crabb showed a firm resolution to resist a North American invasion which they believed imminent.*

Also contributing to the friction between the two nations was the arbitrary conduct of U.S. naval officers charged with patrolling the North Pacific. These men of the Northern Pacific Squadron had vast discretionary powers: they could temporarily appoint consuls and arbitrarily interfere in the domestic affairs of the Latin American states. Naval historian Charles O. Paullin wrote of these men:

...a sailor-diplomat ... preeminently a "shirt-sleeve" diplomat. He is a stranger to the devious and tortuous methods of international statecraft. Being a fighter by profession, he does not underestimate the importance of a display of concrete force when temporarily filling the peaceful office of a diplomat.[36]

By the 1850s, this breed of sea captain regularly anchored in the Sonora port of Guaymas and frequently made intemperate use of their power.

The many problems of land and people, the weakness of both local and national government, and the threat of foreign intervention would continue.

Sonora [was] a land of mourning. Apaches, revolution, filibustering expeditions scourged the people. Mines, haciendas, and ranchos in great numbers . . . abandoned and industry of the State . . . completely paralyzed.[37]

Pesqueira must have been aware of the significance of these problems on August 28, 1857, as he gazed upon the deputies gathered to hear his inaugural address.

La Voz de Sonora, November 16, 1885. This article lamented that Sonora suffered more than any other Mexican state at the hands of the barbarians due to the state's proximity of the United States. Many other such articles were written at this time.

CHAPTER 2

Early Career of the Caudillo

The northern frontier town of Arizpe, formerly the capital of the intendency which comprised Sonora and Sinaloa, stood in a valley irrigated by the Sonora River. The Arizona entrepreneur, Sylvester Mowry, described it as the "garden of Sonora."[1] By 1820, its buildings, among the best constructed and ornamented on the northern frontier, had fallen into disrepair with only vestiges of Arizpe's former wealth and elegance remaining. In colonial times, the city boasted a population of five thousand, but by the 1820s the population had declined to approximately two thousand. Thirty years later, the population dropped to about one thousand.[2]

Arizpe's decline mirrored the depression of the rest of the northern frontier. The Mexican government could no longer supply the presidios with goods and soldiers. This situation enabled the Apache to drive the inhabitants to the center of the state, turning nearby pueblos, such as Fronteras, into ghost towns. John Russell Bartlett, in his *Personal Narrative I*, on pages 265-66, describes Fronteras:

Fronteras was formerly a town of considerable importance. It was established about eighty years ago as a presidio, or garrison, and at one time contained two thousand inhabitants. The view of this from a distance is pleasing. It stands upon a point of table land ... juts into the valley like a promontory in the sea. The Church forms the prominent object in the landscape, and its style is quite picturesque; its effect also is heightened by its somewhat ruined condition. Along the steep sides of its hill, the houses are placed one after another .... Once within the town, one's ideas of the picturesque are soon dissipated by the sight of ruined adobe buildings .... Fronteras, like most military colonies, fell into decay, chiefly from the neglect of the central government to provide properly for the soldiery, in consequence of which the inhabitants were left without protection from the attacks of the savages [the Apaches].

In the absence of state and federal support to the frontier villages, the townspeople had to use their own resources to fend off the Apache. Bartlett on pages 275-76 describes how the pueblos were built to provide for this defense:

At the western extremity of this valley, on a spur of a plateau, stood the village of Bacanuchi. This is a peculiarity of all Mexican towns on the frontier. Farmers do not build their ranchos or houses on their arable lands, but congregate on the desert tableland, elevated from thirty to a hundred feet above the adjacent valley from which they derive their subsistence. The great end of security is thus attained at the sacrifice of all comfort and convenience; no trees or shrubbery grow about the house, nor is a blade of grass to be seen.

The settlers on the northern Sonora frontier of the Apache raids, like the serfs of medieval Europe, looked to local strongmen to defend them, and the recognized Indian fighter soon became a hero. However, conditions were such that the Apache soon overwhelmed the few veteran frontier soldiers. José Carrasco, a veteran of the Apache wars, summed up the frustrations of settler and soldier alike:

It is the old story; our territory is enormous and our government weak. It cannot extend its protecting arms through all portions of the country. Whole provinces are left for years to themselves, except in the matter of taxation, and things run to ruin.[3]

Often in a period of decline, people turn to the past, nostalgically remembering more affluent times. So it must have been with Pesqueira, whose elders often reminded him of Arizpe's legacy of prosperous mines and haciendas. The ruggedness of the land and the precariousness of the environment must have molded Pesqueira's determination and ruthlessness, for, as Stevens says in "Mexico's Forgotten Frontier," ". . .in this cauldron of turmoil and inclemency, a spirit of rugged frontier individualism prevailed," qualities necessary to lead men in nineteenth-century Sonora.[4]

HIS EARLY YEARS

Little is known about the early life of Ignacio Pesqueira. In 1915 Pancho Villa's invading army entered Sonora and burned the Pesqueira ancestral home at the hacienda of Bacanuchi — and with it the family papers. The first Pesqueira in Sonora, Julian Pesqueira, arrived in the 1750s. It is open to conjecture whether he was of Portuguese or Galician ancestry.[5]

In Arizpe, Julian Pesqueira married María Romo de Vívar y Escalante, whose father, José Romo de Vívar, may have been of Sephardic ancestry. In 1772 the Pesqueiras bore a son, José Francisco Pesqueira, in the city of Arizpe. Twenty-four years later, Francisco married María Vicente Bustamante, age thirty, and their union produced Ignacio Pesqueira Sr., the father of Ignacio Pesqueira Jr., Sonora caudillo. Pesqueira Sr. rose to the rank of captain in the Spanish infantry and became commandant of the forts of Tumacacori and Guevavi in what is now southern Arizona. The elder Ignacio Pesqueira married Petra García Tato. The Pesqueira family was not among the more prominent families, but was considered *gente de razón* (people who had a good family name and social status) and of good stock. Ignacio Pesqueira Jr.'s mother, however, belonged to one of the most distinguished families of the day and was the aunt of General Pedro García Conde.[6]

Petra gave birth to Ignacio Pesqueira on December 16, 1820, in Arizpe. At the age of eight, Ignacio left Sonora for Seville, Spain. At this time, his godfather Francisco López, a Spaniard, refused to renounce his status as a

Spanish subject, and chose to leave Mexico. López, married to Pesqueira's aunt, had become very fond of "Nachito," and offered to take him to Spain for a Spanish education. This greatly benefited Pesqueira, since there were few educational opportunities in Sonora beyond the primary level. Sonora's wealthy families usually sent their sons to México D.F. for schooling.

Ignacio matriculated at a Catholic school, majoring in a commercial course. At the age of fourteen, he went to Paris to study painting. After a year, he returned to Seville, where he reputedly took part in the liberal antimonarchist movements that began in 1833 with the death of Fernando VII.[7] The extent of his involvement in these liberal causes is speculative. He must have been exposed to the ideas of the French Revolution, and may have even joined a Masonic lodge while in Europe, according to Fernando Pesqueira, a descendent of Ignacio Pesqueira and a noted Sonora scholar.* In 1838 Ignacio left Spain, arriving in Sonora early the next year.[8] In Arizpe during his early years, he worked in a commercial house, where he allegedly prospered, and cultivated tobacco. Ignacio was also a talented amateur painter. Ironically, even in these early years when he was converted to the cause of liberalism, and consequently anticlerical, most of the subjects of his oils were saints.[9]

EARLY RISE OF PESQUEIRA

Pesqueira joined the local militia, where he learned to fight bravely and drink heavily.[10] He became famous for both, and his affection for mescal gave rise to many stories. In later years, he always carried a ready supply of mescal by mule when he toured the provinces as governor. Partisans say that on these occasions, fun-loving Pesqueira danced and mingled with the common folk.

Pesqueira quickly gained a following and rose rapidly through the ranks of the militia. He became an experienced Apache fighter, receiving guidance from old veterans such as Colonel Rafael Buelna. By 1845 Pesqueira had been promoted to captain, heading a company of forty men. Two years later he enlisted in the state militia, before the expected gringo invasion. While it never materialized, Captain Pesqueira did participate in several expeditions against the Apache.[11]

Pesqueira played an inactive role in the Urrea-Gándara feuds of the 1840s. He is reported to have privately favored Urrea, a native of northern Sonora, but publicly he did not take a stand. On January 11, 1851, Pesqueira was suddenly catapulted from obscurity to state-wide prominence. At Pozo

---

*Ramiro de Garza, "Don Ignacio Pesqueira," pp. 20-21. A. F. Pradeau states that he has records of Masonic lodges in Sonora; Pesqueira's name does not appear among their ledgers.

Hediondo ("Smelly Well") in the district of Moctezuma, Pesqueira encountered the Apache braves under Mangas Coloradas, who allegedly outnumbered his troops three hundred to fifty. The Apache shot Pesqueira's horse from under him and Sonorans abandoned the captain for dead; but he walked all the way to Arizpe where he received a hero's welcome and was publicly lauded by Governor José de Aguilar and Colonel José Carrasco, the Sonora military commander.[12]

After Pozo Hediondo, military authorities promoted him to command the Arizpe urban battalion, and in the same year, his fellow citizens elected him to represent the district in the Sonora legislature. Two years later he returned to his home town, where in September he joined the local militia to once more combat the Apache threat. The following year, Pesqueira was promoted to major. Meanwhile, Ignacio Pesqueira's reputation spread.[13]

Pesqueira reportedly did not become involved in state political fights. He followed the popular majority, even supporting Antonio López de Santa Anna's dictatorship, for which government officials rewarded him with an appointment to the dual post of prefect (sheriff of the district) and military commander of the Ures district.[14] On December 21, 1855, he received a second promotion, to adjutant inspector of the military colonies; this appointment marked the young caudillo's entrance into the regular army.*

At this time, Pesqueira does not appear to have been aligned with any particular faction, although he was on friendly terms with Manuel Gándara.[15] Meanwhile, in 1854, Sonora officials seconded the Plan of Ayutla. The Plan of Ayutla, however, crystalized ideological differences within the state — landed interests versus commercial interests. Gándara was the leader of the former and José de Aguilar led the latter; Pesqueira would come to play an important role in the tug-of-war for control of the state.

SHADOW OF MANUEL MARÍA GÁNDARA

Manuel María Gándara, born in San Juan de Haigame, located in the municipality of La Colorada in 1800, represented the *criollo* establishment which had dominated Sonora since Mexican Independence. His father, Juan Gándara, had migrated to Sonora from Spain in the late eighteenth century, marrying Antonia Gortari. In 1828 most of the Gándara family, with the exception of Manuel María and a brother, left the state in response to the

---

*Eduardo W. Villa, *Galeria de Sonorenses*, p. 138, states that Pesqueira entered into the regular army. Francisco R. Almada, *Diccionario de Historia*, p. 574, states that Pesqueira's commission was not approved by federal authorities and, while he functioned in the position, someone else was actually appointed. There is no proof of Almada's contention. Until May of 1856, Pesqueira signed his correspondence as adjutant inspector.

Spanish Expulsion Act of that year. Soon the family returned to its native Ures, when the elder Gándara died on the high seas; consequently, Manuel María provided for the family.[16]

Manuel María Gándara married Dolores de Aguilar, increasing his wealth, and later acquired the haciendas of Bamure and Topahue near Hermosillo, where he operated a flour mill. In 1829 Gándara entered public life, holding several minor posts, and two years later briefly occupied the post of provisional governor. By 1837 he had risen as leader of the wealthy rancheros, and in recognition of his status, President Anastasio Bustamante appointed him governor of Sonora. Thus began the Gándara years and his role of *cacique máximo.*[17]

An evaluation of the cacique is difficult, since relatively few objective sources are available. He is either Sonora's saviour or her most infamous villain. Most historians brand Gándara as an opportunist, who acted for his own benefit with little regard for the welfare of his party or state. Suggesting proof of his lack of scruples, Gándara is quoted as saying, "I neither hate nor love federalism or centralism. . .as a public functionary, I will adhere to the one. . .adopted by the nation."[18] This statement alone reveals little, for Gándara lived in an age when pragmatism spelled survival.

History does condemn Gándara, however, for his reckless exploitation of the Yaqui, Mayo, and other tribes of the state to further his personal ambition. He catered to these tribes, unleashing them whenever he was threatened. Moreover, Gándara's administrative record was poor, for he failed to bring about order, thus permitting the state's economy to grind to a halt. He favored the rich land owners and the proclerical factions; these groups had formed a coalition to support him and keep him in power. In the process, Gándara had ignored the challenge of the growing merchant and miner class, who were tired of a tax system which favored the landed oligarchy. Gándara wrote on page 4 of *Manifestación* that he came out of retirement because José de Aguilar was taking advantage of the situation. Gándara accused the partisans of Aguilar of moving against people with wealth.

By the 1850s Gándara's enemies had become numerous enough to be heard. Gándara's coalition began to break up and its defects grew more apparent. A contemporary of Gándara's, Captain James Box, stated that Gándara had enriched himself during his stay in office, making many friends by allowing them to accumulate fortunes. Gándara is also alleged to have favored foreigners, which especially angered the rising Mexican capitalist. Captain Box described Gándara's greatest liability as follows: "Moreover, Gándara lacks the grand requisites of a chieftain — courage and confidence. To the greatest ambition he unites the meanest cowardice . . . ."[19]

José de Aguilar, neither a liberal nor conservative, emerged as the leader of the anti-Gándara forces. Ironically, Aguilar was Gándara's brother-in-law.

José Urrea

Manuel M. Gándara

Photos from
Laureano Calvo Berber,
Nociones de Historia de Sonora

José de Aguilar

Aguilar had proven an able, ambitious governor during the years 1849-51. Throughout the early fifties, his ties to the merchants and urban dwellers increased. By 1856 Aguilar must have realized that an open break between the latter and Gándara was inevitable and he must have seen his opportunity to step into the vacuum. By this time rich Sonora merchants were in a position to give Aguilar tangible financial support and must have urged him to challenge Gándara.[20] Nevertheless, Aguilar proved to be faint hearted and, thus, needed a strong ally to unseat Don Manuel María Gándara.

Ignacio Pesqueira, a ruthless frontier fighter, perfectly complemented Aguilar's temerity. In 1856 Pesqueira did not appear to have sufficient stature to play a major role. However, the growing discontent of nonestablishment *criollos*, miners, and merchants of Sonora, along with incredible good fortune, conspired in Pesqueira's favor.* The young caudillo shrewdly assessed the changing times, and boldly sided with Aguilar, bringing to the partnership the image of the "man on horseback." This quality cannot be underestimated in a time when *personalismo* (charismatic leadership) played such an important role.

Sonora historians generally treat Pesqueira favorably. Many of his contemporaries, however, considered his rise lamentable and questioned his integrity. Charles D. Poston of Arizona described Gándara as "a sedate and dignified man with a large fortune who was polite and hospitable to travelers," while he condemned Pesqueira as "an educated savage, without property or position, and [who] naturally coveted his neighbor's goods." [21] Poston's view reflected the feelings of many North Americans as well as older Sonora families.

BIRTH OF THE PESQUEIRISTAS

The Plan of Ayutla of March 1854 stiffened opposition to Gándara. Liberals rallied around the plan and demanded, among other things, the ousting of dictator Antonio López de Santa Anna. By the spring of 1855, the revolution had spread throughout Mexico, and by August 17, 1855, Santa Anna left for Venezúela aboard the steamship *Iturbide*. [22]

The fall of Santa Anna did not automatically insure domestic tranquility. The transition form centralism to federalism tore the nation apart, throwing it into anarchy. Several states reflected the flux, as factional fights broke out for control of the states. The national government played a

---

*Torre Villar, "Notas sobre Sonora," p. 57; Rufus Kay Wyllys, "Henry A. Crabb — A Tragedy of the Sonora Frontier," reprinted for the *Pacific Historical Review*, IX (June 1940), 187. Wyllys wrote that the struggle was between the Elías Aguilar, Pesqueira, and Yñigo group of allied families and followers against other well-entrenched families allied with Gándara.

key role in determining which side won the governorship and who took command of the federal troops within a state. Therefore, in Sonora, the Gandaristas and Aguilaristas both lobbied México D.F. for the mantle of legitimacy and the rod to rule the state.

In reality, neither side had energetically supported the Plan of Ayutla. Although the chicanery of López de Santa Anna embittered many Sonorans who had lost some of their richest land under his administrations and had been victimized by the recent Gadsden Treaty, leaders did not second the Plan of Ayutla until September, 1855.[23] The slowness might have been due to distance and poor communication, but a more realistic explanation is that both factions probably waited to see which side would win before committing themselves. Moreover, this reluctance indicates the obvious weakness of the oppositionist Aguilaristas and that philosophical goals had not jelled.

On the seventeenth of October, the central government appointed Manuel María Gándara to the dual post of governor and federal military commander of Sonora. This appointment indicated that Gándara still had considerable influence in México D.F., for in spite of obvious opposition and his former conservative ties, Gándara was able to convince government officials of his power. The Aguilaristas, including Pesqueira, were angry, but did not protest publicly. Five days later, Gándara, with all the usual rhetoric and without incident, spelled out his plan to restore peace and prosperity. [24]

In the beginning of 1856 the national government reversed itself, appointing José de Aguilar governor and Pedro Espejo federal military commander. Gándara received the orders, but did not make them public for over one month. When he did so on February 19, he still refused to comply with the directive, informing Sonorans that "foreign enemies and barbarians threatened the state," and he would therefore "make a personal sacrifice" and remain in office. The Council of State seconded his action, claiming that the prospect of Aguilar and Espejo taking over alarmed most citizens. Ramón Encinas, spokesman for the council, concluded that if Gándara did not make the sacrifice, all hope of a better social life in the state would end. Encinas also praised Gándara as the "savior of the pueblo."[25] There could be no doubt of the Gandaristas' intention to retain power.

On February 25, Gándara publicly denounced Pedro Espejo, charging that in June, 1855, Espejo had seconded the dictatorship of López de Santa Anna.* By March 19, Gándara felt strong enough to deport Espejo, dismissing criticisms by explaining that he had done so because "he was a

---

*Manuel María Gándara, Circular to the District Prefects, Ures, February 25, 1856, *La Voz de Sonora*, February 29, 1856; also Gándara, *Manifestación*, p. 4, stated that the *Acta* de Ures of September 1, 1855, had called for the removal of Espejo and for General Yáñez to take over the military and political control of the state. This plan named Pesqueira to be second in command. Gándara said that this did not mean a vote of confidence for Pesqueira, but that it was done because Pesqueira was insignificant.

bother to me." At this time Aguilar remained conciliatory. The day before Espejo's expulsion, Aguilar issued a public statement lamenting his brother-in-law's arbitrary actions, but complimenting Gándara for having "struggled against insurmountable difficulties with honor."[26] Soon afterwards, Gándara invited Aguilar to his hacienda at Topahue for a summit meeting.

Although a compromise was effected, Gándara definitely triumphed over Aguilar. The old cacique relinquished the governorship but kept control of the federal forces. The Sonora historian, Eduardo Villa, attributes Gándara's accommodation to the fact that he did not want to incur the wrath of the national government by illegally witholding the governorship any longer.[27] Villa, however, overemphasizes the power of the federal government, and like other historians, is charitable to Aguilar. It is doubtful both that the federal government could have enforced its will and that Gándara feared it. The cacique probably felt that he could continue to bully Aguilar and that time was on his side. Thus he gracefully gave up the governorship which was not legally his and retained the military commandancy to which he was not entitled in the first place.

Gándara's duplicity immediately unfolded. He did not even bother to assume his command; instead he retired to his hacienda and allowed matters to drift. Colonel Ignacio Pesqueira, adjutant inspector of the presidial companies, reported on April 2 that conditions had worsened, and that if immediate action was not taken the consequences would be dire. He also complained that Gándara had not kept him abreast, had compounded confusion with duplicity in feigning illness, and had neglected his duty. Pesqueira further charged that Gándara's actions had broken down discipline among his troops; concluding that the former henceforth would recognize only Aguilar's orders, Pesqueira urged Aguilar to assume command of the army.[28]

Gándara reacted illegally by appointing Colonel Juan Espíndola, head of the garrisons of Guaymas and Hermosillo, to the post occupied by Pesqueira. On April 6, Espíndola sent Pesqueira a letter ordering him to officially recognize his authority. He issued Pesqueira an ultimatum: "two hours. . .to place his troops at Espíndola's disposal." The next day Pesqueira replied, refusing to recognize Gándara's puppet and telling him to "quit his pretensions." Pesqueira then sent Aguilar a letter reporting what had happened. Simultaneously, Pesqueira imprisoned three pro-Gándara battalion commanders for malicious conduct, one of them Colonel Manuel Muñoz, a favorite of Gándara.* Meanwhile, Espíndola, fearing that he would get caught

---

*Manuel María Gándara to José de Aguilar, Santiago, April 22, 1856; a reply from Aguilar to Gándara, Ures, April 22, 1856, *La Voz de Sonora*, April 22, 1856. Further complicating the picture was the apparent lack of information on the part of the national government as to conditions in Sonora. Gándara took advantage of this situation, and on one occasion when correspondence came to him addressed to the governor and commandant general, he wrote to Aguilar informing him of this. Aguilar answered that it was a mistake.

in the middle of an interfamily squabble, left Ures without waiting for further correspondence from Pesqueira. Espíndola did not cause any further problems; in fact, when Aguilar finally assumed the post of commandant general, Espíndola willingly acquiesced and placed his garrisons under Aguilar's command.[29]

Soon after Espíndola left Ures, Aguilar assummed command of the federal forces. Gandaristas protested this action, branding it illegal. On April 16, Battalion Commander Francisco Borunda, commander of the garrison at Hermosillo, revolted against Aguilar. Borunda threatened to invade the capital, marching to the Gándara hacienda at Topahue where he joined other dissidents.[30] Gándara abetted the rebels, even appointing Colonel Manuel Muñoz to lead his forces. Muñoz in turn marched to San Felipe, a short distance from Ures, where he waited for Gándara to arrive with reinforcements.*

These events found Pesqueira in Ures, where he prepared to defend the city. A clash between the old cacique and the parvenu caudillo seemed inevitable. Before the battle, a messenger from México D.F. arrived with a dispatch containing Gándara's appointment to the post of commandant general. Pesqueira allegedly had no recourse but to allow Gándara to enter Ures at the head of a small force. Again the ambivalence of the federal government and the weakness of Aguilaristas were only too apparent.

This did not end the conflict between the two factions. Aguilar moved to consolidate his position by forming a *Consejo de Gobierno* (Council of State). He appointed Pesqueira to the presidency of that body, an important position since it would place the young caudillo next in succession to the governorship.[31] Gándara, in turn, attempted to strengthen his hold over the federal forces and to extend his power to include the state militia which was currently under the governor. He justified the necessity of these actions by alleging that Pesqueira was simultaneously recruiting support on the frontier.

Still Aguilar attempted to avert an open break. He initiated a series of letters with Gándara, which he began by referring to him as "my esteemed brother-in-law," but after a few exchanges grew more formal. Each complained about the other's actions: Aguilar charged that Gándara had used the state militia illegally, for his jurisdiction extended over federal not state troops. The cacique countered by claiming that Aguilar had acted in bad faith and had not recognized his authority from the beginning. He accused Aguilar of conspiring against him. Aguilar again seemed to bend over backwards,

---

*Villa, *Historia de Sonora*, p. 241. Circular issued by José de Aguilar, April 19, 1856, found in the microfilm collection at the University of Arizona of the Archives of the State of Sonora, Hermosillo, entitled Yaqui and Mayo Papers. They were uncatalogued when the author took notes. The circular condemned Muñoz and Borunda as the leaders of the insurrection.

beseeching his brother-in-law not to throw the state into a civil war. Gándara, on April 27, wrote that he did "not aspire to any post nor pretend to any," but that he could not live in fear of revolution and disorder, concluding that the best way to guarantee peace was to assume full control. Aguilar replied that Gándara's actions were illegal, questioning the latter's motivation: why had he deported Espejo, and why did he use the state militia illegally? [32]

The Borunda Revolt continued throughout this correspondence. Borunda's army seemed poised for attack, but again a compromise prolonged the inevitable. Aguilar capitulated and, on April 30, published a circular relating the efforts of his administration to maintain peace and guarantee domestic tranquility.[33] The message was that Gándara had been compensated for ending his illegal revolt: Aguilar placed the state militia under his command.* The cacique still remained unsatisfied.

On the evening of May 8, Gándara unexpectedly left Ures, taking the city's force with him. He moved his base of operations to San José de Guaymas, which almost always was a strategic prelude to a revolt, since the customs of that port were essential for financing a civil war. He further moved to consolidate his position; although he controlled the army, he believed that Pesqueira had many partisans on the frontier. He moved to cut Pesqueira's support by removing much needed soldiers from their frontier posts to concentrate them in San José de Guaymas.† This act dangerously weakened the presidios and encouraged the Apache to increase their attacks. The town of Chinapa – attacked by Apache on May 21 – was a victim of Gándara's perfidy. Colonel of the state militia and prefect of Arizpe, Rafael Angel Corella, rushed to the town's aid, but found it in ruins, with "its streets deserted; scattered here and there were the corpses of men, women, and children who were completely nude, and the ground saturated with blood.[34]

After this, Gándara wound his web of intrigue even tighter. He personally rode to the Yaqui River Valley, appealing to the Indians of that region to support his cause.[35] Gándara also fired Pesqueira as inspector of the military colonies, an action intended to segregate the popular caudillo from his frontier base.

An angry Pesqueira bitterly protested his dismissal, castigating Gándara in a sizzling letter in which he reminded Gándara of the numerous occasions he had praised Pesqueira's dedication to the frontier. Pesqueira, in no

---

*"La Revolución Borunda," La Voz de Sonora, May 2, 1856. Circular to the people from Gándara, May 5, 1856, Yaqui and Mayo Papers, University of Arizona microfilms of the Archives of the State of Sonora, uncatalogued. In this circular, Gándara is thankful that the peace was arrived at as the result of an agreement with the governor and the military class.

†Gándara, Manifestación, p. 10. According to Gándara, he removed the troops to relieve tensions.

uncertain terms, accused Gándara of acting for personal aggrandizement and warned Gándara that he would some day account for his perfidy.[36]

This event threw Pesqueira and Aguilar into a closer league with the governor, who appointed Pesqueira to Colonel Inspector of the national guard.* From his newly acquired post, Pesqueira actively opposed Gándara. The die was cast, and Sonora historian Eduardo Villa romantically marked this occasion as the birth of the liberal party in Sonora under the leadership of "the young caudillo."[37]

Finally, on July 15, the Gandaristas made their move, and under the leadership of "El Chapo," Manuel Dávila, they denounced Governor Aguilar, naming Ramón Encinas governor. Dávila, leading a party of Indians from Aconchi, seized and imprisoned José de Aguilar, and attacked Ures. The Gandaristas then attempted to capture Pesqueira, but he had learned of the events and sped to Arizpe, from where he prepared to defend the Aguilar government.[38]

On the twenty-fifth of July, Aguilar, who had been released, issued a statement approving Pesqueira's actions. Two days later at Baviacora Pesqueira published a statement which condemned Gándara and defended Aguilar's legitimacy. He concluded that, in the governor's absence, he as president of the Council of State would assume the post of chief executive. He urged all Sonorans "to follow him and defend their de jure government."[39]

Fortunately for Pesqueira, the city of Alamos immediately supported him, volunteering four hundred men and funds. Alameños also financed a committee, which was sent to México D.F. to lobby President Ignacio Comonfort on Pesqueira's behalf. All fronts had to be covered; the Pesqueiristas could not afford to be undermined by a bungling national government. Sonorans also realized that General José María Yáñez commanded the federal army of the west, and that Yáñez and Gándara were compadres. It became imperative to neutralize this federal commander, who was at the time stationed in Mazatlán.† Twenty-nine-year-old Bartolomé E. Almada of Alamos headed the committee and did a brilliant job of gaining the federal government's confidence.[40]

Pesqueira moved rapidly and, on August 4, he began the siege of Ures. After four days he entered the city, and then directed his thrust toward

---

*La Voz de Sonora, May 30, 1856; Villa, Historía de Sonora, p. 244. Pesqueira then wrote a letter to Aguilar bitterly attacking the actions of Gándara.

†San Francisco Evening Bulletin, October 29, 1856; "El Sr. Yáñez en Mazatlan," La Voz de Sonora, January 2, 1857. News came from California that Gándara agents in San Francisco were attempting to enlist two to four thousand men to his cause through his agent William Johnson. The later article clearly indicates that Sonorans believed that Yáñez would intervene.

Hermosillo, the commercial center of the state. In route on August 23, on the plains of Dolores near La Misa, he defeated the nucleus of the rebel army under Francisco Borunda. Despite these victories, the rebel forces under Jesús Gándara, the brother of Manuel, continued their opposition around Ures and Magdalena, while the Yaqui and the Mayo continued to threaten Pesqueira. Soon however, it became apparent that the Pesqueiristas had won, and Manuel Gándara fled to Chihuahua.* On November 21, Pesqueira captured, tried, and executed "El Chapo" Dávila; by January 4, 1857, Jesús Gándara had surrendered to the prefect of Guaymas. Thus ended the rebellion, with Pesqueira winning an unexpectedly easy victory.[41]

---

*La Voz de Sonora, September 12, 1856. During this period we also find accusations charging that Gándara was in conspiracy with filibusters; "D. Manuel Gándara," La Voz de Sonora, September 19, 1856; San Francisco Evening Bulletin, November 11, 1856. According to La Voz de Sonora, there was a rumor that Gándara was in México D.F. to be introduced to officials in the capital city by his compadre (godfather of one of Gándara's children), General Yáñez. The Evening Bulletin had an account that Gándara was in Tucson, ready to go to México D.F. with adherents.

CHAPTER 3

The Caudillo and the Filibustero

After peace was restored, Ignacio Pesqueira, the President of the Council of State, offered to return the governorship to José de Aguilar, but the de jure governor declined, stating that Aguilar's health would not permit the ordeal. The young caudillo remained in office, but in an extremely tenuous position. The Gandaristas had been in power for about twenty years, and could still rally substantial support within and outside Sonora. Gándara's supporters included men of wealth, the proclerical factions, and the various Sonora Indian tribes who did not accept the outcome of the war as final.[1]

Pesqueira moved his base of operations from the northern frontier city of Arizpe to the state capital, Ures, which stood close to the center of Sonora. Ures originally had been a mission settlement, founded by the Jesuits in 1636. In 1838 it became the state capital, but in 1842, state officials moved the capital again. Five years later, Ures once more became the seat of government. Ures' growth was artificial, increasing since 1825 with the influx of Sonorans fleeing the Apache in the north.[2]

Ures had about seven thousand inhabitants, and its buildings reflected none of the past splendor of Arizpe. Simple one-story buildings spotted the city; the prison stood out as the only building of note. Like most Spanish and Mexican towns, Ures was laid out in squares, with the plaza holding court to a very plain church.

This capital city was nestled in a valley watered by the Sonora River, whose fertile soil produced wheat, cereals, cotton, and other crops. Important haciendas, such as Santa Rita, Molino, Guadalupe, Topahue, and others, many of which were owned by Gándara or his former partisans, embellished its environs. This area became Ignacio Pesqueira's new home.

THE INFAMOUS FILIBUSTERS

The problem of uniting the citizenry — an almost impossible task in a state as vast as Sonora with so many conflicting economic interests and obstacles to communication between its several districts — remained to be tackled by Pesqueira. Added to this chore was the bitterness of the recent civil war. Pesqueira's chances of uniting Sonorans behind his administration, therefore, appeared very slim. Ironically, in the spring of 1857, an event occurred which united Sonorans behind the young caudillo: a threatened invasion by *filibusteros*. The menace emanated from California in the person of Henry Crabb, who, with a party of about one hundred men, approached

26

Sonora.* A century later Sonorans identify Crabb as a *filibustero* who invaded their soil, wheras many Anglo-American historians contend that Crabb merely led a colonizing party to Sonora at the invitation of the state government. North Americans condemned the brutal treatment of the Crabb party, but they were not aware of the facts surrounding the massacre of Crabb and his men.

In 1848, Sonorans hated, feared, and distrusted North Americans. In a little over twenty years, Mexico had lost 939,968 square miles to its northern neighbor, leaving 767,055 square miles, less than half of its original territory. By the terms of the Gadsden Treaty, Sonora alone lost 45,534 square miles of territory. In the years after the Treaty of Guadalupe, Sonorans had become increasingly exposed to the *yanqui*'s western push.

The 1849 California Gold Rush attracted many immigrants who passed through Sonora's northern borderlands. The boisterous Forty-niners did not hesitate to plunder the lands they traveled through. One gringo leader, Parker H. French, with a party of twenty-five men, stopped at the village of Cieneguita. The village padre welcomed French and his cohorts, and they in turn repaid the priest for his hospitality by hanging him. The padre's life was spared only because his sister told French where the pueblo's treasure was buried. The Honorable Parker H. French later reappeared as a "distinguished member" of the Fifth California Legislative Assembly. To add to Sonora's tribulations, many bandits roamed the poorly policed border, robbing and plundering.[3]

As an outside threat, the neighboring state of Chihuahua offered a bounty for Apache scalps. The scalp hunters did not discriminate, and took the black hair of mestizos to sell it as Apache.

The Apache raids and the aforementioned filibusters — Joseph Morehead, Charles Pindray, Gaston Raousset-Boulbon, and the most notorious of them all, William Walker — compounded the Sonorans' misery. Most of the filibustering expeditions began in California, creating friction between the governments of Mexico and the United States. It is little wonder that Sonorans lived in fear, for they knew their own vulnerability and consequently were suspicious of anything faintly resembling the Texas episode of 1836.

North Americans, on the other hand, boldly and unapologetically bragged about their deeds. California had more than its share of adventurers

---

*A list of these men and their backgrounds can be found in Robert A. Forbes, *Crabb's Filibustering Expedition into Sonora, 1857*, pp. 45-46. Many of the men on the expedition were former members of both houses of the California legislature. One can only speculate why these men would participate in a colonizing party. The *San Francisco Bulletin*, January 22, 1857, wrote that the men had nothing further to gain from Washington D.C., and therefore looked to Mexico.

who wished to emulate the actions of Sam Houston and Charles Frémont.[4] They believed that they followed a natural law, as Horace Bell candidly described it:

The theory of filibustering, or manifest destiny, was: first, that the earth is the Lord's and the fullness thereof, and we are the Lord's people; second, that all Spanish-American governments are worthless, and should be reconstructed, and that such is one mission; that the people of Lower California and Sonora are, or should be, dissatisfied with Mexican rule, and are, or should be, ripe for rebellion, and if not in terror of the Mexican central despotism would cry out for American aid to shake off their galling chains; the *Sonoreños* ought to rise, proclaim their independence, and cry for help from the generous Filibuster, who stood ready to help the downtrodden Mexican and to feather his own nest in particular.[5]

Although the United States government officially committed itself to prosecute filibusters, California authorities openly violated the national policy. To the dismay of the Mexican authorities, California courts acquitted William Walker of filibustering after his invasion of Baja California. Judge Ogden Hoffman of the United States District Court regretfully convicted Colonel H. P. Watkins, Vice President of the Republic of Lower California and Sonora, of the crime of setting foot on Mexican soil during the ill-fated Walker expedition:

From my heart, I sympathize with the accused, but I am sworn to the execution of the law and must discharge my duty whatever my sympathies may be. To the law and to the evidence, then, we must turn our exclusive attention. I may admire the spirited men who have gone forth upon these expeditions to upbuild, as they claim, the brokendown altars and rekindle the extinguished fires of liberty in Mexico or Lower California. It may be that they are not adventurers gone forth to build for themselves a cheap fortune in another land. But even were such my opinion of their purpose, and their objects as glowing and as honorable as depicted by counsel, still, sitting as judge, I should regard only the single question, "Has the law been violated?"[6]

Sonorans knew the sentiments and intentions of these adventurers. By 1857, they realized that they would receive little support from either the Mexican or the United States government in controlling these filibustering expeditions. This set the stage for the Crabb expedition, with Sonorans desperately fighting to ward off the advancing Anglo-Americans.*

*Rufus Kay Wyllys, *The French in Sonora*, 1850-1854, pp. 15, 26, 33. Sonora at this time invited foreign adventurers to its soil. Sonora was helpless, and thought if foreigners would immigrate to the state, a buffer could be formed between Sonora and both the Apache Indians and the North Americans. However, most of these attempts failed, further exposing the state.

Henry Alexander Crabb

Arizona Historical Society

THE HONORABLE HENRY ALEXANDER CRABB

Henry Alexander Crabb would have resented the label "filibuster," for he and his followers believed they had an honorable mission. The majority of the men in the expedition had migrated to California from the American South. Many of them must have believed they were obliged to fulfill a destiny and to extend the sphere of slave states.[7] Added to country and glory was an ill-disguised greed for wealth and fame.

Crabb had been born and raised in Nashville, Tennessee. His father, a brilliant lawyer, rose to the Supreme Court of Tennessee. The younger Crabb also studied law, and was admitted to the bar, after which he set up practice in Vicksburg. During his early years, he formed a close friendship with William Walker. In 1848, Crabb's legal career ended in a duel with Mr. Jenkins, the editor of the *Vicksburg Sentinel*, the local Democratic newspaper. A political disagreement originating at a party rally resulted in Crabb killing Jenkins, for which Crabb was acquitted. The next year Crabb went to California, seeking his fortune in the Gold Rush.[8]

When he arrived in California Crabb was about twenty-six years old. The dark-eyed young Crabb settled in Stockton, rising quickly in politics. Crabb found a natural political base, and in July of 1850, the citizens of Stockton elected him city attorney. From 1851 to 1855 Crabb served in the California Assembly, and from 1853 to 1854 in the state Senate. Politically, Crabb was a Whig, and became popular as an aggressive slavery advocate. In 1853, many of his adversaries alleged that he published a Whig circular proposing the division of the state of California into southern and northern portions.[9]

Crabb married Filomena Ainza, a member of a Spanish family who had immigrated to Sonora from Manila. In Sonora, Filomena's father Agustín had invested a sizeable fortune in mines and other property, but lost these holdings during the state's many civil wars. The family then fled to Los Angeles, and later to the Stockton area. The Ainzas' tales of lost wealth in the Philippine Islands and Sonora must have impressed Crabb. Moreover, the activities of Walker and the French (Pindray and Raousset-Boulbon) in Sonora fanned Crabb's burning ambition.[10]

In October of 1853, Crabb booked passage on the *Carolina* from San Francisco to Guaymas in an attempt to regain some of the Ainzas' lost fortune.[11] Once at sea, however, he realized that the *Carolina* was the same vessel that had transported Walker to Baja, California. Crabb postponed his venture because he feared association with the Walker expedition would damage his cause. After a time he went to the eastern sector of the United States. In February of 1855, he returned to California via the Isthmus of Nicaragua. Although he told his old friend Walker about the prospects in Nicaragua, Crabb decided to run for the United States Senate in California; while there, he became interested in the possibility of leading a filibustering expedition.

Later in 1855, Henry Crabb joined the Know-Nothing party and became a formidable candidate for the Senate, but his proslavery views eliminated him. When it appeared certain that Crabb would not be elected, he withdrew. Meanwhile, Walker had invaded Nicaragua, and was tremendously successful. The news spread to California, which buzzed with stories about Walker. Crabb felt disappointed and humiliated, and in a state of melancholia he turned his attention to Sonora, perhaps to vindicate his tarnished honor. [12]

HENRY A. CRABB IN SONORA, 1856

There can be no doubt that Crabb intended to invade Sonora illegally; events leading to the actual expedition prove this conclusively. These preliminary events, nevertheless, have been ignored by the press and historians.

John Walton Caughey, on pages 304-305 of *California* writes:

Less deserved and consequently more tragic was the fate of the Stockton lawyer and California State Senator, Henry A. Crabb. . . . By a local revolutionist, Ignacio Pesquiera [sic], he was urged to recruit a . . .larger force of Californians to assist in the revolution and to prepare the way for annexation to the United States. . . . Crabb raised 100 men. . . . At the frontier the filibusters encountered unexpected opposition, offered by the very man who had urged their coming. . . partly by superior force and partly by treachery, he was induced to surrender. . . . The . . . prisoners were taken out in batches and butchered.

Caughey then concludes:

It appears that his expedition was more colonizing than filibustering in character, that his followers were high in reputability, that his coming to Sonora was by semi-official invitation, and the opposition to him was motivated by a desire on Pesquiera's [sic] part to cover up his own misdeeds.

Before Crabb left for Sonora, the press criticized him for organizing the Sonora-bound expedition. After his massacre, opinion changed overnight, and suddenly his fellow Californians and others throughout the nation revered him as a martyr. Apparently his massacre salved the conscience of North Americans for all their transgressions against Mexico.

The drama began when early in 1856 Crabb, his wife, and members of her family left California reportedly to visit Sonora to cement old friendships.[13] In Sonora the Crabbs met most of the prominent citizens, including Ignacio Pesqueira and Governor José de Aguilar. The exact particulars of this trip are not known, since the Crabb papers were burned in the San Francisco fire of 1906. An attempt, however, will be made to reconstruct the events. From Juan A. Robinson, long-time resident of Guaymas, merchant, and one-time United States Consul, we learn about the first phase of his trip:

There was a family in Hermosillo by the name of Ainsa [sic]. The father was from Manila, and married a Mexican lady, and they had a number of Daughters. They came up here to San Francisco . . . , and Crabb married one of the Daughters, named Filomena. Sometime after, Crabb took his wife and one of her unmarried sisters, and went down to Guaymas. . . and made a kind of exploring expedition, visiting the Chief places in Sonora, where the Ainsa family was well known.[14]

Meanwhile, an air of tension between Aguilar and Gándara threatened to erupt into hostilities. Crabb must have known this, especially since most of the Ainza acquaintances favored Aguilar. He capitalized on this tension, for Robinson observed:

According to the custom of the country, whenever a respectable family or a single stranger came into a town to stay a while, the chief residents of the place would call upon them as a matter of courtesy and friendship. But in this instance, immediately upon reaching Guaymas, contrary to the usual method of visiting, Crabb and his wife and her sister went around and visited all the prominent families of the place, some of whom were entire strangers to them. The two ladies were very intelligent and cultivated people, and Crabb was a man of elegant address and gentlemanly appearance and manners, and they went about in a stylish way, making their calls. I and my family were quite astonished at receiving a visit from them one morning. After they had finished at Guaymas, they went to Hermosillo, and visited in the same way there, without waiting to be called upon, and then to Ures, the capital of Sonora, and proceeded in the same manner there.

During his visit, Crabb purposely turned his conversations to the subject of factionalism within Sonora. Robinson clearly underscored Crabb's duplicity, stating:

At all of these places, the conversation between them and the people whom they visited frequently turned upon the government of the Mexican people; perhaps the subject was introduced by Crabb and the ladies. At all times there was more or less a complaint on the part of the people against their rules, some spirit of dissatisfaction and criticism, and whenever this was manifested, the Crabb party expressed their sympathy with the complainants, and improved such opportunities to foster and intensify this feeling against those in authority, magnifying the evils complained of, real or imaginary, and thus encouraging a spirit of discontent and sedition to the fullest extent within their power. They represented in glowing colors the advantages which the Government of the United States offered over that of Mexico, and the freedom and happiness of the people of that country in contrast to the inferior conditions of the people of Mexico, and presented and enforced the idea that the Government of the United States might come down and take a portion of Sonora, and assume control of that country.

Robinson concluded that Crabb, after sowing seeds of sedition and attempting to recruit allies, returned to San Francisco, where he circulated news of the Mexicans' dissatisfaction and claimed that even the governor wanted North Americans to take over the state. Therefore Robinson's first-hand observations support the viewpoint that Crabb's ultimate objective was the seizure of Sonora. It is interesting that Robinson does not believe that Pesqueira was involved with Crabb. Robinson was an American businessman and one-time consul of Guaymas, living in that port city.

Exactly when Crabb left Sonora is unknown, but he was in the state as late as May of 1856 in the company of his brother-in-law, Agustín Ainza. They took advantage of the plight of many Mexicans in California who wanted to return to Sonora to escape the Anglo-American persecution. Attempts to organize emigration clubs in California had become popular. Confusion and lack of communication between Sonorans and both Mexican officials and colonizing agents in California thwarted these efforts. Ainza and Crabb portrayed themselves as the champions of the emigrant.[15]

The two brothers-in-law met with Governor José de Aguilar, representing themselves as agents of Jesús Islas, the colonial agent for Sonoran returnees in California. They reported that five hundred colonists readied for the trip to Sonora. Islas asked payment of 13,000 pesos from Aguilar, a sum he claimed the firm Casa Ainsa Hermanos, of San Jose, California, had loaned Islas to outfit the party. Many problems plagued Aguilar at that time, and he could not advance Ainza any money. Nevertheless on May 30, the Minister of Fomento ordered the customshouse at Guaymas to pay Ainza one thousand pesos. It is also very probable that during this time Crabb made a deal with Pesqueira to help him in the event of a Gándara revolt. Pesqueira's position was weak, and it is conceivable he would make a deal with the devil.[16]

Meanwhile, Crabb returned to California. His brother-in-law's subsequent actions, however, clearly implicate Crabb in a conspiracy to overthrow the Sonora government. On June 7, Agustín Ainza left Ures for the villa de Altar to await the colonists from California. Within thirteen days, Ainza revealed his true intentions to state authorities. At the pueblos of Magdalena, Imurís, and San Ignacio, he spread seditious propaganda, confiding his intentions to establish a republic composed of Baja California, Sinaloa, and Sonora, which would later be turned over to the United States in all probability. To accomplish his ends, Ainza would have to solicit the support of Sonora's most influential citizens.[17] Success of his plan was contingent on the immediate arrival of five hundred California colonists, supplemented by the later arrival of North Americans and foreigners living in California.

José María Vélez Escalante Jr. accompanied Ainza. Local officials apprehended them and took them before the prefect of the district of Hermosillo, Colonel Jesús García Morales. The district court charged Ainza with high treason.

Manuel María Gándara took an interest in Ainza's arrest and attempted to have Ainza transferred to the jurisdiction of a special military judge named by him in order to learn the facts surrounding the case. Gándara was unsuccessful, for on July 15, the outbreak of the rebellion which led to Gándara's downfall ended these efforts.*

Sonora historian Laureano Calvo Berber concluded that it would be speculative to implicate any top Sonorans at this point. Yet, the actions of interim Governor Ignacio Pesqueira were questionable. In all probability, Pesqueira conspired with Crabb and Ainza, who apparently pledged their support in Gándara's overthrow. Pesqueira's subsequent actions resemble those of an individual acting covertly. These events began at the end of July, 1856, when state officials appointed Judge Francisco Islas to the case. He, in turn, ordered Ainza's conditional release pending further investigation.[18]

Pesqueira as governor was under obligation to assist the court in its attempt to assemble evidence; however, Pesqueira seems to have frustrated this process. A higher court, the Circuit Tribunal residing in Culiacán, Sinaloa, noted that Ainza's prosecution for complicity with the filibusters to invade Sonora had become stalemated for lack of evidence. The courts in Hermosillo had encountered difficulty in obtaining information from Magdalena, Imurís, and San Ignacio. As late as October 11, 1856, the Hermosillo court had not

---

*La Voz de Sonora, September 12 and 19, 1856. Although there is no proof that Manuel Gándara was involved with Crabb, newspaper accounts continually accused him of this. In "Filibusteros Americanos," La Voz de Sonora, March 6, 1857, the Church Party, which was made up of the followers of Gándara and the privileged classes of the state, was accused of cooperating with Crabb. However, these rumors were propagated by a Pesqueira-controlled press. As mentioned previously, there is a better possibility that Pesqueira, when attempting to overthrow Gándara, actually cooperated with Crabb.

received needed documents from the state government and thus solicited the documents. On November 20, state officials assured the courts that they would send them. By March 5, 1857, the court had still not received the needed information nor any further word from state officials relative to Ainza's case. On June 30, 1857, the court complained that it could not prosecute without the requested evidence.[19]

Calvo Berber alleged that an extensive search of the historical archives of Sonora at Hermosillo failed to uncover any documents relative to Agustín Ainza's case. In fairness to Pesqueira, however, it must be pointed out that Ainza was related by marriage to some of the most influential people in the state. He further had many prominent friends, which may have contributed to the state officials' reluctance to prosecute him.

The Ainza affair must have warned Crabb that Sonora public opinion would not tolerate outside intervention and that anyone connected with Ainza would be tainted with the filibuster's stigma. On August 15, 1856, *La Voz de Sonora* carried an article entitled *"El Filibustero,"* which leaves no doubt that Sonorans considered Ainza a traitor.

Moreoever, this affair revealed Ainza's true intention — secession from the Mexican union. In respect to secession, another article in *La Voz de Sonora*, July 4, 1856, entitled *"D. Agustín Ainza y Su Proyecto,"* by C. Ramírez, condemned Ainza's conspiracy, adding that it would be impossible to "separate one finger's breadth of land from the Mexican Union." Pesqueira must have had second thoughts about any deal he might have made with Crabb and might have informed Ainza's agents that the original commitment, if there had been any, could not be honored.* Pesqueira may have had many faults, but he could never be accused of fostering secession. In fact, Pesqueira always fought efforts to secede, both in Sonora and in neighboring Sinaloa.

By the fall of 1856, the outcome of the war favored Pesqueira in his plot to replace Gándara. By early 1857, Pesqueira had won. Pesqueira's position, however, remained tenuous, and any complicity with the filibusters would have been fatal. By this time, there could be no doubt that Ainza and Crabb did not intend to lead a peaceful colonizing party to Sonora.

Sonora's reaction to Ainza's arrest must have warned Crabb. The articles in *La Voz de Sonora* were definite in their condemnation of Ainza

---

*A typical letter that questions the relationship of Pesqueira and Gándara with Crabb was S. Llaguno to Jesús García Morales, Commandant of Baja California, San Francisco, February 15, 1857, in Fernando Pesqueira, "Documentos Para la Historia de Sonora," Primera Serie, Tomo VI. Llaguno warned García of the invasion of Crabb, telling García to alert Pesqueira. Llaguno warned of the possibility of subversion from within, and did not believe that Pesqueira was involved in the conspiracy or that he invited Crabb to Sonora. But Llaguno did suggest the possibility that some of Pesqueira's partisans, in an effort to get rid of Gándara, could have made such a deal. As to Gándara, Llaguno did not think that even Manuel Gándara would deliver the state to the filibusters.

and the projected expedition. Since this was the official mouthpiece of the state government, it should have been definite to Crabb that the governor would not and could not tolerate his coming to Sonora.

Documents in the Sonora historical archives indicate that the Sonorans closely followed the events in California and read its newspapers, which reported that Crabb's venture was more than a colonizing party. There are numerous clippings from San Francisco newspapers in the Archivo Histórico del Estado de Sonora, Hermosillo, Gaveta 3-2, 233, 3/6. A clipping from an undated issue of the *San Francisco Herald* draws an analogy between Crabb's expedition and Walker's to the point that Crabb left San Francisco with fifty-six men as Walker had when the latter left for Nicaragua. Another clipping from the *Alta California* called Crabb a filibuster, and said that his expedition would only delay the eventual acquisition of this territory. These and other articles appeared translated into Spanish. An article in the San Francisco *Evening Bulletin*, March 2, 1857, stated that Crabb was leaving California to join Gándara, and drew a parallel between Crabb and Walker. Headlines in the San Francisco *Evening Bulletin*, March 13 and 20, 1857, read: "Filibusterism Ogling Sonora" and "Sonora Filibusters." Informed citizens knew that Crabb would depart for Sonora leading a filibustering expedition. In addition, many letters from former Sonorans to relatives told about the invasion.

Crabb, in a letter dated December 9, 1856, wrote: "Suffice to say, that the people of Sonora desire to be independent of Mexico and have called upon me for assistance, and I intend to render that assistance in the most effective manner."[20] In view of these facts, there can be no doubt as to the status of Crabb's expedition.

What course of action Pesqueira would take could also be predicted. Crabb must have known about Governor Pesqueira's circular to the people of Sonora notifying them that the military commander at Mazatlán had warned him about an invasion from California. In it, Pesqueira reaffirmed his intention to defend Sonora. Thus, Sonorans had notified Crabb that all previous agreements no longer had validity.[21]

CRABB AND HIS ARMY

In California, meanwhile, Crabb ignored these danger signals and prepared to return to Sonora. He left San Francisco on January 21, 1857, with a contingent of volunteers. The group landed in San Pedro, California, assembling in El Monte, which at that time formed the only Anglo-American town in predominantly Spanish-speaking southern California.[22] Soon afterwards Crabb left California, organizing his party into military companies A, B, and C, with a full complement of officers and men. They marched overland to northwestern Sonora. At Sonoita, Sonora, the prefect told them to return to the United States and indicated Sonorans' readiness to resist Crabb's entry.

On March 26, 1857, Henry Crabb wrote an insolent letter to José María Redondo, prefect of the district of Altar:

In conformance with the laws of Colonization of Mexico, and because of positive invitations of some of the most prominent citizens of Sonora, I have crossed into your state with one hundred companions and the vanguard of nine hundred more, with the hope of finding among you a place to make our homes. I have not come with the intention of offending anyone; I did not come because of private nor public intrigue. Since my arrival at this place I have given no indication of sinister plans, but on the contrary, I have only made friendly propositions. It is true that I am well supplied with arms and munitions, but you know very well that it is not the custom in America or any other civilized population to travel without arms; in addition, remember that we have had to travel across regions infested with Apaches; and because of these circumstances I imagine, to my surprise, you are preparing and organizing a force to exterminate me with my companions. I am well informed that you have given an order to poison the wells and that you are taking more vile and cowardly measures against us.

But beware, Sir, because if we suffer for any reason, vengeance will fall upon your head and those who assist you. I never would have imagined you to be so degraded that you would put such extreme measures into effect! I know also that you intend to set our good friends the Papagoes against us, but it is very probable, because of the position I am in, that this effort will be in vain. I have come to your country because I have the right to come and spread ideas of civilization. I have come, which I can completely prove, expecting to be received with open arms, but today, I believe that I am going to find death at the hands of a savage enemy. But before my companions who find themselves at my side and those who are to come, I protest against this act. Finally, you should realize and have it known, that if blood is spilt, this will fall upon your head and not on mine. Anyway, you should guard yourself against continuing with hostilities: for my part, I immediately continue my march to where I have for sometime planned to go. I am the leader and it is my intent to work in accordance with the natural laws of survival.

Meanwhile, we will see each other in Altar, I remain your obedient servant.

Henry A. Crabb [23]

Redondo replied within two days, stating he would send Crabb's letter to the governor, but in the meantime, Crabb must proceed no further or he would be met with resistance.[24] On March 30 Pesqueira received the letter and reacted immediately. He activated the national guard, issuing instructions to resist the invaders, and published a broadside to acquaint the public:

Free Sonorans! To arms all!!!

The hour has sounded which I lately told you, about which you would have to prepare for the bloody struggle you are about to enter upon. In that arrogant letter you have just heard a most explicit declaration of war was made by the chief of invaders. What reply does it merit? That we march to meet him. Let us fly then, with all the fury of hearts intolerant of oppression, to chastise the savage filibuster who has dared, in unhappy hour, to tread our national soil and to provoke, insensate! our rage. Show no mercy, no generous sentiments toward these hounds.

Let them die like wild beasts who, daring to trample under foot the law of nations, the right of states, and all social institutions, dare to invoke the law of nature as their only guide, and to appeal to brute force alone.

Sonorans, let our conciliation become sincere in a common hatred of this accursed horde of pirates, destitute of country, religion, or honor.

Let the tri-colored ribbon, sublime creation of the genius of Iguala, be our only distinctive mark, to protect us from the enemy's bullets as well as from humiliation and affront. Upon it let us write the beautiful words "Liberty or Death" and henceforth it shall bear for us one more sentiment, the powerful, invincible bond that now united the two parties of our state lately divided by civil war.

We shall soon return covered with glory, having forever secured the welfare of Sonora, and having, in defiance of tyranny, established in indelible characters this principle: the people who want liberty will have it.

Meanwhile, citizens, relieve your hearts by giving free scope to the enthusiasm that oppresses them.

Viva Mexico! Death to the Filibusters.[25]

Crabb did not falter in the face of opposition; he pressed forward to Caborca, south of Sonoita.[26] Crabb fully expected reinforcements to reach him any day. His agents recruited men in California and the Santa Cruz Valley of southern Arizona. Crabb departed from Sonoita with a vanguard party of sixty-nine men, leaving twenty at the pueblo to follow within a few days.

On the eleventh of April, at eleven in the morning, Crabb's party arrived at Caborca. He entered the town, proceeding slowly; however, once inside the pueblo, Mexican troops prepared to ambush Crabb's party. After seven days of bitter fighting, Crabb and his survivors surrendered. The Mexican's treatment of the party appears extremely harsh in contrast to that meted out to previous filibusters: Sonorans tried and executed the survivors. They severed Crabb's head from his body and exhibited it to the crowd. Some authorities report that Sonorans then preserved Crabb's head in alcohol. An eye witness alleged that officials left the corpses of Crabb's men for the hogs and coyotes to gnaw at, and after several days, they dumped them into a trench.

Accounts of the execution differ according to the sources consulted. Mexican sources play down the execution, while North American historians overplay it. The latter account is generally based on the word of the expedition's sole survivor, Charles Evans, a boy of sixteen whom Pesqueira spared because of his youth. Sixteen of the twenty men Crabb had left behind at Sonoita departed for Caborca. Sonorans intercepted them outside Caborca, where they surrendered. The prisoners were taken to Caborca, where they were tried and executed.

AFTER THE CRABB MASSACRE

The violence of the Crabb execution cannot be condoned, but it can be understood. Fed up with the invasions of the filibusters, the Sonorans moved to stop them.[27] After the Crabb incident, major filibustering threats from California ceased.

The incident increased bitterness between North Americans and Sonorans.* For a time, rumors that there would be another expedition to avenge Crabb persisted. The United States Minister to Mexico, John Forsyth, vigorously protested the action to the Mexican government; and the President of the United States sent a report to Congress reviewing the facts of the case. North Americans and Mexicans along the border refought the Crabb massacre: to the Anglos, Crabb became a martyr; Sonorans branded him a pirate.[28]

According to a contemporary Arizonan, Charles Poston, the mines of southern Arizona ground to a standstill as the result of the Crabb controversy. Sonoran miners and laborers for a time abandoned their work, paralyzing business in southern Arizona. The importance of Mexican labor is clearly documented by Joseph Park of the University of Arizona, who contends in his "History of Mexican Labor" that without the labor of the Mexican, Arizona's growth would have been impossible. The dependence on this labor played a major part in cooling North American tempers in Arizona.

The Crabb incident became so intense that it created a cleavage between many friends. The following exchange of letters between two former friends dramatically reflects the position of both peoples, the North American and the Sonoran† :

Letter of Hernández, the Executioner
Dr. Hammond,

I have not had time to answer your letter. I have received few of the medicine you send me, and am much obliged, to you for so doing. I spose you are very well Know of your Americans got whip here With us: Dr the Americans came here with a great hostile indignation, in a nomber of 100 men or 119, they fought desperately, but in vain our nomber was 150 men in all, three officers, Rodriguez, Ganilendo and me. Rodriguez was kill by Crabb, but I had the opportunity to cut Crabb's head off and I have got it in a preserve to remember the piratcle action of Crabbism. Then after a days fight, los on each side the filibusters few of them surrender a discretion, and

---

*San Francisco Bulletin, May 27, 1857, reported the Crabb saga. This account recorded that he was surrounded by fifteen hundred men. A more sobering account was in a letter to the editor a week earlier (May 22), by a W.W.D., who objected to the efforts of the California press to build up sympathy for Crabb. He stated that Crabb was clearly a filibuster, and asked why there was no sympathy for families of the two hundred patriots who were reported to have been killed by Crabb and his army.

†Spelling errors are those in the original.

in a few hours of coort martial I was commissioned with my company to have all shot, which I did. Dr, we Mexicans do not inten to fight like in the past. Good many of the American population has treat us badly, and we intent to do the same in war. I have no duet you may be sorry of your country men, but as I think you are gentlemen you cannot never have the Idea of protecting Robbers. Dr, stay always at home, never come to forren contray, we do not like Yankees no more on account of their bad action. I have plenty medicine Now but filibusters Brought me all I want, therefore I am obliged for your comedation. Mr. Crabb and fifteen others cry like children before they were condem to be shot – great great disgrace for you Americans. Yankee of no kind has no show now here.

Yours,
J.S. Hernández

Hammond replied from Fort Yuma:

We have reliable information that your force consisted of between 300 and 400 men, or more; also, from an eye witness, that the men whom you butchered after they surrendered, died bravely. So the two items in your letter with regard to these points I consider totally false.

Hoping that your *bravely* earned medicines may do you much good, I remain,

Geo. Hammond, M.D.

P.S. I have the charity to think that since you have written to me in English, you do not know what you say; for I cannot believe that a man who pretends to have the sentiments of a gentleman could write so barbarous a letter as yours.

G.H. [29]

The routing of Crabb insured Ignacio Pesqueira's status as Sonora's defender. Forbes, p. 43, after examining mostly American sources, concluded:

Crabb was a restless adventurer visionary, attracted by an opportunity for intrigue that proved too deep for him, leading him and his duped followers into a trap from which there was no escape. The severity with which these transgressors against the peace of a neighboring state were treated proved discouraging to similar undertakings, and this was the last of the southwestern filibustering expeditions.

Pesqueira's vigorous actions against the filibusters in immediately activating the national guard and his mobilization of the Sonorans made him a patriot. He appeared to be the man of action for whose leadership Sonorans had been waiting, for he had personally prepared to head the army in the event others invaded the state. Sonorans, who for a long time had resented the humiliation they suffered at the hands of North Americans, finally had a source of pride. They were united in their belief that what they had done was right.

CHAPTER 4

The Man on Horseback

In an ambiance of peace and pride in their state, Sonorans prepared for elections in accordance with the Constitution of 1857. Ignacio Pesqueira, as expected, ran for the governorship. On May 5, 1857, he returned the government to José de Aguilar, retiring to his hacienda at "Las Delicias" in the district of Arizpe, and waited for his election. Sonorans gave Pesqueira an overwhelming vote of confidence. On August 15, the constitutionally elected legislature convened and confirmed Pesqueira's election as well as that of his substitute governor, Miguel Urrea from Alamos. Urrea's financial aid had been essential to Pesqueira's rise.[1]

Ignacio Pesqueira's inauguration on August 28 signalled rebellion. Most Sonora Indians had remained loyal to Manuel Gándara, and approximately one hundred and fifty at Onavas and Tónichi went on the warpath, calling for the return of Don Manuel. The revolt was not serious, and on November 22, state forces defeated the rebels, driving them into the Yaqui River Valley, where they sought the protection of the Yaqui Indians.[2]

Meanwhile, Jesús Gándara actively stirred discontent among the Yaqui. Sonora authorities countered the threat by sending Colonel Antonio Campuzano of Guaymas to the Yaqui Valley with about three hundred men. At Pitaya, during the first days of December, a force of Indians intercepted and defeated Campuzano. Campuzano's rout signalled an all-out Gandarista uprising in the leading cities and pueblos. Soon Yaqui raids expanded, threatening the port of Guaymas itself. Although for a time the situation appeared serious, the state militia turned back the Yaqui on December 17. In Ures, Jesús Gándara remained active and continued attacking the Pesqueiristas.[3]

Jesús Gándara led the revolution, acting as field commander and the rallying force behind the Gandaristas. He more than compensated for his brother's apparent battle-shyness. When news of the Plan of Tacubaya reached Sonora during the last part of December, 1857, Jesús Gándara immediately seconded the conservative cause.[4] His activity centered around Ures, where he defeated government forces near Santiago; Gándara then turned on Ures, attacking the plaza on December 30 and 31, and again on New Year's Day.

Many expected the intervention of General José María Yáñez, the military commander of the Federal Army of the West. Jesús Gándara circulated rumors to this effect. In reply to persistent rumors, Yáñez, in a letter dated October 20, 1857, denied his intention to intervene in Sonora's affairs. But, after the Plan of Tacubaya, Sonorans braced themselves for the worst.[5]

After the first of the year, Jesús Gándara increased his attacks, forcing Pesqueira to take to the field. Pesqueira inspired government partisans, and on January 8, 1858, at El Bajadero, he routed Jesús Gándara's army, after a difficult battle in which Pesqueira reportedly fought bravely.[6] This battle, however, did not break Gandarista resistance. Their allies, the Yaqui, marauded in the valley around Guaymas, and although government forces under Captain Nemesio Merino dispersed them on February 1, they continued their resistance.

Jesús Gándara continued operations in the districts of Ures and Sahuaripa. Governor Pesqueira asked the legislature for extraordinary powers to end the rebellion. The legislature granted these powers, whereupon the governor personally led a large army against the Indians and Jesús Gándara.

Pesqueira sought out the enemy, and on the twenty-fourth met the rebels under Gándara at El Saucito near the pueblo of Bacanora. Each side numbered about seven hundred men. After a pitched battle, Pesqueira's army defeated the Gandaristas, who lost more than a battle; their leader Jesús Gándara was mortally wounded.[7]

The end of the Gandarista revolt did not quell the Yaqui and the Mayo, who remained on the warpath, routing a garrison near Santa Cruz. Pesqueira sent Jesús García Morales to sweep the Yaqui Valley and Rafael Corella to patrol the Mayo River Valley; both commanders had large forces. Many skirmishes followed and, while state troopers won most of them, the Indians refused to submit. This set the stage for Pesqueira to make another dramatic entrance in which he marched to the aid of his compatriots. Again the additional forces and Pesqueira's stepping up of operations overwhelmed the Indians.* By May of 1858, the Sonora militia had almost completely demoralized the Mayo and Yaqui. Peace finally settled over Sonora.[8]

In retrospect, it is tempting to give Pesqueira too much credit for his role in the subduing of the Indian rebels; contemporaries did not recognize him as a superior military planner. They considered García Morales, for example, a better military strategist than Pesqueira, for García Morales in reality led Pesqueira's most important campaigns. Pesqueira, however, inspired his soldiers, possessing undefinable charisma. His entrances gave the soldiers a well-timed lift and demoralized the already beaten opponent.

In June, 1858, Pesqueira addressed Sonorans. He sought to permanently subdue the Yaqui Valley. The governor issued standing orders stating

---

*Fernando Pesqueira, ed., "Documentos para la Historia de Sonora," Cuarta Serie, Tomo II, typewritten copy in the Biblioteca y Museo de Sonora, Hermosillo, Sonora. On May 26, 1858, Pesqueira complained that the war was a hangover of the Gandarista Revolt of 1856.

the Yaqui could not carry arms without a license, they must bank their guns in the villages, and these armaments would be placed under proper supervision. Violation of these orders would be considered a crime, punishable by imprisonment and hard labor.[9] The governor took such measures because he felt that there could be no peace in Sonora without total control of Yaqui Indians. He also wanted to exploit the rich lands of the Yaqui and Mayo valleys, and thus repay his political debt to the powerful Alameño merchants who coveted these rich valleys.

Meanwhile, rumors had reached Sonora that President Comonfort planned to sell Sonora as a means of settling the nation's financial responsibilities. Pesqueira vigorously protested any possible sale of Sonora, proclaiming he would defend the state's integrity. To this end, on October 9, 1857, the governor recommended to the state legislature that the deputies draft a letter to the Juárez government, informing it that Sonora would resist segregation from the Mexican nation.[10]

The arrogance of California newspapers further inflamed Sonorans, for they urged the immediate annexation of Sonora. On July 30, 1858, *La Voz de Sonora* vehemently protested the California periodicals, proclaiming *"No queremos ser americanos."* (We do not want to be Americans.)[11]

By the time the War of Reform raged in the rest of the nation, hostilities within Sonora drew to an end. The Gandaristas' revolt had begun before the Plan of Tacubaya, and by the time they seconded the proclamation, the Pesqueira forces had almost won. Throughout the War of Reform, Sonora stood away from the centers of agitation so as not to become embroiled in it. Shielded by its natural boundaries, Sonora could have used this isolation as a safeguard and refrained from the war. The state could have consolidated its resources. An ambitious governor, however, was piloting the ship of state.

THE WAR OF REFORM: THE MEXICAN NATION

During the early years of the republic, Mexico's feudal economy permitted domination by special interest groups. The War of Independence had failed to destroy this feudalism, merely substituting one class for another, with the *criollo* (full-blooded Spaniard born in America) assuming the role of the *peninsulare* (Spaniard born in Spain). To rid itself of feudalism, Mexico had to revolutionize those institutions and customs that prevented political, social, and economic participation of a wider range of people. This break could be accomplished only by a War of Reform.

The Constitution of 1857 had struck at some of the nation's most powerful institutions, for the framers were intent upon ending the special privileges enjoyed by the hacienda owners, the church, and the military, which hampered commercial and business progress in Mexico. The constitution was the end product of the Plan of Ayutla, which had begun with the revolt against Antonio López de Santa Anna in February, 1854. The revolt had succeeded by August, 1854, when Santa Anna resigned. Under the leadership of middle-class liberals, the assault against special privilege began: in November, 1855, the *Ley Juárez* suppressed all special courts except ecclesiastical and military, denying however even these jurisdictions over civil matters. The church interpreted this as an attack and raised the cry " *¡Religion y fueras!* " (Religion and privilege!). In June, 1856, the *Ley Lerdo* again attempted to limit the power of the church by prohibiting civil or religious corporations from holding real estate not directly used for religious worship. It is estimated that the church at that time held over half the land of Mexico. Other laws were passed against the church: the liberals took cemeteries out of its control, regulated the fees of baptisms and marriages, and limited the clergy's political activity. The federal Constitution of 1857 climaxed these acts of reform, guaranteeing personal liberties, abolishing all special courts and monopolies, and refusing to recognize the Catholic Church as the state religion.

Predictably, special interest groups reacted violently to such an abrupt break with the past. In the spring of 1857, the constitution became law, with Ignacio Comonfort taking the presidential oath of office. Many of the clergy declared an informal war, closing the churches and barring Comonfort and his cabinet from the sacraments. These actions naturally unsettled many Mexicans.

President Comonfort moved to conciliate both reformers and clericals. In the autumn of 1857, Comonfort attempted to placate the conservatives, requesting Congress to suspend civil guarantees and revise the entire Constitution of 1857. A liberal- and moderate-dominated congress suspected that Comonfort had sold out to the conservatives and refused his request. On December 17, 1857, Félix Zuloaga, commander at Tacubaya, seized that city and announced the Plan of Tacubaya. This proclamation called for a Comonfort dictatorship and another constitutional convention.

Comonfort again vacillated and yielded to the conservatives. The Archbishop of Mexico and many of the clergy seconded the plan, with many of the faithful following. At Querétaro, seventy congressmen declared their faith in principles of the constitution and prepared to defend it. This assembly accused Comonfort of breaking the constitutional oath, and the deputies declared Benito Juárez, Chief Justice of the Supreme Court and consequently under the Mexican constitution the successor to the president, the President of Mexico. Comonfort, not in accord, jailed Juárez.

Shortly thereafter, Comonfort changed his mind and released Juárez; Comonfort then left the country. Juárez, defender of the Constitution of 1857, was now President of Mexico.

Thus began the War of the Reform. Juaristas centered themselves around Veracruz, as this port brought in the only customs taxes. The conservatives centered their base of operation around México D.F. The federal government abandoned the individual states to fend for themselves — the defenders of the constitution versus the defenders of the faith. It also became a war between the local strong men in the several Mexican states who either supported the constitution or defended the privileges of the church. The War of Reform lasted until January 11, 1861, at which time Juárez made his entrance into México D.F.[12]

GOVERNOR PESQUEIRA
AND THE WAR OF REFORM

In Sonora Pesqueira, championing the cause of constitutionalism, prepared to defend his state against the possible threats of the conservatives. On March 23, 1858, the legislature authorized Pesqueira to act as deemed necessary — independent of the federal government if need be. On July 6, he received extraordinary powers from the legislature.[13] The governor consolidated affairs within Sonora; he reorganized Sonora's administration, strengthened the military, and shored up frontier defenses. Pesqueira realized that his position must be secure before he could involve himself beyond the borders of Sonora.

The church remained a source of danger during this period. It had many defenders in Sonora, as in the rest of the nation. Most volatile were the Indians, who remained fanatically religious, and would defend the clergy when incited by them. The role the church actually played is open to conjecture as sources are contradictory. An article appeared on July 16, 1858, in *La Voz de Sonora*, which denied reports in a California newspaper that the church remained a power in the state.[14] To the contrary, however, there is proof that Sonora's higher clergy enjoyed considerable prestige, often effectively working against reforms. Leaflets were circulated accusing Pesqueira of conspiring with William Walker.* But there is no evidence that the church itself led any vehement campaign against the liberal government during the first days of the War of Reform.

A review of materials reveals that anticlericalism did not reach the same degree of bitterness in Sonora as in the rest of the nation. In fact, there is little evidence that Pesqueira directly participated in attacks on the clergy. When the Archbishop of Sonora went on an inspection tour in late 1858,

---

La Estrella de Occidente, August 12, 1859. Note the change of name of the official newspaper of the state of Sonora from *La Voz de Sonora* to *La Estrella de Occidente*. This is probably an indication of Pesqueira's expanding perspective.

Pesqueira instructed the prefects to insure the Archbishop's personal security and bade him "Godspeed."[15]

This does not imply that no friction existed between government and clergy. At the time of independence from Spain, the clergy had been very powerful.[16] It remained a force to be reckoned with, and as the war dragged on, the clergy's opposition grew. Carlota Miles, in her book, *Almada of Alamos*, describes the panic of many Sonorans during aurora borealis (the time when the midnight sun lit the skies in September 1859, giving the entire city a ghostlike atmosphere). Many people believed that it was a sign from heaven. Miles also describes the doleful ringing of the bells, and the priests and acolytes marching in procession. On the sixteenth of September, this activity stopped with the priests refusing to celebrate the *Te Deum* masses traditional with national independence. Anticipating persecution, they went into hiding.

The war increased the existing bitterness between factions. Sonorans were Catholics and, like the rest of Mexico, their loyalties were split. As aforementioned, the extent of the church's influence is open to conjecture. United States consular records at Guaymas state that Consul Lewis Dent believed Pesqueira's hold over the people was precarious since most of them belonged to the church or conservative party.[17] Other accounts do not substantiate Dent's observation. If the church party had had more power, they probably would have openly revolted against the Pesqueira government, however, no documentation exists of a revolt.

Liberals in other states such as Sinaloa did not enjoy such relatively cordial relations with the clergy. The strongly anticlerical Sinaloan governor, Placido Vega, exiled Archbishop José de Jesús Loza from Sinaloa in December, 1859. Loza went to Sonora, but returned in January of 1860, whereupon Vega attempted to capture and imprison him. Loza escaped again to Sonora but this time Igancio Pesqueira, reportedly on the advice of others, arrested Loza and sent him back to Culiacán, the capital of Sinaloa.[18]

The conservative threat predictably did not come from within Sonora, but from its neighbor to the south. Sinaloa was a hotbed of reactionaries, and, as expected, on˙ January 1, 1858, conservatives revolted against the Reform government. Sinaloan commanding general Pedro Espejo affiliated himself with the Plan of Tacubaya and with the commander of the Army of the West, General José María Yáñez; the two became the overall conservative leaders.[19] In turn, they threatened Sonora's peace.*

---

*Manual María Gándara to General D. Luis G. Osolla, Mazatlán, March 29, 1858, *La Voz de Sonora*, August 20, 1858. Shortly after this time, Gándara arrived in Mazatlán where he was received by Yáñez. He wrote a letter to a friend stating that he had been in Mazatlán for ten days, and that he had heard about the death of his brother Jesús at the hands of the treacherous Pesqueira. He had also heard that Pesqueira had seven hundred men, versus his brother's two hundred partisans. Gándara praised the Plan of Tacubaya and stated that his brother Jesús had seconded it immediately.

Ignacio Pesqueira undoubtedly watched the events in Sinaloa with interest. He proceeded cautiously, however, and even when liberals under Placido Vega denounced the Plan of Tacubaya at the Villa Fuerte on August 17, 1858, preparing to fight, Pesqueira remained quiet. Vega's document, written to induce Pesqueira to intervene, included an offer to command Sinaloa's liberal forces, which the governor refused. Instead, he sent his trusted aide, Colonel Jesús García Morales, to represent Sonora.[20]

On October 6, 1858, García Morales left Alamos for Sinaloa with four hundred men. The Sonorans met with immediate success; twenty-three days later, they defeated the conservative army at La Noria. On the first of November, the Sonorans again defeated the rebels at Culiacán. At this battle, conservatives wounded García Morales, who by this time had won the esteem of the Sinaloans. They gave him a hero's welcome when he entered Culiacán. Meanwhile Pesqueira supplied the liberals in Sinaloa with men, arms, and supplies.[21]

In Sonora, Pesqueira took measures to strengthen his position, for he could not leave the state at the mercy of the Yaqui and Mayo.[22] In the latter part of the year, Pesqueira left for Alamos, preparing to invade Sinaloa. In retrospect, Pesqueira acted prematurely, for as later eruptions will prove, dissident elements within Sonora had not been brought under control. At the time of his departure for Sinaloa, many observers concluded that Pesqueira put personal glory before the welfare of the state. Sonora needed peace and tranquility. A war in Sinaloa would leave the frontier forces weakened; money needed to reconstruct the state would be spent outside its borders. Pesqueira, however, "charged to the sound of the guns," again playing the man on horseback.

PESQUEIRA LEAVES FOR ALAMOS

Pesqueira arrived in Alamos in the latter part of 1858 and intended to remain for a few days before leaving for Sinaloa. He probably was aware of the opposition to his projected venture and, therefore, one of his objectives must have been political conciliation. The Alameños idolized him; after all, under the sponsorship of this city, he had overthrown Gándara. The people hoped he would bring a break with the past and provide the ambiance for economic growth.

The population of Alamos numbered about six thousand inhabitants. Located a short distance from the foothills of the Sierra Tarahumara in the southernmost portion of Sonora, it was considered by many to be Sonora's most powerful city. Formerly one of the state's richest mining centers, Alamos, in its decline, continued to play an important role in the politics between Sonora and Sinaloa.[23]

The colonial architecture of the buildings — many constructed of stone — reflected the former wealth of Alamos. The city was renown for cleanliness and beauty, and particularly the grandeur of its palm tree plaza. From Europe and other parts of the Americas, Alameños imported trees — especially impressive in an arid and treeless state.[24] The isolation of Alamos, however, strangled its potential. The Mayo and the Yaqui often impeded communication with the interior, and the roads were infested with highwaymen. These dangers made transportation of the city's bullion hazardous.

Alamos, a city jealous of its memories, dreamed of recapturing its past. Proud, beautiful, and powerful, it still exerted considerable influence. Pesqueira knew its history and undoubtedly was grateful to the Alameños. In great part, he owed his political survival to the townspeople.

Alamos welcomed Pesqueira in a gay and hospitable mood: "They received him with triumphal arches, flowers, parades, speeches, banquets and balls, and seated him under a canopy decorated with white clouds." Poor and rich alike came to pay tribute to Sonora's hero, the conqueror of Gándara and Crabb. They courted him, playing "La Indita," which became the military march for Pesqueira's soldiers. Its lyrics were:

> *Indita, que haremos ahora,*
> *nos hallaron platicando,*
> *diles que tu me llamaste,*
> *y yo te estaba cantando.*
> *Para cantar esta Indita*
> *se necesita talento,*
> *asi la canto Pesqueira*
> *cuando iba pa tierra adentro.* *

> Little Indian, what shall we do now,
> they found us chatting,
> tell them that you called me,
> And I was singing for you.
> To sing for this little Indian
> takes talent.
> Thus sang for her Pesqueira
> when he went into the interior.

Fun-loving Pesqueira enjoyed the attention; basking in glory he is reported to have remarked: " *¡Ojalá no se huberia nunca borrado del corazón entusiasta de aquellos habitantes!* " (I hope the enthusiasm of those inhabitants will never end!)[25]

The Alameños' festive mood soon changed when Pesqueira told the leading citizens that he planned to depart for Sinaloa and entrust the state government to Miguel Urrea. Although Pesqueira's most influential Alameño

---

*Miles, p. 21. Both Spanish and English are direct quotations.

friends backed Urrea, the decision met with definite resistance and Urrea refused the office.[26] However, Pesqueira did not waver.

The Alameños resented Pesqueira's arbitrary decision.* They believed that Sonora had sufficient problems without Pesqueira becoming involved in Sinaloa's plight. This objection, although partially based on the rivalry between the two states, was primarily one of rational self-interest. The menace of the Gandaristas had not disappeared, the Apache still threatened to burn the entire state, and, furthermore, Alamos, one of Sonora's richest cities, would be taxed heavily to finance Pesqueira's Sinaloa venture. To Alameños, Pesqueira's actions appeared designed solely to further his own career.[27]

Many Sonora cities and pueblos expressed similar disapproval. There is no record of Pesqueira's reaction, although he did attempt to placate Alamos by opening the port of Santa Cruz on the Mayo River, not far from Alamos. He noted the hazards of shipping through Guaymas and Mazatlán. Moreover, he projected colonies in both the Mayo and Yaqui river valleys. The administration urged Ures, Hermosillo, and Guaymas to contribute to this venture.[28]

In the last analysis, however, Pesqueira did as he pleased. He named his secretary and member of the legislature, Manuel Monteverde, to administer the state while he would be away. On December 18, 1858, Pesqueira marched from Alamos toward Mazatlán.[29]

Sinaloa and Sonora had had a common history until their separation in 1831.[30] This history joined the politics of the two states, and, although rivalries persisted, they had many interests in common.

Sinaloa, unlike Sonora, is not isolated from the rest of the nation; it has access to the sea and is bordered by Chihuahua, Durango, and Nayarit. Consequently, Sinaloa was closer to the center of the Reform movement — Jalisco — and the frequent revolutions initiated in that state affected Sinaloa; in turn, Sinaloa could not help but affect Sonora.[31]

With the church party much stronger in Sinaloa, the liberal-conservative ferment reached greater proportions than in Sonora. Culiacán, with an estimated population of eleven thousand, housed the episcopal seat.[32] Mazatlán, the other city of note in Sinaloa, had an important sea port, and its customshouse attracted revolutionary groups.

As has been stated, José María Yáñez headed the conservative forces. An old warrior familiar to Sonorans, Yáñez had been the state's military

---

*Fernando Pesqueira, "Documentos para la Historia de Sonora," Tercera Serie, Tomo IX. Note that in May of that same year Ignacio Pesqueira had appealed for voluntary contributions in the war against the Apache. In his own words, the war had been neglected and he needed money to prosecute it more actively. Pesqueira therefore altered his plans to use the much-needed money both in and out of state.

commander and had gained fame as the hero of Guaymas for his defeat of Count Gaston de Raousset de Boulbon in 1854. Also present was Pedro Espejo, a veteran soldier who had participated in the Apache wars and had been governor and military commander of Sonora under General Santa Anna. Manuel Gándara had also joined Yáñez, and, together with other leaders of the Plan of Tacubaya at the port of Mazatlán, prepared to defend Sinaloa against the Sonora Pesqueiristas.[33]

The Pesqueiristas recognized as their main ally Colonel Plácido Vega, the personable, likable, but erratic leader of the liberals in Sinaloa. Often arbitrary, spurning criticism, and very ambitious, Vega became quite friendly toward Pesqueira.[34]

On December 18, 1858, Pesqueira left for Mazatlán, Sinaloa's principal city and port,* arriving at its outskirts on January 4, 1859, with about five hundred men. The liberals rejoiced, recognizing Pesqueira as Sinaloa's provisional governor and military commander. Further, the Juarista government made him military commander of the armies of Sonora, Sinaloa, and Baja California. Pesqueira next attempted to lay siege to Mazatlán; failing, he fell back because, in his own words, he lacked "the necessary elements of war."[35]

Pesqueira's failure, however, must be considered a setback rather than a defeat. Pesqueira retreated to Cosala where two thousand men and twenty pieces of artillery comprised the nucleus of his force. Aware that he would have to be well prepared to capture the city, he waited for more supplies, training his men and consolidating his forces.[36]

While in Cosala, Governor Pesqueira suffered another near-setback. He learned of President James Buchanan's 1858 message to the Congress of the United States asking permission to enter Chihuahua and Sonora under the pretext of pursuing the Apache war more effectively. Pesqueira opposed any encroachments on Sonora territory and sent a strongly worded directive to the Sonora prefects. He commanded the prefects to prepare for a Yanqui invasion. Activating more state militia, Pesqueira prepared to return to Sonora in the event of gringo ingression. Fortunately, the North Americans did not violate Sonora; however, their attempt only made the U.S. intentions more apparent. On March 10, reinforcements from Durango strengthened Pesqueira's forces, hastening his decision to attack Mazatlán again; the liberal forces laid siege to the port on the third of the following month.[37] After a

---

*Archivo Histórico del Estado de Sonora, Hermosillo, Gaveta 14-3, 330. The unreasonable attitude of Pesqueira in pursuing the war in Sinaloa is illustrated in a letter dated December 10, 1858, to the Commander of the frontier forces; in this letter written before leaving for Sinaloa, Pesqueira indicated that he feared the invasion of filibusters. On December 13, 1858, from Alamos, he again alerted this commander to the possibility of filibusters.

bloody battle, conservative forces fled. Advancing liberal forces almost captured some of the top conservative leaders who had escaped, seeking refuge on the *Alarm*, a British frigate anchored in the harbor. Generals Pedro Espejo, José Yáñez, and Manuel María Gándara numbered among the leaders. Their escape minimized Pesqueira's moment of glory, but nevertheless, this must have been his finest hour. Pesqueira's popularity zoomed to its zenith, volunteers rallied around him, and his numbers increased to more than three thousand men.

In Mazatlán, Pesqueira learned of the Pablo Lagarma plot — a plan to eliminate Pesqueira and other liberal leaders — and was successful in suffocating the conspiracy in its infancy. Pesqueira next projected a campaign into Jalisco. He thought that this venture would, in all probability, make him one of the foremost defenders of the constitution and enhance his national reputation. The threat of civil war in Sonora, however, ended Pesqueira's plans for a triumphant march into the interior.[38]

The Opata, under Juan and Refugio Tánori, sided with Manuel Gándara and the Apache continued their marauding; therefore, Pesqueira decided to return to Sonora and declared Plácido Vega provisional governor of Sinaloa.* Pesqueira left for Guaymas aboard the American ship *Santa Cruz* on June 4, arriving in Guaymas on the fifteenth. On the twenty-sixth, he marched to Hermosillo where the citizens accorded him a hero's welcome. Once in Sonora, he began the task of reorganizing the government. He pursued a strict policy, blaming the new upheavals on his laxness in dealing with the Gandaristas in 1856.[39]

Pesqueira controlled the Gandaristas without much difficulty for their support had grown thin. The Indians, however, presented a more serious threat as they continued to ravage the state. Pesqueira pressed a relentless war against the Indians on the southern and northern frontiers in an attempt to end hostilities.

During this war, Pesqueira sent the trusted García Morales with five hundred men and five pieces of artillery to pursue the Yaqui and the Mayo. This show of strength forced them into their valleys, but it did not end the threat. The Yaqui and the Mayo did not sue for peace until December, 1859.[40] The Apache campaign also raged, continuing throughout the Pesqueira years. Nevertheless, relative peace returned to the state, with internal unrest reaching a manageable level.

At this point, Pesqueira could have returned to private life with the appreciation of most Sonorans. He had returned from Sinaloa covered with

---

*Ignacio Pesqueira to Sinaloenses, Mazatlán, June 4, 1859, *La Estrella de Occidente*, September 2, 1859. He gave a passionate farewell to the citizens and inspired them to continue the struggle. He delivered the government to Plácido Vega and predicted great success for the expedition into Jalisco.

laurels and had energetically defended the Constitution of 1857, bringing honor to his state. Furthermore, he had carried this defense beyond the borders of Sonora. Pesqueira's popularity had climbed to its zenith and his control of Sonora would not be seriously threatened until the end of the war, in the beginning of 1861.

His Sinaloa venture, however, had earned Pesqueira the opposition of Miguel Urrea and the powerful Alameños. In disregarding their advice he had alienated many partisans in that city. His driving ambition had surfaced, and people gradually began to question whether Pesqueira valued Sonora or personal aggrandizement first.

Doubts concerning Pesqueira's sincerity were not without foundation. Had he chosen, Pesqueira could have kept Sonora out of the conflict, using funds to combat the Apache and consolidate the state. Considering Sonora's turbulent condition, few people would have criticized him. Instead, he chose the role of the man on horseback, riding to the sound of the guns.

CHAPTER 5

Pesqueira and the St. Mary's Affair

The War of Reform did not seriously threaten Sonora throughout 1859. Sonora's primary problem continued to be the Indian menace, which Pesqueira never fully controlled. These wars drained the state, and made it more vulnerable to the intrigues of its northern neighbor, whom many Sonorans accused of inciting the Indians on the northern frontier to attack Mexican settlements. This problem, combined with the liberal government's desperate attempts to raise funds through the survey and sale of public lands, resulted in a confrontation between Pesqueira and a North American naval captain. The incident, called the *"St. Mary's Affair,"* took place in the Port of Guaymas.

Nature favored Guaymas, making it potentially the most important town in Sonora, and the one where intrusions such as *St. Mary's* would most likely occur. Its customshouse produced the major source of revenue for the state, and in periods of national turmoil, these custom duties would revert almost exclusively to the Sonora governor. During the many rebellions, the Guaymas customshouse became the prize of those wishing to finance their uprising. Guaymas, an important port of entry to the Sonora interior and to southern Arizona, harbored the ships of many nations, bringing trade and communication from Arizona-Sonora to the outside world. Many people in Arizona, therefore, considered U.S. ownership of this port essential to the future growth of their state.

Guaymas' growth began in the 1820s with Mexican Independence, which ended the Veracruz and Acapulco monopoly. Foreign trade could thus be conducted directly through Guaymas, and the town mushroomed from a hamlet with one home in 1820 to a villa of about three thousand in the 1850s. During this period, the legislature officially designated it as a villa, and its swelling population attracted many merchants who added to its importance. On July 13, 1859, Governor Pesqueira recognized the growing influence of Guaymas by elevating it to the status of a city.

Guaymas stands on the eastern shore of the Gulf of Cortés, and the surrounding mountains completely shut off its harbor. These mountains are located both on the shore and on the offshore islands, forming a natural cover which protects the ships in the bay. Guaymas is often considered the best port on the Mexican Pacific Coast. North American officials fully appreciated the port's potential, and expected Guaymas to become the Pacific terminus for a railroad, linking Arizona and the Southwest to the ocean.

Near this bay, where Yaqui fishermen caught shrimp, crab, lobster, oysters, and fish, stands the town of Guaymas. It hugs the margin of the bay, occupying a strip of land about one mile in length, and not exceeding one-fourth of a mile in width. Mountains surround the town, hemming it in. The town could be entered by the north, and an avenue that ran through the center of the community traversed it. This main street had small intersecting streets that ran into the sea.

Off the dusty main road, small adobe homes dotted the landscape, and occasionally some brick and stone homes could be seen.[1] In the best section of the port, close to the ocean, the rich Guaymas merchants occupied plastered houses.

The most striking feature of Guaymas, although surrounded by the sea, was its lack of fresh water. The inhabitants obtained their water supply from the town wells. The donkeys, laden with leather water bags bulging at their sides, trod down the *caminos.* Water wagons carried the brackish but very necessary water to the people.

The visitor to Guaymas easily deduced that the value of the port city was not in its land, for few gardens embellished the city. The port held the key survival, for Guaymas opened the gate to the Sonora interior. Logically, intruders would appear in Guaymas. It was the *St. Mary's*, anchored there in October of 1859, that brought another crisis to the already strife-ridden Sonora.

BACKGOUND OF THE *ST. MARY'S* INCIDENT

The *St. Mary's* incident was the by-product of concerted attempts by both U.S. and European capitalists to gain control of Sonora's vast underdeveloped lands. The interplay involved North American and French bankers, as well as Mexican associates who recognized Sonora's potential and wanted to exploit it. Mexico's inability to control its states or to develop their potential encouraged the aggressions of warships like the *U.S.S. St. Mary's.* In Sonora's case, local entrepreneurs resisted the central government's attempts to contract with foreign interests to exploit Sonora public lands. They backed Pesqueira's decision to block the terms of a contract between the national government and the Jecker-Torre Company to survey, map, and exploit these lands.

The contract's legality cannot be questioned, for the national government clearly had the power to execute such contracts. Historically, the unused lands belonged to the central government, but in the years after independence, México D.F. had done little to unify the nation or to fulfill its obligations to the frontier states. Sonora especially had suffered the national government's alienation of large portions of its lands. Sonora lost the Arizona portion of its northern frontier through the Treaty of Guadalupe Hidalgo and the Gadsden Treaty. In turn, when she asked the central government for assistance, it could not render aid. A typical example occurred in the early 1850s, when Sonora Governor José de Aguilar solicited the Mexican government's assistance to help control the Apache raids. All that Sonora received from the national government were rhetorical proclamations and grandiose plans for the establishment of military colonies. Mexico's weakness and its inability to execute these plans condemned the projects to failure.[2] Thus, when the national government negotiated contracts affecting the state's future, the state felt little obligation to support them.

Most knowledgeable Sonorans knew that Mexican officials intrigued with foreign businessmen and negotiated with them to exploit the nation's natural resources. These foreign capitalists coveted the fabled mines of northern Sonora. In October, 1850, the Jecker-Torre Company had entered into a contract with the Mexican government to develop the mines in what is today southern Arizona.[3] This began an abortive attempt of the French in California to colonize in Sonora, beginning with the Pindray and ending with the Raousset-Boulbon tragedy. These incidents highlighted the instability of the local officials, who after first approving these ventures, turned on the colonizers. The Jecker-Torre Company must have therefore known that Sonorans would be hostile to outside attempts to exploit their lands.

With Pesqueira's rise, Sonorans grew increasingly independent, for he represented the rising regional aspirations. The new entrepreneur class, who had hoisted him into power, jealously guarded their right to exploit Sonora. During this time, Pesqueira's friends — personal, political, and military — became the beneficiaries of the wealth. These local parvenus especially wanted the Yaqui and Mayo valleys.* To this end, on October 24, 1858, they formed La Junta de Colonización de los Ríos Yaqui. Pesqueira wanted to use these lands as patronage for his backers in Alamos, who conspired to use the power of the state government to encroach on the owners of the richest lands in Sonora. He franchised the first colony, Colonia Agrícola Pesqueira, to establish a settlement between the pueblos of Santa Cruz and Navojoa on the Mayo River. Colonel Rafael Angel Corella led the operation. In September of the same year, Pesqueira granted his cousin, Jesús García Morales, and his friend, Crispín de S. Palomares, a similar franchise to plant another colony on the Yaqui River.[4]

These projects, although they failed largely due to internal problems, did indicate the Sonorans' intention to develop their own land. Moreover, they did not confine this activity to the southern half of the state, for Pesqueira himself expanded his personal holdings on the northern frontier.

*Governor Pesqueira's encroachments of Indian lands were in fact the main cause of the Yaqui and Mayo uprisings.

The Jecker contract's generous terms, therefore, must have shocked Sonorans who believed the state was their private domain. Moreover, the Sonora entrepreneurs became suspicious when they learned that the Jecker associates had assigned a major portion of the contract to United States' interests.

JECKER CONTRACT

Sonorans knew the Jecker-Torre Company. The company's misfortune has already been noted, with the explanation of the ill-fated French adventures in the early 1850s. The principal agent of the Jecker-Torre Company, Juan Jecker, born in Porrentry, France, immigrated to Mexico during the first part of the nineteenth century and took up residence in México D.F.[5] Mexicans described him as a Swiss banker, although his exact nationality is unknown. This shrewd businessman had a stormy career, claiming and receiving the French government's assistance whenever he had difficulty, thus evoking Mexican suspicion.

The name of the Jecker-Torre Company alerted Sonora hostility, and this hostility increased when they learned that North Americans would implement the contract terms. The contract stipulated that the San Francisco capitalists would receive 50 percent of the Jecker claim to lands surveyed. The group included L. W. Inge, James E. Calhoun, and Captain Isham.[6] The subcontract obligated them to finance and direct the parties conducting the survey. Thus, its San Francisco affiliation tainted this expedition from the beginning, for Sonorans remembered that San Francisco capitalists had financed many filibustering expeditions bound for Sonora and Lower California. Therefore, with 50 percent of the land belonging to the North Americans, Sonorans became increasingly alarmed.

Ongoing border conflicts between Sonorans and Arizonans added to the tension. Since the Crabb expedition, relations between the two peoples had been explosive. Remarks made by prominent North Americans such as Sylvester Mowry added fuel to the fire. In a speech before the Geographical Society in New York on February 3, 1859, Mowry clearly showed the intentions of Anglo-Americans in Arizona. He stated:

The Apache Indian is preparing Sonora for the rule of a higher civilization than the Mexican. In the past half century the Mexican element has disappeared from that which is now called Arizona, before the devastating career of the Apache. It is every day retreating farther south, leaving to us (when the time is ripe for our own possession) the territory without the population.[7]

The feelings of Mowry and his contemporaries naturally placed Sonorans on the defensive; thus when they learned about the terms of the Jecker contract, Sonora leaders prepared for the worst and were determined to counter it.

The Jecker contract broke the proverbial camel's back. It had been negotiated between the already distrusted Comonfort and the Jecker-Torre Company. The fact that the contract had been entered into without Sonora's official consent added insult to injury. Under the terms of the contract, signed on August 14, 1856, Jecker-Torre Company promised to survey and map Sonora's public lands within a period of three years. In consideration of this service, the subject company would receive title to one-third of the lands it surveyed, with the other two parts remaining vested in the national government. In the event of the sale of the parts belonging to the national government, Jecker-Torre Company would have the option of buying another third at the sale price.[8] The central government had the obligation to insure Sonora's compliance with the terms of the contract. In pursuance of the agreement and in accordance with the law of the land, the federal government named a special judge to accompany the survey commission.

CHARLES P. STONE AND THE SURVEYING COMMISSION

In pursuance of the contract, San Francisco interests directed Charles P. Stone, an engineer, to survey the lands in question. This project began on March 16, 1858, with three sections of engineers departing California for Sonora. Stone planned to send one section to the state's northwestern region under a Mr. Whiting, who upon completing the task would proceed to Guaymas, and Stone appointed other groups to survey the outlying areas. State matters preoccupied Pesqueira and at this time he did not overtly challenge the activities of the party. Until he was ready to survey the state's interior, Stone could ignore Pesqueira, but in the interior Pesqueira exercised undisputed control. Stone, therefore, requested permission to continue with the project.[9]

On April 13, 1858, Stone entered Guaymas and, confident that the Mexican government would support him, announced his plans to local authorities. Two days later, as head of the survey commission, he formally requested permission from Pesqueira to proceed with the survey in accordance with the terms of the Jecker contract. Governor Ignacio Pesqueira replied that he did not have the authority to allow the survey and informed Stone that a ruling from the national government on certain observations made by him was necessary. Before he did this, Pesqueira added, he must submit the matter to the state legislature. Pesqueira emphasized that the people's wishes must be considered, and he could and would not risk upsetting the state's tranquility. He apologized, but stated that he could not allow Stone to continue his project. Pesqueira was firm in his decision, and a few days later refused to recognized the authority of Judge Antonio María Viscayno who had requested permission to proceed with the survey. The state legislature seconded the governor's actions, denying Jecker-Torre Company the concession to survey the public lands.[10]

Stone alienated officials in Guaymas almost from the moment he arrived: they resented Stone's arrogant and officious manner. Conditions in Sonora remained uncertain, with Pesqueira becoming increasingly involved with both events in Sinaloa and his defense of the Constitution of 1857. He, however, was aware of the North American threat, and must have realized that his opposition to the North American survey party would most certainly incur the wrath of the United States Pacific Squadron. The *St. Mary's* had previously anchored in Guaymas, reportedly to liberate Jesús Ainza, who had been held in complicity with the Crabb filibuster. But Pesqueira did not waver, maintaining the illegality of the Jecker contract.* He asked Stone to leave.[11]

Stone ignored Pesqueira, continuing his survey with a team of about forty men.[12] At this point, some historians have marvelled at Stone's audacity and his willingness to confront Pesqueira on his own ground. Years later Charles Poston, the Arizona entrepreneur, shed light on Stone's aggressiveness. On a trip to Washington D.C. in the winter of 1857-58, he learned that eastern capitalists had won the ear of President James Buchanan and interested him in the possibility of seizing Sonora in order to exploit her mineral wealth. Poston remarked in the *Arizona Weekly Star* of February 26, 1880:

Among other secrets it may now be told that President Buchanan and his cabinet, at the instigation of powerful capitalists in New York and England, had agreed to occupy northern Sonora by the regular army, and submit the matter to Congress afterwards. Ben McCullough was sent out as agent to select the military line, and Robert Rose was sent as consul to Guaymas with an American flag prepared expressly to hoist over that interesting seaport upon receiving proper orders.

As conditions deteriorated with the arrival of Robert Rose in Guaymas in November of 1858, Rose used the excuse of the state officials' refusal to recognize his exequatur to precipitate more trouble. At the same time, the *St. Mary's* remained near Guaymas, attempting to intimidate Sonorans. On December 16, 1858, its captain appointed the now infamous Charles P. Stone to the post of acting consul to represent American interests in Guaymas. In this capacity Stone wrote to Lewis Cass, United States Secretary of State:

I have carefully studied the country and people for eight months past, in which time I have had an excellent opportunity of gaining information from my position in the Survey of the Public lands, and I feel confident that the

---

*Jecker and Company to Pesqueira, *La Voz de Sonora*, July 30, 1858. Jecker and Company attempted to convince Pesqueira of the benefits of conforming to the contract.

only means of saving this state from a return to almost barbarism will be found to be its annexation to the United States. In this opinion I only agree with the most intelligent inhabitants of the state, both native and foreign. [13]

In the meantime, the *St. Mary's*, under Captain Charles Henry Davis, aided and abetted dissident United States citizens. Clearly Stone and Davis wanted to provoke an incident. They were no doubt influenced by Sam Houston's attempts to force the U.S. to annex Mexico.* Pesqueira, in turn, prepared to leave Sonora, and could not devote his full attention to the matter, preferring to fight in Sinaloa. In retrospect, Pesqueira can be criticized for allowing events to drift in view of what was happening in Washington D.C. There President Buchanan pressed his annexation views. On December 6, 1858, he reviewed in detail the problem of the lack of law and order in Mexico and the depredations of the Apache. Buchanan recommended:

I can imagine no possible remedy for these evils, and no mode of restoring law and order on that remote and unsettled frontier, but for the government of the United States to assume a temporary protectorate over the northern portions of Chihuahua and Sonora and to establish military posts within the same; and this I earnestly recommend to Congress.

Fortunately, Congress did not accede to his requests. Nevertheless, reactions in Sonora and Arizona further polarized the states.

In spite of this incident, during the first part of 1859 Pesqueira did nothing to check Stone, who continued in the capacity of acting consul. Stone defended every act of United States citizens, even to the point of the ridiculous. One case, for instance, involved Samuel Murphy, whom Mexican officials arrested when a bullet from his gun grazed a Mexican woman's arm and injured a child. Murphy's transgression, although accidental, showed a lack of regard for the safety of Mexicans. He was annoyed with a barking dog and decided to silence the dog by shooting it. Murphy, not distinguished as a marksman, missed the dog, and his bullet glanced off another object, grazing the woman and child. This act outraged Mexican officials, who jailed Murphy, and refused to release him. Stone could not understand their attitude: it had been an accident, Murphy had apologized, and, after all, he was a United States citizen.

The matter remained a source of irritation even after Robert Rose later replaced Stone as consul. State officials did not recognize Rose, but nevertheless, he assumed the duties because Captain Davis of the United

---

*On February 17, 1858, Senator Sam Houston had presented a resolution to establish a U.S. protectorate over Mexico, Nicaragua, Costa Rica, Guatemala, Honduras, and San Salvador to insure "order and good government" there. It was later amended to include only Mexico. On June 2, 1858, Houston insisted that a vote be taken on his resolution. The Senate voted against it 16 to 32. Joseph Park, curator of the University of Arizona Library Western Collection, points out that eight senators from northern states voted for the resolution. He attributes this vote to New England capitalist influences. "Mexican Labor," pp. 29-30; also conversations with Park on this subject.

States vessel of war — the *St. Mary's* — bestowed this power upon him. Like his predecessor, Rose as consul, acted arrogantly toward Sonora authorities, and he, too, attempted to force Murphy's release. Rose favored a tough line with the Sonorans, and wrote Lewis Cass, the Secretary of State, that the interests of the United States demanded a man-of-war in the Gulf of California to protect United States citizens in Sonora in case of open rebellion. Rose emphasized: "There is no place on the entire Pacific Coast where such protection is so much needed as here." Rose reported that anti-American feeling ran high in Sonora. In this same letter Rose mentioned that Stone had left Sonora temporarily. (Stone left only for a short time, however, and by the end of February he had returned to Guaymas.)[14]

Interested parties lobbied in México D.F. and Washington D.C. to force compliance with the contract, and to encourage the annexation of Lower California and Sonora. L.W. Inge, a member of the San Francisco capitalist group which held 50 percent of the Jecker contract, wrote to Robert McLane, United States Minister to Mexico, on April 20, 1859: "The man who accomplishes that great object [the annexation of Sonora and Lower California] will gain a high place in the esteem of the American people." He concluded: "We expect to be protected and indemnified through the agency of our government to the extent set forth in the letter to Mr. Jecker."[15]

Stone continued his belligerency. *La Estrella de Occidente*, on June 10, 1859, reflecting the attitude of Sonorans, questioned whether Stone was in fact making himself obnoxious in order to create an international incident and, thus, give Washington D.C. a motive to declare war. Pesqueira therefore, made his move and, on May 18, 1859, ordered Stone to leave the state. About this time, U.S. consuls again changed when Rose, unexpectedly, had to return to Washington. Before leaving, Rose appointed Farrelly Allden, a native of Pittsburgh, Pennsylvania, to replace him. Before his departure, Rose protested Stone's expulsion. Meanwhile, Stone prepared to leave for Fort Buchanan in Arizona to meet Robert Whiting, his chief engineer. Stone wrote a letter to the Jecker Company, reporting that he enjoyed the mass support of Sonorans, and in particular the state's rancheros, and giving the impression that everyone except Pesqueira supported him.[16]

Evidence, however, clearly shows that Stone was his own worst enemy. American sources blamed his failure largely on his arrogance and stated that he created a milieu of distrust. Edwin Conner, United States Consul at Mazatlán, on May 26, 1859, reported to Secretary of State Lewis Cass that public pressure existed to expel Stone. Conner feared that if Washington allowed Stone to continue his activities serious consequences would develop. He pointed out that tension was mounting between Mexicans and North Americans in Sonora and reported:

From conversation with respectable individuals here, I am disposed to think that the opposition to Capt. Stone is greatly increased by public and open display of Military discipline which I am informed he preserves with management of his party.[17]

Stone frequently marched his men about Guaymas, which probably reminded the Guaymas citizens of Count Gaston de Raousset-Boulbon.

The activities of other North Americans in Sonora complicated relations between Mexicans and North Americans. About the time of Stone's eviction, Sonoran officials expelled a group of United States citizens from Hermosillo. A skirmish between these North Americans and Mexican officials in the Sonoita Valley followed. During this altercation, Anglo-Americans allegedly killed thirty Mexicans.[18]

A barrage of inflammatory articles in the North American press added to the tension. In the *Weekly Arizonan* of March 3, 1859, an article appeared prophesying: "The seizure of Sonora can be but a question of time. Its possession is virtually necessary to the settlement and development of all the great expanse of country between the Colorado and the Rio Grande." [19] Stone's expulsion in May did not end his threat as he continued to taunt Sonora officials from Arizona. On June 15, 1859, when Pesqueira returned to Sonora, the matter came to a climax.

In the meantime, the San Francisco group lobbied in Washington D.C. and México D.F. Jaspar S. Whiting met with Benito Juárez and Melchor Ocampo. Reportedly these Mexican officials were receptive and admitted the Jecker contract's legality. In addition, they reputedly recognized the damages caused by Pesqueira's rejection of the contract.[20]

Inge pressed the claims, alleging on August 15, 1859, that $100,000 had thus far been expended in furtherance of the contract. He implored the United States Minister in Mexico: "I beg you to represent in a proper manner to the government of President Juárez." The attitude of the Mexican government was ambivalent. Roy de la Reintrie, Secretary of the United States Legation, on October 1, 1859, wrote Lewis Cass from Veracruz that he considered President Benito Juárez favorably disposed toward United States interests in said contract. The records, however, do not indicate that Juárez gave United States interests anything more than lip service. In fact, his government resorted to delaying tactics, for on September 28, 1859, Juan Antonio de la Fuente wrote to Henry R. de la Reintrie that work on the contract should be reestablished by legal means, but that he first wanted reports from all of the interested parties, including Pesqueira.[21] Throughout the affair, the Mexican national government conciliated all sides and never really pressured Pesqueira to accede to the terms of the aggreement it had contracted.*

---

*Degollado to Pesqueira, January 30, 1860, Archivo Historico del Estado de Sonora, Hermosillo, Gaveta 15-2, 366. After the *St. Mary's* incident, Degollado, Secretaria del Estado y del Despacho de Relaciones Exteriores, wrote to Pesqueira that the esteemed president was grieved about the affair and would extend any help required. He also said that the Mexican minister in Washington was instructed to protest the actions of Porter.

At this time, rumors persisted that Sonora would be either sold along with Chihuahua and part of Tamaulipas, or that intervention was imminent. Sonorans, hearing about negotiations of the McLane-Ocampo Treaty, angrily opposed them. An editorial in *La Estrella de Occidente*, "*¿Por Fin, Se Nos Vende?*" dated August 19, 1859, expressed the frustration of Sonorans:

Poor Sonora! All the elements of misfortune conspire to ruin you: everywhere you hear terrifying threats against your political existence. The mother country has been a step mother to you, and in the chief executive power of the nation you have witnessed only merchants preoccupied with selling the national territory piece by piece. Where will your eyes turn to, poor Sonora?

Negotiations between U.S. Minister Robert McLane and Liberal Minister Melchor Ocampo, concluded in December of 1859, added fire to rumors. Under the treaty's terms, Mexico would receive a loan of four million dollars and, in consideration of this, the United States would be granted

a perpetual right of way across the Isthmus of Tehuantepec, with two railroad routes across northern Mexico to the Gulf of California, free ports at their terminal, the right to protect the transit with troops, and to intervene, in cases of extreme danger, without even the consent of Mexico.

Some have charged that the treaty in effect made Mexico a protectorate of the United States and eventually would have led to the occupation of Mexico. During the negotiations, rumors exaggerated to proportions far beyond the actual written word inflamed Sonorans. Fortunately, the U.S. Senate rejected the treaty, twenty-seven to eighteen.[22]

Upon his return, Pesqueira consolidated his position within the state, remaining unyielding to the pressure exerted to recognize the legality of the Jecker contract. Public opinion supported him; the press revealed its belief that foreign capitalists were interested only in exploiting Sonora's mines. The *Estrella de Occidente* recalled the Raousset-Boulbon venture.[23]

Pesqueira braced himself, for he must have known that Stone's expulsion would not end the Jecker survey party problem. Jecker and his associates would not allow such valuable property to slip through their hands. The *San Francisco Herald* reported a conspiracy in an article on October 2, 1859, stating that Washington officials had met with Captain William H. Porter of the *St. Mary's* and apprised him of the course of action he must take. Three days later, the *St. Mary's* appeared in Guaymas, vehemently protesting Charles P. Stone's expulsion by Governor Ignacio Pesqueira.[24]

ST. MARY'S INCIDENT

The *St. Mary's* appearance made it evident that the United States government had yielded to pressures from San Francisco interests to intervene in the Jecker affair. It was also evident that Buchanan had not given up hope of annexing Sonora. Although Stone's expulsion had taken place in May of 1859, it was not until October 5 of the same year that North American authorities acted. Almost immediately a communication breakdown resulted. Porter charged that Pesqueira had broken a treaty between the two nations by expelling consulate officials and U.S. citizens. Meanwhile, United States authorities at Fort Buchanan sent R.S. Ewell from Arizona allegedly to investigate the friction between the *St. Mary's* Porter and Sonora officials and possibly to defend Stone's position.[25] A mediator's appearance however, further complicated an already embroiled situation.

Ewell, in route through Sonora to Guaymas, clashed with state officials over a mule he acquired, which formerly belonged to a Mr. Lacarra. This animal had been stolen, and therefore was confiscated when Ewell reached Hermosillo, Sonora. Immediately tempers flared. Ewell refused to compromise or admit that the mule had been stolen, rejecting Lacarra's offer to lend him the mule if Ewell promised to deliver it to Onofre Navarro when he returned to Arizona. Ewell also refused to submit to the jurisdiction of the courts, and instead marched to Guaymas protesting the Sonora officials' conduct to the *St. Mary's* Captain William Porter. Porter only too anxiously made an issue out of this misunderstanding and demanded the return of the mule to Ewell.* Sonora officials, however, refused to yield to Porter's demands and threats, informing him that no decision could be made without first hearing from the prefect of Hermosillo. Tension continued to mount, and on October 25, Pesqueira arrived in Guaymas with eighty dragoons.[26] The Sonorans' reaction to the events and to the aggressiveness of the North American agents can be summed up by a quotation from *La Estrella de Occidente* (October 28, 1859, "¡Un Vice-Consul Por Fuera!") which observed: *"Bravo vecinitos son los nuestros!"* (What bullying neighbors we have!)

Porter's arrogance aggravated tensions between Sonorans and North Americans. He acted condescendingly, making little effort to use the minimum of tact. In a letter to Governor Pesqueira dated October 5, Porter not only strongly protested Stone's expulsion, but also insulted Pesqueira, adding that, "with a little cultivation...with the help of an industrious population, who was addicted to the law, energetic and intelligent," Sonora could be transformed into one of the richest states in the Republic of Mexico. Porter further rattled his sabers by telling Pesqueira that the Pacific Squadron was powerful and virtually sovereign in the Pacific.[27] Throughout the month of October, he browbeat and intimidated Sonora officials as if to attempt to create an incident.. Events reached a climax when Porter demanded an interview with Pesqueira.

---

*Ironically, Ewell was a diplomat who was supposed to quell tensions.

The governor agreed to the meeting, but before it actually took place, Porter landed one hundred men and two pieces of artillery, placing them about one hundred meters from the appointed meeting place. During the meeting, Pesqueira refused to back down; afterwards he prepared to meet the expected invasion. Porter then retired to the *St. Mary's*, from where he threatened to blockade the port. So flagrant was this American commander's retort that the French and Spanish consuls protested Porter's action.[28]

Stone's intimidation of Pesqueira enraged Guaymas residents, and tension mounted. Captain Porter and the North American consular officials, although they knew of the possibilities of violence, continued in their attempts to bully Pesqueira and other Sonora officials. They demanded the right to fly the U.S. flag on national holidays of the U.S. and of Mexico. Most U.S. consulates had attempted to secure this right since the Mexican-American War, but anti-American sentiment in Sonora made compliance imprudent. Nevertheless, state officials granted permission, and the U.S. flag was flown over the U.S. Consulate at Guaymas. While the U.S. officials at the port had the right to fly their flag, especially since the consuls of other nations did the same, the timing was ill-considered. At one o'clock in the afternoon on November 18, Mexicans invaded the U.S. Consulate and tore down the American flag. The enraged people of Guaymas rioted in the streets, shouting, " *¡Muerte a los Americanos!* " (Death to the Americans!). During the tumult, Sonorans assaulted U.S. Consul Farrelly Allden and trampled the American flag. Allden protested that the Mexicans almost killed him.[29]

Pesqueira had not been a party to this demonstration, nor is there any indication that he encouraged it, for he acted promptly to restore order to the port. The governor and the Guaymas prefect apologized to the U.S. Consul and took the desecrated flag to the U.S. Consulate in person. He delivered it to Farrelly Allden and firmly commanded the people to obey the law.[30]

Porter, not satisfied with the apology, threatened to bombard Guaymas, triggering the *St. Mary's* affair. Pesqueira, remaining calm in the face of Porter's threat, informed the U.S. naval officer that if he fired one shot over Guaymas, Pesqueira would not be responsible for North American life or property in Sonora. In the face of this threat and aware of the intensity of anti-American feeling, Porter prepared to leave Guaymas immediately, requesting only Ewell's baggage.[31]

Officially this ended the *St. Mary's* incident, although the Jecker-Torre Company and associates continued lobbying to restore the claim. These events affected Pesqueira, whose attitude toward North Americans before the *St. Mary's* affair appeared to have been softening; after this incident he became markedly anti-American. As late as October 31, U.S. Consul Farrelly

Allden had written to Secretary of State Lewis Cass, "Govn. Pesqueira is peaceably disposed towards all Americans as well as Cap. Stone's surveying party," adding that Pesqueira had responded to advisors who resented Stone. In Allden's opinion, pressure exerted by Sonorans upon Pesqueira to assume a hawk-like attitude resulted from their desire to be annexed by the U.S., but this is doubtful. Porter's show of force shocked Pesqueira into the realization that the Manifest Destiny of North Americans still thrived and, furthermore, could not be deterred.[32]

The *St. Mary's* departure ended the annoyance of the Stone surveying party. Next Pesqueria turned his attention to the threat of the McLane-Ocampo Treaty; he became anxious over President James Buchanan's growing aggressiveness and took steps to prevent diplomatic seizure, removing federal units and replacing them with state officials. Pesqueira knew that the state's vulnerability lay in (1) the northern frontier which was open to the threat of military attack, and (2) the perfidy of México D.F., which would bargain away Sonora's sovereignty and territory by treaty.[33] Pesqueira prepared to defend against these threats by usurping federal control of the northern garrisons, infiltrating them with state forces.

Sonora feared the possibility of the sale of its territory. The official state newspaper, *La Estrella de Occidente*, documented this apprehension. More than one issue of this official state newspaper reported the threat, and declared Sonora's intention to fight.[34] One editorial, February 25, 1860, questioned the federal government's legal right to sell the territory, for the newspaper reasoned that if the liberal government had the license to alienate territory, so should the conservative government. During this soul-searching, even Benito Juárez became the object of criticism in an article in *La Estrella*, March 30, 1860, questioning, "How could Juárez forget the sentiment of the people? " But fortunately, as aforementioned, the U.S. refused to approve the McLane-Ocampo Treaty.

Once again, Sonorans approved of their caudillo's defiance of México D.F. and his success in defending the state against the northern intruders. The *St. Mary's* affair added to his defense of the national constitution and increased his popularity. With the termination of the Jecker threat, Pesqueira and Sonorans must have believed that they would have an opportunity to rebuild. But peace did not come to Sonora, for the turbulence of the sixties would involve both Pesqueira and Sonorans.

CHAPTER 6

Beginning of the Turbulent 1860s

The 1860s brought Sonora continuing problems of the 1850s. Internal rebellions and intrusions by foreigners still threatened the state. In 1861, Sonorans reelected Pesqueira, and for most of the 1860s he dominated the state. Pesqueira governed by decree, since he did not have any major political rivals. According to Arizona entrepreneur Charles Poston, Pesqueira held Sonora "in a state of quasi-independence from Mexico."[1]

Although Pesqueira ruled Sonora, he could not control it. In March of 1860, the Yaqui and Mayo again took to the warpath, protesting against the encroachment of the *yoris*. The Pima Indians, under Juan and Refugio Tánori, joined them. The Indian threat increased, and Pesqueira soon found it necessary to impose an additional assessment of $40,000 to finance a large scale operation. He sent García Morales against the Yaqui and Mayo and prepared to lead the military operations himself.[2]

The Yaqui repelled the Sonora troops sent against them. On July 14, 1860, the Yaqui routed a force under Colonel Crispín de Palomares, a contingent of about two hundred men which broke under the savage attack of the Yaqui near Potam in the Yaqui Valley. In late August, Pesqueira marched to the Yaqui Valley to reinforce García Morales. En route, a large number of Yaqui overwhelmed his small force. Pesqueira and his men allegedly fought valiantly, but the Yaqui defeated them. During the battle, the Yaqui shot Pesqueira's horse from under him, and only the quick action of his adjutant, José Montijo, who mounted the governor on his own horse, saved the caudillo.[3]

Pesqueira reassembled his men, and fought his way out of the ambush, retreating to Hacienda La Misa, which lay about fifteen miles from Las Guasimas. There he joined Colonel Jesús García Morales and his main army, and returned to Ures. In the Sonora capital, he postponed a scheduled session of the state legislature because of the Indian threat.[4]

At Ures, Pesqueira turned his attention to the Apache menace. Sonora bled profusely from the wounds inflicted by their incessant raids upon the ranchos, haciendas, and other population centers, and consequently, northern Sonorans feared and hated the Apache. According to Sylvester Mowry, an Arizona miner: "The State of Sonora has suffered much, having several intestine wars, occasional rebellions of half-civilized Indians that inhabit it, and being overrun by the Apaches."[5]

A traveler in the region, John Ross Browne, in his *Adventures in Apache Country*, wrote:

I saw on the road between San Xavier and Tubac, a distance of forty miles, almost as many graves of the white men murdered by the Apache within the past few years. Literally the road side was marked by the burial places of these unfortunates.[6]

During his trip, Browne painted a clear but prejudiced picture of the stolid attitude of Sonorans, about whom he wrote, "The future seems to have been crushed out of the people," and added, "All day long they sit by the doors of their filthy huts, making *cigarritos* and playing cards."[7]

Pesqueira knew that the Apache situation had improved little since he took office in 1856. Nevertheless, he was powerless to subdue the Apache effectively,* for he did not have sufficient troops or money to carry on a meaningful campaign.

Sonora direly needed a period of peace, during which time officials could deal with the Indian problem. These Apache, along with the Yaqui, crippled the state psychologically and economically. In addition to the Indian depredations from 1860 to 1862, two damaging civil wars and an intrusion of the British warship, *The Mutiny*, would plague Sonora. The first important threat came on September 28, 1860, from the northern Sonora pueblo of Magdalena.[8]

PLAN OF MAGDALENA

In the north of Sonora, south of the rancho of Nogales and north of the pueblo of Santa Ana, stood the villa of Santa María de Magdalena, which Father Eusebio Kino founded in 1698. As a mission site, it grew in importance. During Pesqueira's era, Magdalena, an important northern supply depot, stood in the path of Sonora-Arizona traffic. Some of Sonora's most prosperous ranches surrounded the villa. The district's prefect, the judge of the district, and other government administrators resided in Magdalena.[9]

On October fourth every year, Magdaleños celebrate their famous Fiesta of San Francisco. In Pesqueira's time, the town's estimated population of fifteen hundred inhabitants swelled to several times its size since the fiesta

---

*La Estrella de Occidente, June 29, 1860, stated that Pesqueira proposed to make peace with the Apache. There were negotiations during this period. *La Estrella de Occidente*, July 13, 1860, noted that negotiations also took place at Fort Buchanan in Arizona with officials at the fort. *La Estrella de Occidente*, July 27, 1860, pointed out that Sonorans wanted peace with the Apache and did not want to fight a war of extermination.

attracted visitors from the entire state. James Bartlett, the famous boundary commissioner, described this quaint village:

La Magdalena is the best built town we had yet seen; the houses are chiefly of adobe, though some are of brick, and nearly all are stuccoed and white washed. Many are colored yellow and otherwise ornamented, in a manner exhibiting considerable taste.[10]

On September 28, 1860, Remigio Rivera, Hilario García, Antonio and Francisco Gándara, and Captain Hilario Gabilondo, the commandant of presidio Santa Cruz, announced the Plan of Magdalena. This plan questioned the Pesqueira administration's constitutional legitimacy, naming Dionisio Rivera provisional governor of Sonora. It contained the customary list of grievances and imputations against Pesqueira, alleging that the governor acted arbitrarily and did not respect Sonora citizens. The document especially condemned the odious tax levies imposed by Pesqueira.

The hostilities began when Dionisio Rivera, with a force of two hundred men, left the villa of Magdalena, destined for the Yaqui Valley to enlist the Indians to his cause. Since the Yaqui had already rebelled, Rivera expected their support. On September 30, a party of rebels numbering about one hundred men under Refugio Tánori's leadership attacked Ures at nine o'clock in the morning; the attack was unsuccessful as the state militia forced the rebels into retreat. On the seventh of October, the band under Rivera attacked again without success; they were warded off by the defenders of the pueblo of San Marcial. The rebels then continued their march to the Yaqui Valley, for it was evident that their only hope was to enlist Yaqui aid.[11]

By this time, many of Gándara's former partisans had joined the revolt and consequently the Rivera rebels gradually gained strength. In the Yaqui Valley, they incorporated a force of about sixteen hundred Yaqui who were mostly unarmed. Rivera now led an army large enough to challenge Pesqueira; nevertheless, Rivera would have a difficult time controlling this large and undisciplined group.[12]

Meanwhile, Colonel Jesús García Morales had assembled five hundred men and two pieces of artillery at the Hacienda Aguilar, a distance about twelve miles from the enemy's camp. When Rivera's Yaqui partisans learned that García Morales was camped near them, the shout went up to go to attack García Morales. The Indians shouted: "¡Vamos a atacarlo! ¡a vencerlo! " (Let's go to attack him! To defeat him!)[13]

Rivera did not want to confront García Morales, but the insistent Yaqui demands forced him to communicate with García. Before leaving, he made up his mind to bypass García Morales if the latter did not surrender or chose to resist. On October 15, Rivera arrived at García Morales' camp. Rivera contacted the colonel, attempting to cajole him into joining the rebellion. García Morales refused to cooperate, and prepared his forces. Not wanting to risk a fight with García Morales' well-entrenched troops, Rivera retreated.[14]

Rivera's attention then turned to Hermosillo, where Pesqueira was recruiting militia. The rebels had learned that Pesqueira was ill-prepared and therefore they believed they could defeat him without difficulty. Rivera hesitated, but he yielded to the pressure of his disorganized mob. The rebel leader knew that it would have been useless to oppose the Yaqui, for he did not have enough loyal men to control the Indians. Rivera attempted to keep the Yaqui in line by catering to them in hope that he would meet more of his followers on the road to Hermosillo. The march began on the eighteenth, and two days later the army arrived at a Seri pueblo on the outskirts of Hermosillo.[15]

Rivera must have been perplexed by his dilemma: he could have been the victorious if he so desired, although the price would be the destruction of Hermosillo, Sonora's first city. This prosperous city, founded in colonial times, stood on the right bank of the Sonora River. It had been established to control the Seri Indians who menaced the territory. In 1828, officials changed the name from Pitic to Hermosillo in honor of the Mexican Independence hero José María González de Hermosillo. That same year they officially declared it a city. Intermittently until 1847 Hermosillo was the state capital, but throughout Pesqueira's days the capital was Ures.

Other than Alamos, many judged Hermosillo the best constructed town in Sonora. Large substantial dwellings lined the streets; colored and plaster-coated homes livened the landscape. Orange trees and flowering shrubs filled the city's courtyards; other kinds of trees, notably the palm, graced Hermosillo. The city generally reflected the good taste of its inhabitants. Even John Ross Browne, who never passed up an opportunity to criticize and ridicule Sonorans or Mexicans, described Hermosillo as "one of the most beautiful cities in the northern part of Mexico, if not the whole continent of America."[16]

Hermosillo's central location, which places it at the center of Sonora's trade routes, contributed to its growth. In Pesqueira's time, the city had approximately twenty thousand inhabitants.[17] Hermosillo is surrounded by one of Sonora's most productive valleys in which the majority of the state's wheat is grown. Hermosillo's destruction, therefore, would have meant the destruction of Sonora's leading city, a blow from which the state might never recover.

Rivera knew that he could easily defeat Pesqueira's small band, for the governor's popularity in Hermosillo had declined to a low ebb. Rivera, however, lacked the ruthlessness necessary to ignore the consequences. He knew that he could not control his Yaqui troops and if allowed to enter the city, they would probably plunder. Consequently, Rivera decided against attacking Hermosillo; he stalled the Yaqui, allowing García Morales sufficient opportunity to reach him at El Buey. On October 22, the state troops defeated the rebels, ending the Magdalena Rebellion.[18]

This revolt indicated substantial discontent with Pesqueira among a sufficient number of the most respected men in Sonora, not only among Gandaristas, conservatives, and their Indian allies. Men such as Hilario Gabilondo and Dionisio Rivera prepared to sacrifice their personal careers in the interest of Sonora. Rivera had revolted against Pesqueira because he sincerely believed the governor to be a tyrant; others joined the rebellion for the same reason. Rivera's sacrifice at Hermosillo proved his commitment to the state and his unquestionable honor. Would Gándara or Pesqueira have done the same? The rebel leader's decision also proved that only the ruthless could lead in Sonora. Rivera rose to great heights when he said of his decision not to sack Hermosillo: *"Pero no me pesa, porque nunca me ha pesado hacer el bien, aún a costo de grandes sacrificios."* (But I do not regret it, because I have never regretted doing the right thing, even at the cost of great sacrifices.)[19]

After El Buey, the Yaqui continued on the warpath, with Pesqueira personally pursuing them.[20] By the beginning of 1861, he still had not subdued the Yaqui. His failure to bring order contributed to the Sonorans' discontent with him. In 1861, Pesqueira had to stand for reelection; therefore, he began a whirlwind of activity to soothe political discord.

END OF PESQUEIRA'S FIRST TERM

On December 17, 1860, the Sonora legislature convened for the first time in two years.* At this session Pesqueira announced a series of measures designed to bring prosperity to Sonora. Pesqueira recognized the necessity of improving communication between Sonora and the other Mexican states; the governor therefore informed the legislature of the solicitation for a railroad by General Angel Trías,† who acted as agent for an American-Mexican company based in New York. The group proposed to build a railroad that would link Sonora with Chihuahua and North American railroads. The legislature granted the concession on March 5, 1861, but the company defaulted in 1863. Pesqueira also announced to the Sonora legislature that on

---

*Calvo Berber, p. 218, states that during this time there were persistent rumors that Pesqueira was involved in plots to segregate Sonora from the Mexican nation.

†Carlota Miles, *Almada of Alamos*, p. 41. General Trías had been in Sonora for some time. Pesqueira must have had extensive negotiations, for he had been with Trías on Indian campaigns. Trías was with Pesqueira at Las Guasimas.

December 7, 1860, he had contracted with the mint of Hermosillo to coin copper money at its face value in order to replace money already in circulation. Necessity made this measure imperative, since large quantities of counterfeit money circulated, contributing to Sonora's instability and seriously crippling her finances.[21]

Shortly after his address to the legislature, Pesqueira planned to campaign personally against the Yaqui and the Mayo. On February 1, 1861, he established general quarters at San Marcial, from where the Sonorans marched to Agua Caliente, penetrating deep into Yaqui territory to the pueblo of Torín. The Sonora army occupied the Yaqui region, and the militia drove the Indians back. The Indians, forced to yield to Pesqueira's large numbers of well-equipped forces, eventually sued for peace — the Yaqui in May, 1861, and the Mayo the following month.[22]

Meanwhile, Pesqueira promulgated the Constitution of 1857 in an attempt to return civil rule to Sonora. He extended amnesty to the rebels on March 17 in Agua Caliente, hoping to alleviate the bitterness caused by the Magdalena Revolt. Unwisely, he did not include the principal revolutionary leaders. In retrospect, Pesqueira made a major blunder for in failing to conciliate his opposition, he made bitter enemies not only of the rebel leaders, but also of members of their extended families, many of whom returned during the French Intervention to oppose Pesqueira.[23]

In 1861 Pesqueira's first term ended. Ignacio Pesqueira had accomplished something unique in Sonora and Mexican politics: he had completed his first term in office, becoming the first governor since the state's separation from Sinaloa to accomplish this. And, although many problems plagued Sonora, there could be no doubt who governed the state.

In four years Pesqueira compiled an impressive record, repulsing Crabb's invasion, waging vigorous campaigns against the Apache, Yaqui, Mayo, and other Indians, and attempting to repopulate the frontier. He had protected the state against foreign intruders, such as the agents of Jecker-Torre Company, and had overcome the Gandaristas. Foremost among Pesqueira's accomplishments was his defense of the Constitution of 1857, not only victoriously defending it at home, but also carrying the struggle to Sinaloa.

Once again, retirement at this point would have raised Ignacio Pesqueira to the level of a statesman, but instead he chose to run for another term. And while Sonorans were grateful to their caudillo, signs of discontent increased. No doubt existed that opposition to Pesqueira would become more intense during the coming elections. The main opposition to the governor would come from the city of Alamos in southern Sonora. The city's antagonism would become significant, spreading to other portions of the state as time passed; Alameño opposition would never cease throughout the Pesqueira years.

During the election campaign, Pesqueira made efforts to reconcile former supporters, promising dissidents that he would suspend debts to the treasury, overhaul the public treasury, and make no further forced loans. The election took place in June of 1861. The respected Guaymas businessman, former governor Fernando Cubillas, opposed Pesqueira. Historian Francisco Almada wrote that conservatives sponsored the Cubillas candidacy. This contention, however, is an oversimplification; the issue was no longer "Pesqueira versus Gándara" or "Pesqueira versus conservatives." Opposition to the governor crossed political philosophies and became embroiled in family rivalries and regional grievances. Fernando Cubillas, a partner in the Manuel Iñigo Company of Guaymas, had married María Iñigo. The Iñigo family held extensive commercial and agricultural holdings, as did Cubillas. Moreover, the Iñigos were closely related to former Governor José de Aguilar, head of the Aguilarista party, which counted among its ranks the state's richest merchants. The Aguilaristas, by marriage or family relationship, were also related to many other leading Sonora families. It should be remembered that this same group had sponsored Pesqueira's rise; however in 1861, it appeared that they had withdrawn their support from the ambitious governor.[24]

In addition to Cubillas' allies and friends, many leading Alameños, who previously had been strong supporters of Pesqueira, opposed him. Because of the governor's fiscal policies and tendency to run the state for an oligarchy of friends, Alameños and other merchants had become disaffected.

Recognizing the discontent, Pesqueira went to Alamos before the election, where he made concessions to leading citizens and special efforts to placate the rich. Former deputy governor Miguel Urrea resented Pesqueira's fiscal policies, for much of their burden fell upon the Alameño merchants, miners, and ranchers, many of whom charged that Pesqueira considered the city "an inexhaustible source of government income."[25]

The governor's last-minute goodwill efforts proved successful, for Sonorans reelected him by a two-thirds majority.[26] And, although considerable discontent with Pesqueira had emerged, unified opposition to his candidacy did not materialize. Some Sonorans still believed his promises, or perhaps feared that chaos was the alternative to Pesqueira. Above all, Sonora needed a period of prolonged peace.

ESTÉVEZ REVOLT

Events, however, conspired against the state, for the national government had inherited a host of problems as a consequence of the War of Reform. Conservatives still aspired to power; in July of 1861, when Juárez declared payment on foreign debts suspended for a period of two years, they seized the opportunity to spread seeds of discontent.[27] Sonora, like the other Mexican states, was factionalized, and dissidents took advantage of growing dissatisfaction with Pesqueira; yet, they lacked enough power to mount an intensive campaign.

On August 2, 1861, events in Sinaloa disturbed the peace in Sonora. Colonel Antonio Estévez, at the villa Fuerte Sinaloa, resurrected the Plan of Tacubaya and rallied conservatives in an effort to unseat the liberal governments of Sinaloa and Sonora. Although this small rebellion never threatened Pesqueira, it had far-reaching repercussions in Sonora. On the nineteenth, approximately two hundred Tacubayas, as the rebels became known, crossed the border into Sonora.[28] Their immediate objective was the wealthy city of Alamos where they expected to solicit enough money to finance the revolt.

Alamos braced itself for the attack; many of its citizens panicked at the prospect of rebels sacking and plundering the city. Colonel Crispín de Palomares and José Tiburcio Otero, the Alamos prefect, marched out of the city to confront the invaders. The defending army was not equal to the well-disciplined invading troops. The rebels defeated Sonora's defenders at El Salitral, where, under a stiff attack by the Tacubayas, their rear guard deserted them, resulting in a running retreat by the Sonorans.[29] The desertion left Alamos undefended, and at the mercy of the Tacubayas.

The Sinaloa rebels entered Alamos without any resistance, finding the city deserted. Carlota Miles, in *Almada of Alamos*, describes the Sinaloans' entrance into the city, writing that Estévez found Alamos "frightening in the moonlight in its stillness and desertion." She adds that this awesomeness tempted Estévez to turn and flee, but not before he extracted a forced loan of thirty thousand pesos.[30] In Alamos, Estévez published a denunciation of Pesqueira and sought to enlist some of the city's more influential men.

As Alameños grew disenchanted with Pesqueira their loyalties changed. Most Alameño leaders had been loyal to the liberal cause during the War of Reform and, although dissatisfied with Pesqueira, they wisely abstained from enlisting. The judgement of these more sober citizens proved correct for Pesqueira quickly stamped out the threat. José María Tranquilino Almada, the most famous of José María's sons, refused Estévez' offer; however, two of his younger sons joined the revolution. Estévez promoted Toribio Almada, age twenty-one, and his younger brother Vincent Almada to the rank of captain. José María Almada was undoubtedly the strongest and most influential of the Alameños. In fact, the wealthy miner and owner of ranches in Sonora and Sinaloa was considered the patriarch of the city. He had thirty-six children and innumerable relatives, including Bartolomé Almada, who was a strong liberal.[31]

On the afternoon of September 7, after forcing tribute from Alamos, the main body of Tacubayas, consisting of about four hundred men and fourteen cannons, marched into Sonora's interior. They moved through the Mayo and Yaqui valleys, inciting the Indians. Pesqueira immediately countered the rebels, sending Crispín de Palomares with a section of the state militia; on September 11, Palomares captured the Alamos plaza.[32]

Meanwhile, the rebels approached the state's center recruiting dissidents. One of these dissidents was Lorenzo Avilés, who on October 5 declared in favor of the rebels. His defection surprised the Pesqueiristas, since Avilés had been a distinguished officer of the national guard who had served honorably during the War of the Reform, taking part in the now-famous Sinaloa campaign of 1859.[33]

Pesqueira established his headquarters in Hermosillo, organizing his defenses, alerting the national guard, and strengthening the city's fortifications. Most of his defenses centered around the plaza. On October 15, 1861, the rebels arrived with a force numbering about five hundred.* The Tacubayas attacked with vigor, but Pesqueira and a force of about three hundred successfully repelled the invaders after five hours of fighting. Pesqueira completely routed the rebels, capturing approximately one hundred prisoners and ten pieces of artillery.[34]

Pesqueira then marched to Alamos to rid Sonora of the remaining Tacubayas in that sector. In Alamos, Sinaloa Governor Plácido Vega had arrived to assist Pesqueira and began mop-up operations before Pesqueira's arrival. Pesqueira had ordered many prominent Alameños arrested. When Pesqueira finally arrived in Alamos, he delivered the prisoners taken at Hermosillo to Governor Vega.[35]

With the revolt suppressed, Pesqueira would have been wise to take time to assess the situation. Instead, he moved quickly and vengefully, hunting down escaped rebels previously captured by the state militia — Toribio Almada and Juan Nepomuceno Escobosa, the secretary of Estévez, and their men in the mountains of Chihuahua — and bringing them back. On November 24, the captors delivered the prisoners to Pesqueira. He released all prisoners except Toribio and Escobosa, whom he had sentenced to execution on November 29, 1861.

Pesqueira's unexpected lack of clemency shocked Alameños. After all, Toribio was an Almada, and in Alamos the Almadas stood next to God. Liberals and conservatives alike believed that "a wrong choice did not warrant capital punishment! "[36]

---

*Corral, p. 42. Allden to U.S. Secretary of State, Guaymas, October 13, 1861, "Despatches from U.S. Consuls in Guaymas," describes an insurrection in Guaymas on October 6 which was quickly put down. He wrote that Estévez had nine hundred men and was expected to overthrow Pesqueira. He also complained of another 50,000 pesos loan imposed by Pesqueira.

In *Almada of Alamos* Carlota Miles describes the agony of the execution:

Toribio sent desperate messages to Don Bartolomé to obtain pardon for him. His mother and his young wife, Nelita, tried again and again to gain access to the Governor's mansion, but in vain. In order not to hear the crying and pleading before his windows, the inexorable Governor ordered his men to sound horns and drums. The execution was to take place in the Alameda, but such a crowd had gathered there that Pesqueira feared rioting. The condemned men were taken from the jail early in the morning and driven to the cemetery without being allowed to take leave from their relatives. Toribio's parents were inconsolable. His wife, Nelita, ran crying after the death carriage with her newborn baby in her arms. Deadly silence reigned in the streets. The windows and doors were shuttered, the whole town wore the black of mourning. (p. 30)

After the execution, the cleavage between Pesqueira and Alameños widened. The wounds inflicted by the execution cut too deeply to heal, for all the drums and bugles that Pesqueira could muster would not drown out the cries of Toribio's young wife nor the Alamadas' vengeful vows.

Pesqueira had compounded his error by arresting the elder José María Almada on October 3. He charged the elder Almada with inciting the Indians against the government, basing his charge on mere circumstantial evidence. He rationalized that since Almada wielded considerable influence with the Mayo, he had incited them. The state never proved the charges, and they finally had to release José María Almada. Alameños could never forgive the tragedies Pesqueira forced upon the patriarch: his humiliating imprisonment despite his illness, the bitterness caused by his son's death, and Pesqueira's failure to release the grand old man until the family paid blackmail of 10,000 pesos all aroused the town's righteous indignation.[37]

Undaunted, Pesqueira added insult to injury with a rash of arrests after Toribio's death. Relatives of the city's leading citizens were thrown into prison or dungeons.[38] Most of these families remembered Pesqueira's "generosity" and the governor became a persona non grata. No longer would the song *"Indita"* be played in his honor.

The Estévez revolt lasted only a few months and had been quelled with a minimum of effort. Pesqueira's lack of mercy would have far-reaching repercussions. Many who had once been committed to the liberal cause and loyal to the governor would now become vehemently anti-Pesqueira, going to any ends to unseat him.

THE INTRUDERS – 1862

Early in 1862, French, Spanish, and English armies landed in Mexico in accordance with a treaty negotiated in October of 1861. These armies had instructions to collect debts and damages that Mexico owed to their merchants and capitalists. England and Spain soon left when it became apparent that France, contrary to the terms of the treaty, intended to violate Mexico's territorial and political integrity.[39] Thus began the French intervention, which would ultimately affect all parts of Mexico including Sonora.

The French occupation did not directly involve Sonora during most of 1862. The peace of the state was however disturbed by another foreign threat, one which involved a British sea captain who protested the Mexican government's right to tax foreigners. On December 26, 1861, the federal Congress passed a bill which taxed Mexican and foreign interests alike two percent of their capital. As anticipated Mexican and foreign merchants complained that the tax would ruin them since it was added to an already long list of taxes. While Mexican merchants had no one to champion them, foreign merchants could and did appeal to their consuls.

In Sonora the reaction was especially vehement since Pesqueira had levied numerous contributions and forced loans to pay for the Estévez Revolt and his expensive program. Many Sonorans and foreigners considered Pesqueira's use of his taxing power arbitrary and openly accused the governor of lining his own pockets. This situation was aggravated by the state's already unsettled currency. Sonora copper coins had diminished in value, declining to sixty cents on the dollar. Therefore, when state officials refused to accept copper money in payment of taxes, demanding only gold and silver, fuel was added to the fire.[40]

Thus, when the federal government passed its two percent tax, merchants opposed it. The failure of many states to comply with the government order complicated this confusion. Pesqueira, however, upheld the justice and legality of this tax, ordering officials to collect it.[41] Some merchants in Guaymas then complained to Captain William Graham who, on March 28, 1862, arrived in that port in command of Her Majesty's ship, the *Mutiny*.

Captain Graham's actions reminded Mexican citizens of the behavior of the *St. Mary's* Captain William Porter. Graham immediately complained to the governor about the treatment of a certain Lieutenant Bruce, who had allegedly been assaulted and insulted by a sentry when he had gone ashore at Guaymas.[42] (There is no indication that Bruce was from the *Mutiny*, and the incident probably took place some time before Graham arrived in Guaymas.) The matter of the two percent tax which Captain Graham demanded be suspended, however, soon became obscured. Graham rationalized that the states of Guerrero and Sinaloa had suspended the tax; and, therefore, Pesqueira should follow suit. Graham also demanded that Pesqueira return the tax money that had already been collected, or at least hold it in trust until the tax's legality could be determined by the Juárez government.

Governor Pesqueira disagreed with Graham's rationale that condemned the tax as inconsistent and nonapplicable to foreigners. He also objected to Graham's pretensions in questioning the legality of the tax. Graham protested Pesqueira's resolution, but temporarily withdrew.[43] The governor in turn grew more determined than ever to enforce the order of December 26, 1861.

On April 7, 1862, Graham, thinking that a Mexican pilot boat, the *Angelita*, carried seven bars of silver, captured the boat. The silver, however, had been taken off the boat at Santa Cruz on the Mayo River. The Guaymas officials protested this act, and condemned it as a violation of international law.[44]

Captain Graham hovered off the Sonora coast near Guaymas. Soon, federal officials precipitated another incident when they attempted to tax Juan A. Robinson, a North American resident, fourteen hundred pesos as his share of the two percent tax. Robinson asked and received Graham's protection. Ironically, Robinson up to this point had been loyal to Sonora officials. During the *St. Mary's* incident, his son, a Mexican citizen, had been the Guaymas prefect, and Robinson had refused to cooperate with Captain William Porter. Robinson, now a wealthy man, headed the annexationist party, which also had ties with the Aguilaristas, the state's richest merchants.[45]

It is alleged that Robinson offered to pay the tax in state currency, but that state officials refused; Robinson thereafter refused to pay. Governor Pesqueira, learning of this defiance, instructed Guaymas prefect Jesús E. Nuño to collect the tax. Graham impeded this collection by placing Robinson under his protection and ordering the tax not be paid.[46]

The prefect proceeded cautiously, attempting to stall Graham by telling him that he had to confer with the governor, and then notified Pesqueira regarding what had transpired. Before Pesqueira could reply, Captain Graham landed one hundred men from the *Chameleon*, a sister ship of the *Mutiny*, during the morning hours of May 2. They surrounded Robinson's house, preventing government officials from collecting the tax. Prefect Nuño reacted immediately and firmly. At ten that morning, he sent a letter to Graham condemning his landing soldiers on Mexican soil to prevent the collection of taxes. Nuño stated that this action was "contrary to proscribed law and national dignity." The prefect ordered Graham to leave by twelve noon, or he would be ejected by force. Graham answered Nuño's letter in a very defensive and evasive manner; nevertheless, before the appointed hour of twelve noon, Graham removed his troops.[47]

Graham's departure, however, did not settle the question of taxes. During May and June, British subjects refused to pay their monthly tax, and another British sea captain came to support the British merchants. Captain

William Hays of the *Tartar* protested the fining of British subjects, but this crisis soon passed. Meanwhile, U.S. officials in Sonora charged that Pesqueira had made an agreement with a Captain Harding of the *Chameleon* to suspend the British subject's monthly levies.* The U.S. Consul protested this alleged discrimination against North Americans, demanding that U.S. citizens be afforded equal treatment.† The consul also wrote to the U.S. Secretary of State William Seward, with the same protest.[48]

The demands and protests of the U.S. Consul apparently did not budge Pesqueira, who refused to respond to his letters or accusations. The governor continued to collect the taxes. During this same period, Pesqueira also refused the U.S. Consul permission to fly the U.S. flag over the consulate,[49] further straining relations. Fortunately, an incident did not result. In fact, relations between the United States and Pesqueira improved, with the former becoming more conciliatory during its own Civil War.

About the middle of May, Sonorans learned that Mexican forces had clashed with the French at Cumbrés de Acultzingo. The war of the French intervention now became a reality. Although Sonorans rallied to the defense of their Republic, there appeared to be little immediate danger to Sonora. For the present, Pesqueira's participation would be limited to sending a contingent of Sonorans to fight outside the state.[50]

---

*It is not known when, or, if indeed, such a deal was made. It is however highly probable.

†Baker to Pesqueira, Guaymas, July 11, 1862, Archivo Historico del Estado de Sonora, Hermosillo, Gaveta 16-1, 384. Baker complained that he had been officially informed that the monthly levies against the British had been suspended and demanded equal treatment for North Americans.

CHAPTER 7

French Intervention in Sonora

The French intervention lasted from 1861 through 1867. Most Mexican histories focus on its progress in the nation's interior, while the story of this foreign intrusion into the northern borderlands, for the most part, remains hidden in the archives of the state capitals of the northern region.

The actual conflict did not affect Sonora itself until 1864. Prior to this time, Sonorans limited their involvement to organizing patriotic clubs, such as *Independencia* and *Libertad O Muerte*, which mobilized public opinion behind the war effort and raised money to help finance the liberal cause.[1] An effort was made to send Sonoran volunteers to the interior — to fight side by side with the republican forces. It was a venture that ended in disgrace, and, in retrospect, predicted the fate of Pesqueira when the French finally arrived in Sonora.

On June 19, 1862, the relative peace was broken; Pesqueira sent García Morales to Sinaloa at the head of the First Battalion, numbering about five hundred men. One month later, Colonel Gabriel Corella left for Sinaloa with an additional five hundred men. Sonorans and Sinaloans made much fanfare over this force, with President Juárez personally thanking Pesqueira for his prompt assistance. These great expectations soon ended when Pesqueira received his first major setback at the port of Mazatlán: almost all the Sonora troops and their officers deserted.[2] This so-called act of treason personally embarrassed the governor, both at the local and federal levels, discouraging his own participation outside the state.

The desertion at Mazatlán furthermore explodes the belief that there was widespread support for either Pesqueira or the liberal cause in Sonora. Most Sonorans were concerned with eking out a living. Their local village was the center of their lives. México D.F. was thousands of miles away — foreign to most of them. Most Sonorans had little contact with the central government, other than suffering its taxes. In return, they received few services and less protection. Small wonder that these same voiceless citizens would be less enthusiastic about the war than their governor. It is also significant that most of the rank and file had been forcibly conscripted. At the same time, the army lacked money and supplies, and therefore could not even buy the loyalty of its troops.

Pesqueira, it is reasonable to speculate, did not see the desertion in these terms. To his credit he remained in Sonora, personally leading operations against the Apache, Yaqui, and Mayo. During this period, conditions had worsened on the Indian frontiers. This was especially true in the north, where the removal of Union troops from Arizona to fight in the east had emboldened the Apache. If this were not enough, Pesqueira now had to deal with the intrigues and pressures of both Union and Confederate agents.

THE UNION AND THE CONFEDERACY

Although the Juárez government professed neutrality, Juárez favored the Lincoln government from the beginning. The Mexican Congress granted a Union request for the privilege of transporting troops and supplies from Guaymas across Sonora to attack the Confederates in New Mexico. J.T. Pickett, Confederate agent in Mexico, protested this action, threatening that if Mexico did not nullify the decree, the Confederate states would invade northern Mexico. The liberals merely ignored him. His pugnacious manner only alienated the Juárez administration, which continued openly to favor the Union. The objective of Pickett's mission to Mexico had been to negotiate a treaty of friendship, commerce, and navigation; in this endeavor, however, he failed.[3]

In reality, the federal government had limited power, for the regional caudillos of northern Mexico ruled independently. Men like Santiago Vidaurri, who had united Coahuila and Nuevo León, administered them as independent entities within the Mexican nation. In 1861, he nominally supported Juárez. Vidaurri, an ambitious man, toyed with the idea of a Republic of Sierra Madre in northern Mexico and therefore played all sides. Luis Terrazas of Chihuahua also ruled his state independently of México D.F. Finally, in Sonora, Ignacio Pesqueira dictated to his subjects. All three caudillos often ignored the national government and the decrees of the Mexican Congress. Nevertheless, Terrazas and Pesqueira professed their loyalty to liberalism and, like Juárez, favored the republic and the Constitution of 1857.[4]

Pesqueira also favored the Union over the Confederacy. However, because of his tenuous position, he was forced to conciliate both sides. Also during this period, he moderated his stance toward North Americans in the state, liberalizing his commercial regulations and ameliorating tensions by relaxing his taxation policies.[5]

Meanwhile, Brigadier General H.H. Sibley of the Confederate Army and Commander of the Army of New Mexico, sent Colonel James Riley to Sonora to form an alliance with Pesqueira and negotiate a concession to establish a port of deposit at Guaymas. After conference in Sonora, Governor Pesqueira refused Riley's requests, emphasizing his policy of neutrality.[6]

In spite of his professed neutrality, Pesqueira clearly favored the Union, forming a close friendship with Colonel James H. Carleton, who had gone out of his way not only to remove trade restrictions but also to cultivate the friendship of Pesqueira. In an exchange of letters, he warned Pesqueira about Confederate agents. The caudillo replied by thanking Carleton for his interest and assuring him: "My political sympathies have been and always will be with those nations which are so fortunate to be governed by purely democratic institutions." Pesqueira told Carleton of his talks with Riley, adding that the assertions circulated by the Confederate were exaggerated and admitting only that he had offered Riley the rights of neutrals. Forced by necessity, the Carleton-Pesqueira friendship flourished throughout the U.S. Civil War and the French intervention.[7]

THE YEAR 1863

The war of the French intervention raged in the interior of Mexico throughout 1863. It did not, however, affect Sonora or Pesqueira, whose only link with the war remained Sinaloa.

In September of 1863, Sonorans again elected Pesqueira by an absolute majority. Whereupon, Pesqueira named commissioners for all the districts to collect donations for the hospitals of the central army, established a branch of public education and a college preparatory school under Professor Leocadio Salcedo, and protested the establishment of the Maximilian monarchy. No major problems broke out during this period, other than Pesqueira's continuing battles against the Indians. Conditions in the Sonora of 1863 remained calm, without major incident.[8]

During the first days of 1864, a French warship briefly blockaded Guaymas, raising speculation that the French intended to invade Sonora. In response, the Sonora Congress granted Pesqueira extraordinary powers, and the governor in turn mobilized the national guard to repel the invaders.[9] However, the expected invasion did not materialize.

THE FRENCH TEMPT PESQUEIRA

On September 12, 1863, Napoleon III wrote General Francois-Achille Bazaine requesting a confidential report on the Sonora mines and asked whether the state could be occupied. Napoleon's interest in Sonora increased, and on December 16, 1863, he again wrote to General Bazaine inquiring about mines. Nevertheless, the French did not immediately try to invade the state of Sonora. Instead, they attempted to persuade – without having to commit troops — Pesqueira to join them. The French knew that this task would require delicacy and tact.[10]

Opportunity came from Panama. At this time, the presence of foreign agents and numerous Spanish-American exiles made Panama a city of intrigue. Arturo de Zeltner represented both the French government and the regency as consul. In Panama, Zeltner had met Pablo de Fourniel, who had been a businessman in Sonora. For his anti-republican politics, the latter had been forced to leave his friends and relatives in Sonora, one of whom was Ignacio Pesqueira. Impressed with Fourniel, Zeltner wrote to J.M. Arroyo, secretary of the regency, about Fourniel.[11]

Arroyo agreed to Zeltner's plan to send Fourniel to Sonora. Zeltner arranged to transport Fourniel, and the regency authorized Fourniel to negotiate with Pesqueira in its name. Pablo de Fourniel accepted the commission, profusely thanking Zeltner. All parties to the project — Zeltner, Arroyo, and Fourniel — seemed sure of success. On May 3, 1864, Fourniel left Panama for Acapulco, where he transferred to another ship destined for Sonora. Upon arriving at San Blas, Fourniel wrote a letter to Arroyo in which he expressed doubts about the arrangements Arroyo had made. Fourniel's lack of authority especially troubled him, for it was based on a mere directive from the Consul of Panama. He sensed the insecurity of his position, but continued his mission, taking the frigate *D'Assas* to Sonora.[12]

On the morning of July 3, 1864, the frigate arrived in La Paz, Baja California. There the Frenchman was well received by Navarrete, governor of the territory. Fourniel wrote to Arroyo that the territorial government had problems and could not withstand an attack; he doubted, in fact, if any force would be necessary. On July 9, 1864, the *D'Assas* continued on to Guaymas. Fourniel immediately wrote to Governor Pesqueira informing him of his mission.[13]

On July 11, 1864, Pesqueira answered Fourniel that it would be useless to talk for Sonora, like the other states of the union, "will have the glory of fighting for our country in perpetual opposition to the figurehead empire established in the Capital of the Republic." On the same day he wrote a more seething letter to Fourniel, berating him for assuming that he, Pesqueira, would cooperate with the Frenchman's request, especially when Fourniel knew of Pesqueira's commitment to the republican cause. Pesqueira closed his denunciation by declaring that he would sacrifice all for the independence of his country.[14]

On July 20, 1864, Fourniel wrote to Arroyo that he had been denied the right to travel into the interior of Sonora. The French agent learned that the authorities had special instructions not to allow him into the plaza. In this letter, he keenly appraised the Sonora situation, surmising that authorities were worried about revolts in Ures and Hermosillo. Fourniel recommended invasion of Sonora, suggesting a blockade of Guaymas, where he said North American merchants had alarmed the populace against the French. Fourniel advised against giving special consideration to the Americanos, warning Arroyo not to trust them. He also presented a blueprint for the conquest of Sonora, cautioning that first Sinaloa had to be pacified, and then Sonora had to be invaded and subdued. Fourniel accurately evaluated the breach between Alamos and Pesqueira, prophesying the easy occupation of the principal commercial centers of the state.

Fourniel predicted that with the occupation of the main centers, Pesqueira would be forced to retreat to the pueblos of Banamiche, Senaquipe, and Arizpe, where his only alternative would be guerilla warfare. The imperialists would then have to force Pesqueira into the open and destroy him. The Frenchman stated that Sonora would become a prosperous state without Pesqueira's arbitrary rule, and encouraged its immediate invasion. [15] The importance of Fourniel's correspondence was that it predicted the problems confronting Pesqueira, and indicated that the governor's control had not been as complete as Sonora's historians have portrayed. Fourniel's departure signalled the beginning of the French intervention in Sonora.

MOUNTING FRENCH INTEREST IN SONORA

Napoleon III wanted the mines of Baja California and Sonora as his bounty for assisting the emperor of Mexico. The French emperor asked Maximilian to ratify a former agreement between the Marquis de Monthalon, the French Minister to Mexico, and Luis de Arroyo, who represented the regency in New York, whereby Sonora would be ceded to France. Maximilian, however, rejected the idea of giving any territory to France. Numerous reports on Sonora sent to Napoleon during 1864 further dramatized French interest. Nye's English version of Velasco's statistical study on Sonora was even translated into French. Zeltner dwells on the rich Sonora mines in his preface to the Velasco translation. In October, 1864, an anonymous author sent a report to Maximilian on the mines of Sonora, Chihuahua, and California. It was recommended that Chihuahua be attacked immediately, since the last of the Juaristas had sought refuge there. The report then went on to praise the mines and agricultural lands of Chihuahua and Sonora, emphasizing the proximity of Sonora to California and the potential for trade and colonization.[16]

At this time, imperialist sentiment and anti-Pesqueira feelings in Sonora intensified. Manuel Gándara had attended the court of the Mexican emperor to induce him to invade Sonora. The old caudillo had not given up hope of regaining control of Sonora. In the first days of November, 1864, simultaneously in the districts of Ures and Magdalena, Pedro Flores and Jesús Salgado, partisans of Gándara, seconded the empire. The rebellion failed, and rebel leaders were executed by the national guard.[17]

In November, 1864, the French occupied Mazatlán, threatening to invade Sonora. In Chihuahua, Juárez declared Sonora in a state of siege on November 25, 1864, making Pesqueira both governor and military commander of the state and granting him all necessary powers to defend her. Pesqueira rallied Sonorans, calling upon them to resist, declaring, "It is a Holy War: it is a War for National Independence: it is the same cause our fathers fought in 1810 against the Power of Spain." The end of 1864 saw the imperial forces in control of three quarters of the nation. Only Chiapas, Guerrero, southern Michoacán, Chihuahua, and Sonora remained under the republican regime. The Juaristas were no match for the highly disciplined French troops who swept Mexico.[18]

EVENTS OF 1864

The governor remained resolute in defending the liberal cause. He had rebuked Fourniel, strengthening his position within the state by proving his dedication to Juárez. The latter was documented on January 14, 1864, when General Manuel Doblado and others asked Juárez to resign. Other commanders – General Luis Terrazas of Chihuahua, General José María Patoni of Durango, and General Ignacio Pesqueira of Sonora – vigorously opposed Doblado. Their support must have played an important part in keeping Juárez in office, for they actually controlled most of the northern part of the republic.[19] Juárez' resignation would have weakened the liberal cause and dangerously divided the union.

During this period, several filibustering expeditions threatened Sonora, the most notorious being that of former Senator William Gwinn, who had gone before Napoleon III and told the emperor of his project to colonize Sonora with southerners loyal to the empire. Gwinn had been in Paris in 1863, where he received a letter of recommendation from the French emperor on June 2, 1864. For a time Gwinn's proposed expedition created excitement: Rumors circulated throughout California and Arizona that he intended to become the duke of Sonora.* Many believed these rumors, since the Maximilian government sympathized with the Confederacy. It followed, logically, that it would be to Maximilian's advantage to encourage Gwinn, but Gwinn's Sonora expedition never materialized. The caution of French officials as much as Gwinn's failure to produce contributed to the resulting fiasco.[20]

The year 1864 also saw the last stages of the U.S. Civil War. North American adventurers from everywhere flooded into Arizona, lured by stories of free land and mining bonanzas. Sonora's precarious position also

---

*Coleman, "Senator Gwinn's Plan," p. 498. Bazaine to Napoleon III, warns and cautions, but does not discourage, Napoleon on colonization of Sonora and Chihuahua. Sarah Yorke Stevenson, *Maximilian in Mexico* p. 179, writes that Maximilian was unwilling to harbor Confederate refugees because it would hamper U.S. recognition.

concerned U.S. authorities more and more.* Pesqueira's relations with James H. Carleton, now a brigadier general, remained excellent. Pesqueira also struck up a friendship with Lieutenant Colonel Coult. Through letters, the governor granted the latter both the privilege of shipping supplies and munitions through Sonora and permission to pursue the Apache into Sonora. These letters, however, revealed a weakness in Pesqueira's position. Carleton had stepped up operations against the Apache and requested Pesqueira's assistance. Pesqueira replied that while he was interested in coordinating efforts with Carleton, he could not take a very active part, for at that time the defense of the coast from possible French attack had priority.[21]

Carleton must have realized Sonora's perilous position. Lieutenant Colonel Theodore Coult, stationed at Tucson, allegedly had made a private bargain with Pesqueira to raise the stars and stripes over Sonora in the event the French marched into the state. Reputedly Carleton transmitted the agreement to Major General Halleck, General-in-Chief of the United States. Carleton wrote: "Our country will never be perfectly adjusted. . . until we have a port and naval station on the Gulf of California." Washington, however, did not share Carleton's enthusiasm. The Civil War preoccupied Lincoln and he did not desire involvment in territorial skirmishes that would endanger the neutrality of the United States.[22]

The year 1864 closed with the certainty of Sonora's invasion by imperialist forces. Pesqueira, although prepared to defend the state, would be in an unfavorable position against the veteran French troops.

FRENCH INVASION OF SONORA

In the early part of 1865, the forces of the empire under Armand Alexandre Castagny gradually crept up the western coast of Mexico. Most of the towns in Sinaloa fell to his well-disciplined veteran troops. He made a concerted attempt to drive Juárez out of Mexico and planned to move into Sonora to prevent Juárez from escaping through that route. Meanwhile, Colonel Agustín Henri Brencourt would invade Chihuahua. On February 16, 1865, General Castagny wrote to General Bazaine from Mazatlán, complaining that the citizens in that port opposed the French. He reported rumors that the U.S. had projected the annexation of Baja California, Sonora, and Sinaloa. The general explained his project to invade Sonora, adding that he did not anticipate resistance since Pesqueira was "a weak man and a drunkard."[23]

---

*C.H. Bell to C.H. Poor, Flagship Lancaster in Callao, September 13, 1864, in United States Navy, *Official Records*, Series I, Vol. III, p. 214, found in Dabbs, p. 143, note 30. "As early as 1864 the American (Federal) naval vessel, the *Sarnac*, patrolled the Gulf of California and maintained communication with Juarist officials like General Pesqueira."

Finally in the middle of March, 1865, the French arrived in Sonora. Four French ships cast anchor at Guaymas, carrying a contingent of about twelve hundred men. As predicted, even though Pesqueira had a sizeable force of about three thousand men, his troops were inexperienced and inadequately armed – in spite of the fact that he had had three years to prepare for the French invasion. Pesqueira, in the face of the French landing, retreated to a point called La Pasión, about eighteen miles from Guaymas, where he was to suffer the worst setback of his career.[24]

Most of Pesqueira's trusted followers, including Jesús García Morales, accompanied him to La Pasión.[25] They prepared to push the French into the sea, but many inexperienced volunteers weakened the Sonora army. In the face of the invasion, the army withdrew. Pesqueira should have prepared for any emergency, yet his officers allegedly were lax and did not take even minimal precautions. Historians of the state blame the ensuing rout on Pesqueira's negligence, for his officers allowed themselves to be surprised by a small contingent of French. Dr. A.F. Pradeau, in his unpublished manuscript, "The History of Guaymas," contradicts this viewpoint, and writes that he interviewed a survivor of La Pasión in 1914 who reported that the Sonorans were not surprised. The old veteran contended that the ammunition was old and defective; therefore, when the French attacked and the guns would not fire, the republicans fled in terror.

After the battle, the French broke the spirit of the Juaristas. Some even accused the general of treason and of supplying the French with information; however, there is no indication of this. Pesqueira retreated to Hermosillo with a small force. At this city, anti-Pesqueira sentiments within the republican ranks came to the surface. Some dissident elements wanted to replace the general with Francisco Serna, but the latter refused their offer, knowing the obvious consequences the coup would have in further dividing the already cleaved republicans.[26]

The defeat at La Pasión also signalled the conservative uprisings within the state. The Yaqui revolted under José María Marquín, and the Mayo joined. In Alamos, "El Chato," José María Tranquilino Almada, revolted; in Moctezuma, Antonio Terán y Barrios and Salvador Vásquez; in Altar, José Moreno Bustamente; in Sahuaripa, Concepción Alegría; and finally the Opata and the Pima under Refugio Tánori seconded the empire.

Soon the French occupation spread throughout Sonora, panicking the Mexican citizenry. The French moved to pacify the populace, and intentionally did not disrupt mining in an effort to make friends with the proprietors. General Castagny addressed Sonorans:

Sonorans! I come to protect you, but if you refuse my protection I shall invade your cities, I shall offend the honor of your wives and daughters and I shall deliver you to certain death, such as I have accomplished in Sinaloa. [27]

Courtesy of Guillermo Pesqueira Serrano

Ignacio Pesqueira and his family in the 1850s. From left: Dolores, Ramona García Morales (Pesqueira's first wife and sister of Jesús García Morales), Manuel, Ramón, and Ignacio holding his son Ignacio.

The imperialists launched an aggressive offensive. On June 10, 1865, Francisco Gándara attacked Ures, defended by García Morales, who successfully repelled the attack. Meanwhile, Colonel Isidoro Teódulo Garnier marched toward Hermosillo in hope of taking advantage of Pesqueira's mentally and physically weakened condition, thereby ending the resistance with his capture. When Pesqueira evacuated the city, retreating toward Ures, French troops entered Hermosillo without firing a shot.[28]

Imperial forces then pursued Pesqueira to the state's capital, Ures, on July 13, where they attacked. Finally, on July 30, the imperialists won control of the capital. On August 15, 1865, Garnier entered the city on the same day that Brincourt entered Chihuahua City, sending Juárez fleeing to the city of El Paso del Norte, which is today Ciudad Juárez.[29]

Pesqueira, with a force of about four hundred, retreated to the hacienda of La Concepción called El Molinote. Pesqueira, completely demoralized, disbanded his troops and commenced a leave of absence. At this point Pesqueira was psychologically exhausted, for added to his political setbacks was the death of his eleven-year-old son, Manuel, in the town of Arizpe.[30]

Pesqueira crossed the boundary line into Arizona, proceeding toward Tubac with his wife Ramona García Morales de Pesqueira. On route to their destination, the party crossed a river where his ailing wife was forced to abandon the carriage. In fording the river Ramona got wet, aggravating her illness. In the Calabasas area, Captain M.H. Calderwood of the California Volunteers granted Pesqueira permission to encamp. North American officials in Arizona extended their protection to Pesqueira because they sympathized with the Juarista cause and self-interest dictated that Arizonans prevent foreign occupation of her borders. In the home of Colonel Lewis of Fort Mason, the condition of Ramona Pesqueira worsened. Moreover, word came that the French had sent a force of about two hundred to capture Pesqueira; whereupon Colonel Lewis announced his intention of resisting the invaders and continued to harbor Pesqueira.[31]

Historian Almada described Pesqueira's plight while in Tubac:

Seriously ill with a cerebral congestion from which he miraculously recovered and hardly had he forgotten this illness, than he was attacked by enteritis to such an extent that during several months he could not be moved.[32]

His wife died on October 25, 1865. This personal tragedy, added to his physical incapacity, prevented the general from leading the republican struggle.[33]

SONORA'S RESISTANCE

Once Pesqueira left the state, the French attempted to control Sonora. García Morales led the liberal opposition in guerilla warfare which was noted for its bitterness and, as in the rest of the nation, was cruel and implacable. In turn, imperialists commenced a reign of terror in which the liberal families of Arizpe and Matupe were persecuted. Many of them were taken to Ures and mistreated to the point of death.[34]

The tenacious Jesús García Morales, the state's foremost hero and Pesqueira's brother-in-law, now led the republicans, harassing persistently the enemy at every turn. The official imperialist newspaper described him as dangerous — to be treated as an outlaw. But the discontent in Sonora worked to the advantage of the French. Had Sonorans been united, the state could not have been occupied. Most of the ranchers had firearms, and it would have been impossible to disarm them. In other Mexican states, this had been a major problem; in Sonora, the ranchers did not hamper the imperialists, for they had been Gandaristas and vehemently anti-Pesqueira; therefore, they remained neutral.[35]

The French divided Sonora into four military districts, with the first at Altar and Magdalena, the second at Oposura and Arizpe, the third at Ures and Hermosillo, and the fourth at Alamos. In these districts, according to the

French, they had loyal commanders. Captain Guillet gave the breakdown of manpower as follows:

	Men
Permanent guard of Yaqui and Mayo chiefs	40
Five companies of thirty men, one each (Altar, Magdalena, Arizpe, Oposura, and Ures)	150
Two companies of fifty men (Hermosillo and Alamos)	100
Three sections of mountain troops of fifteen men (Altar, Ures, Alamos)	45
Two companies of fifty men at the orders of Tánori	100
Two squadrons of forty men (Altar and Hermosillo)	80
Total: 435 plus 80 cavalry	515

In addition to these forces, Guillet estimated another thousand auxiliaries. [36] During the remainder of 1865, the imperialists controlled Sonora.

The only threat to the imperialists came from Sinaloa when General Antonio Rosales, a former governor of Sinaloa, attacked the district of Alamos during the first days of September 1865. "El Chato" Almada headed this district, where in addition to regular troops he could count on fifteen hundred Yaqui and Mayo. The two armies maneuvered for position, each attempting to gain control; the struggle centered on the outskirts of Alamos.[37]

Rosales finally took possession of the city, but on September 22, 1865, the imperialists counterattacked with a force numbering about two thousand. A fierce battle followed in which the liberals suffered a decisive defeat. The Indians had rallied to the support of "El Chato." During this battle, the imperialists mortally wounded General Rosales, who had fought valiantly in hand to hand combat in the streets of Alamos.[38]

Liberals and imperialists alike admired the valor of Rosales. After the battle, Almada gallantly permitted him a funeral with full military honors. After a city-wide wake, they buried Rosales' body in the municipal cemetery of Alamos. Many years later, a grateful Mexican government transferred Rosales' remains to the Rotonda de Hombres Ilustres in México D.F.[39]

After this incident, Almada's control over Alamos was complete. The French named him prefect of the department of Alamos and awarded him the highest imperialist decoration, the Order of Guadalupe. At the time, most of the other major cities of Mexico were controlled by the imperialists.[40]

The situation in Sonora, as in most of Mexico, appeared hopeless, with liberal guerrillas struggling against insurmountable odds. In the autumn of

1865, both United States' pressure and the growing tenseness of Europe, caused in part by the rise of Prussia, encouraged Napoleon III to reevaluate his commitment. He instructed Francois Archille Bazaine to order the withdrawal of French troops to the center of Mexico.[41] Ironically, the French at that time came very close to consolidating their control of the northern frontier including Sonora. Instead of grasping victory, they withdrew.

TURNING THE TIDE

On January 3, 1866, the imperialists won their last significant battle at Nácori Grande near Matape. There the combined forces of Francisco Gándara and Refugio Tánori defeated Jesús García Morales. Four days later, General Angel Martínez and his famous *macheteros* entered Sonora and directed themselves against the forces of "El Chato." Twenty-eight-year-old Martínez was completely dedicated to drive the French out of Mexico. General Ramón Corona, in charge of the Federal Army of the West, sent Martínez to Sonora, ordering him to operate in northern Sinaloa and Sonora. His men had been nicknamed the "*macheteros*" because of the machetes they carried. Their reputation as ferocious fighters had spread to Sonora, where Carlota Miles described the panic of the Alameños and the terrifying fervor of the *macheteros.*

With terrifying war whoops they would charge into the enemy and cut down men, women, and children alike. When Martínez was approaching Alamos, Almada decided to wait in the city for the attack. Trenches were dug and fortifications were built in the surrounding hills; Guadalupe Hill in the center of town was strongly fortified. . .
The adherents of the Imperium were seized with panic and emigrated *en masse.* [42]

Martínez and his men attacked Alamos, fighting their way into the city; the imperialists defended their city, combating hand to hand with the invaders. Martínez, however, overwhelmed the imperialists, who were forced to abandon the city. The *macheteros* plundered and destroyed; respecting nothing, they broke into churches on horseback and stole valuable religious objects. The *macheteros* fully enjoyed the spoils of the war, with their screams and laughter often breaking the silence of the night.[43]

Angel Martínez became Sonora's most successful field commander, forcing Almada to retreat to the Mayan pueblos where "El Chato" recruited more men and rearmed his army. Almada counterattacked Martínez and his forces, only to meet defeat again. The *macheteros'* savagery reached new depths as they followed the Indians into their river valleys. More battles ensued, with the Indians fighting gallantly against the ruthless Mexican patriots. Meanwhile, the central command summoned Almada to Guaymas where he incorporated his forces with those of Emilio Lamberg, then Commander of the imperial army in Sonora.[44]

With Alamos under his control, Angel Martínez reorganized its administration. He divided the local army into three battalions: "Cazadores del Occidente," "Defensores de Sonora," and "Libres de Sonora." At the head of these battalions he appointed Jesús Toledo, José T. Otero, and Adolfo Alcántara, respectively.

Pesqueira viewed the events with interest from Tubac, Arizona. Martínez' victories encouraged the former governor and the liberals throughout the state. On February 28, 1866, twenty-five officers under Jesús García Morales, with the commander's approval, issued a petition requesting Pesqueira to return and resume command of the Sonora troops. Ignacio Pesqueira, heartened by Martínez' success, resolved to return to his native state and to the fight.[45]

Pesqueira's return was symbolic of Sonora's independence,[46] and a rallying point for the masses. Many of his partisans, however, must have questioned his return to assume command. After all, he had deserted Sonora in her hour of need. The governor, nevertheless, still had many partisans who welcomed his return.

A succession of events followed: on March 1, 1866, federal officials promoted Martínez to the rank of major general and put him in command of the united brigades of Sonora, Sinaloa, and Jalisco; three days later Pesqueira returned to Los Broncos, Sonora, near his native town of Arizpe. There Pesqueira took command of a guerrilla band under Major Bernardo Zúñiga, after which Pesqueira set out to unite liberal bands. As he marched, partisans joined him, and by the first of April, his force had swelled to three hundred men. At Buenavista, he once more assumed the offices of governor and commanding general of Sonora. All other liberal leaders recognized his leadership.[47]

On April 6, 1866, Jesús García Morales attacked the plaza of the villa of Magdalena and won another battle. Over one hundred men under Lieutenant Colonel Manuel I. Castro's command defended the pueblo, and after two hours of hard fighting, surrendered. With this success, García Morales' band swelled.[48]

During April, García Morales' and Martínez' forces operated independently: Martínez roamed Sonora, leaving the district of Alamos under the charge of Commandant Lorenzo Torres.* On May 4, 1866, Martínez attacked and routed Almada at Hermosillo, who had held the city with four hundred men. In Hermosillo, Martínez expropriated large quantities of arms and

---

*Almada, pp. 791-792. Lorenzo Torres (1836-1912) later became governor of Sonora. Up until the time of French intervention, Torres was not well known in Sonora.

munitions from the enemy, sacked the city, and slaughtered the opposition.* Martínez did not rest, and when he learned from his scouts that the enemy had marched on Hermosillo, he went out to meet them with a small cavalry force. He discovered the enemy force just outside the city, but did not expect eight hundred troops. The imperialists, commanded by Lamberg, Tánori, and Salvador Vásquez, forced Martínez to retreat to San Marcial, where he joined the rest of his army. The *macheteros'* morale suffered from this defeat.

After reorganizing his troops, Martínez renewed his raids throughout the state, taking the plaza of Ures by surprise with a force of about three hundred horsemen. He skirmished with the army led by Lamberg and Tánori, with neither side winning. Soon afterwards, he incorporated his band with the forces of Pesqueira and García Morales at San Marcial.[49]

Beginning in June, the Juarists made incessant raids, disrupting communications between Ures and Hermosillo. The liberal headquarters were established at San Marcial. The intensity of the liberal operations increased, and by mid-year their fortunes had improved greatly. Liberals controlled the district of Alamos, the strategic northern villa of Magdalena, and numerous other pueblos. The imperialists controlled Sahuaripa, Moctezuma, Arizpe, Guaymas, Altar, Ures, and part of the district of Hermosillo.[50]

Maximilian's armies lost ground during the next two months, although they still controlled key districts.† Pesqueira and Martínez stepped up their raids, and on August 14, Martínez captured Hermosillo and allegedly slaughtered all Frenchmen. By this time the action centered in and around Hermosillo and the initiative had passed to the liberals, setting the stage for the Battle of Guadalupe.[51]

BATTLE OF GUADALUPE

The Battle of Guadalupe proved the turning point of the war, making possible the invasion and capture of Ures and ending the French threat in Sonora.[52] The battle began during the first days of September, with republican forces mobilizing over Ures, defended by General Lamberg. During the second and third days of September, operations began with the imperialists forming their line of defense at the pueblo of Guadalupe. Hostilities broke out on September 4, with intense fighting on both sides. By

---

*Bancroft, *Northern Mexican States*, II, 697. Lamberg to Sonorans, May 7, 1866, in Fernando Pesqueira, "Documentos Para la Historia de Sonora," Segunda Serie, Tomo IV, accused Martínez, García Morales, and Pesqueira of crimes and killings. He decreed the death penalty for anyone aiding or not reporting their whereabouts.

†B.R. Carman to Seward, Mazatlán, July 1, 1866, "Despatches from U.S. Consuls in Mazatlán," complained that every day the French were more and more aware of the mistake that they had made in coming to Mexico. He wrote that the French were very anti-North American.

the afternoon, the imperialists' defense had been broken and the imperialists hastily retreated in all directions, leaving General Lamberg's corpse behind.

On the fifth, the republican forces prepared to attack Ures, which had been weakened on the day before. By the sixth, Ures fell to the republicans. On the next day, Pesqueira installed the Ayuntamiento of Ures, presided over by Cirilo Ramírez, an old-time supporter of the governor.

Pesqueira then dispatched Jesús García Morales in pursuit of enemies in the district of Moctezuma, where he captured and executed Terán y Barrios. Angel Martínez marched to Guaymas, and on September 14, the French, in retreat, embarked taking Sonora prisoners with them. This ended the French occupation of Sonora, leaving thousands of sympathetic families at the mercy of Martínez, who occupied Guaymas on September 15.[53]

The threat of monarchy ended in Sonora, with the remaining imperialists retreating to the Yaqui and Mayo river valleys. There the Indians remained loyal to the imperialist cause and continued to fight.[54] The struggle ended with the republicans in control. The republicans, who by this time received North American aid, quickly subdued the imperialists, who were without French troops and supplies.

"El Chato" knew that all was lost; therefore, he attempted to escape to Baja California. At Médano he took a French schooner with his two sons Salvador and José, his chiefs of staff, and the faithful Refugio Tánori. Martínez learned of the escape and sent a pursuit ship from Guaymas to intercept the escapees. The republicans captured the ship in the middle of the Gulf of California.

Abato Avilés executed Almada on the spot.* He then returned the other captives to Guaymas where officials courtmartialed and executed them. Among them, Refugio Tánori had remained loyal to the emperor to the last. At his execution he shouted defiantly to the executioners as they raised their muskets:

I am going to die for defending the cause of the Empire, which enlarges the social regeneration of my country, its independence, its honor. . . I die, well satisfied, for having complied with my obligations as a Mexican. Long live the Emperor.[55]

---

*A.F. Pradeau relates an interesting sidelight told to him by Lauro Quiroz, the captain in charge of the firing squad which executed Lorenzo Avilés. Almada took Lorenzo, along with his secretary – a boy of sixteen – prisoner, and when Avilés attempted to defend the boy, Almada arbitrarily stated: "Enough of this comedy, execute him." Before Avilés was executed, he gave Quiroz his watch and fob but made him promise that he would take his bloody shirt to his mother – Loreta Encinas de Avilés in Guaymas. Quiroz did so, telling his mother what had happened and offering to return the watch to her. She replied that she would not accept the watch and fob because her son wanted him to have it. In front of the imperialist officer, she called in her three other sons and made them swear that they would revenge the death of Lorenzo – popularly known as El Manzano ("the apple," because his cheeks were always so rosy).

The thunder of the bullets drowned out the cry of the Opata, who fell to the ground dead. Thus ended the career of the Indian rebel and signalled the close of the French intervention in Sonora.

Sonora had suffered greatly from this intervention.* The civil war within the state had split families. The plundering and depredations by both sides had ravaged Sonora's properties. Liberals fell victims of the wrath of Castagny, who had warned them that he would rape and plunder if they did not obey him; the reign of terror imposed on Arizpe and Matape mirrored this perfidy. On the other hand, the whoops of Angel Martínez and his *macheteros*, as they raced through the state resembling the hordes of Attila the Hun, would not soon be forgotten. It now remained for Pesqueira to consolidate Sonora, for once more he reigned as her unchallenged caudillo.[56]

---

*Pesqueira to Sonorans, Ures, October 1, 1866, *La Estrella de Occidente,* October 19, 1866. Pesqueira formally addressed the citizens of Sonora declaring the peace and giving credit for the victory to Martínez and Jesús García Morales on October 1, 1866.

CHAPTER 8

Last of the 1860s

In 1867, the last French troops withdrew from Mexico, beginning the end of the imperial government of Mexico. On February 3, 1867, Marshall Bazaine, in the name of the army, addressed the Mexican people:

During the four years that they have stayed in your beautiful capital, they could only congratulate themselves in the sympathetic relations that were established between themselves and the people.

So in the name of the French army under his orders and in his own name the Marshall of France takes his leave of you.

I tender you all our best wishes for the welfare of the chivalrous Mexican nation.

All our efforts have tended to establish internal peace. Rest assured of that; and I assure you at this moment of leaving you, that our mission has never had any other object, and it has never entered the intentions of France to impose upon you any form of government contrary to your will.[1]

On February 5, the French raised and lowered the tricolor for the last time in the Mexican capital. The troops then marched out toward the eastern Mexican coast where they boarded ships bound for France. On March 12, the last two French ships left Veracruz, leaving Maximilian at the mercy of Benito Juárez.[2]

After the departure of the French Army from México D.F., Maximilian also abandoned the capital and marched to Querétaro where he arrived on February 13. There he prepared for his last stand. On March 4 the troops of Generals Ramón Corona and Mariano Escobedo arrived at Querétaro and prepared to besiege the city.[3]

Escobedo headed the Juarista forces; Generals Miguel Miramón and Tómas Mejía commanded the imperialists. The Juaristas laid a savage seige, but the protagonist of the empire fought valiantly against insurmountable odds. Finally, on May 15, Querétaro fell and Maximilian was taken prisoner. The emperor surrendered to General Bibiano Dávalos, who delivered him to Corona, then to Escobedo, who accepted Maximilian's sword.[4]

A Council of War tried and found Emperor Maximilian guilty, and on the morning of June 19, 1867, at the Cerro de las Campanas, the republicans executed Maximilian together with his faithful generals, Mejía and Miramón. He stood between the two men — Mejía, who could have evaded this moment but had purposely marched to Querétaro to be with his emperor to the end, and the handsome Miguel Miramón, the outstanding conservative general of his time. The shots from Juárez' soldiers' guns sounded the end of the French intervention in Mexico.[5]

Pesqueira attempted to restore order to Sonora. Guerilla wars had ravaged for over two years and, consequently, conditions were critical. In the latter stages of the war, Pesqueira did not help the Juarista forces to any great extent, because he needed the men and resources at home. He did, however, contribute twenty thousand pesos to Ramón Corona and his Army of the West.[6] When the war ended, the governor had a difficult problem to solve — reviving a bankrupt state.

A BANKRUPT SONORA

The French intervention marked a turning point in Ignacio Pesqueira's career. Even before the war, opposition was growing among the very groups who had sponsored his governorship. He had remained in power only through the grace of the state militia and capable coworkers such as Jesús García Morales. Pesqueira's image as a strong leader also contributed to his success. But his abandonment of Sonora during the French intervention had tarnished his image, encouraging many to oppose him.

After the departure of the French, Pesqueira once more had an opportunity to reestablish his reputation. Overwhelming problems confronted him, but perhaps his experience as a leader could have brought order. At first, he appeared attentive to fiscal problems. He attacked the most pressing barrier to Sonora's economic progress — the lack of a stable currency. The root of much of this trouble was that Sonora's currency was based on copper coins, an unstable specie, due to its extreme fluctuation. Its value was uncertain — usually 37 percent of its face value — and considered good when at 40 to 50 centavos on the peso. The great number of counterfeit copper coins in circulation added to the weakness of the currency. Such counterfeiting badly shook the people's confidence. This uncertainty led to the operation of Gresham's law: Large quantities of silver and gold were hoarded, removing large quantities of coins from circulation, constricting the flow of money, and depressing the economy.[7]

In an attempt to alleviate this problem, Pesqueira limited the circulation of copper coins, stopping the coinage of the metal, and redeemed the copper coins with silver. On June 19 in Hermosillo, he imposed a forced loan of forty-five thousand pesos on the more prosperous citizens of Hermosillo, Guaymas, and Ures. This move was designed to finance the withdrawal of copper specie, most of whose circulation centered in Hermosillo and Ures. Although Pesqueira knew that forced loans would evoke opposition, he felt this step was necessary in order to avoid a calamity. In an editorial featured in the official state newspaper, *La Estrella de Occidente*, on June 21, 1867, the government issued a patriotic appeal to the wealthy capitalists of Sonora, urging them to loan the government silver to finance the exchange for the copper currency. Pesqueira also granted Hermosillo capitalists the power to issue more money in an attempt to increase money circulation and stimulate industry.[8]

Another problem was the minting of the bullion mined within the state. Since Sonora stood so far from the commercial centers of Mexico, out-of-state minting proved expensive. The ores could not be transported over the bandit infested highways because the losses were high. Shipping costs were prohibitive; therefore, Pesqueira attempted to increase the minting of more money at the Casas de Moneda in Alamos and Hermosillo.[9]

The many trade and travel restrictions within Sonora presented barriers to the free flow of capital: Oppressive interior duties drove up the cost of goods; Indians and highwaymen made the roads of the state unsafe; State law required citizens to carry passports, primarily designed to control the people in times of turmoil and to prevent the evasion of forced conscription. Pesqueira moved to eliminate these barriers, however, he did not effectively meet the challenge.

CONFLICT WITH FEDERAL OFFICIALS

Pesqueira needed money to finance his programs, and local sources proved limited. The rancheros were land poor; the miners and merchants were already overtaxed. In reality the federal customshouse at Guaymas proved the only consistent source of revenue. During the French intervention, it had been placed under the direction of Governor Pesqueira and he used the funds at his discretion. After the war, he fully expected to continue controlling imports and exports and using these taxes to finance state programs.

In August of 1867, however, the federal government resumed control of the customshouse. That same month a dispute broke out between the officials of the customshouse and Pesqueira. The governor attempted to requisition funds from the federal officials with the excuse that he sorely needed the money to carry out his wars against the Indians. When Pesqueira asked for the money, the custom's collector, Bartolomé E. Almada, refused the request. Almada had remained loyal to Pesqueira and the liberal cause throughout the French intervention and, in fact, had been appointed to this post by the governor himself. Now he was placed in the position where he had to oppose his benefactor. In her biography of Almada, *Almada of Alamos*, Carlota Miles describes this incident:

. . .an office [the Collector of Customs] for which he was well-equipped with previous experience in Mazatlán. His business correspondence is preserved, including many letters to President Juárez, which testify to his sound judgment and unswerving honesty. It was on matters of principle that he got into difficulties with Pesqueira, who dismissed him when he refused to conform with the Governor's arbitrary use of the customs proceeds. (p. 180)

Whether Pesqueira had used these funds arbitrarily is open to conjecture, for Sonora did need the money and the federal government would not and could not give the support needed to subdue the Indians. Once funds left the state, very little, if any, trickled back. Almada must have realized this, and knew that peace could not be restored without funds.[10] But Almada, a dedicated man with a strong sense of duty, under the direct authority of the federal government, automatically obeyed the federal authority which was superior to Pesqueira's. Moreover, Almada, like the rest of Sonora, had become dissatisfied with Pesqueira's rule.

In December of 1867, Pesqueira brought matters to a crisis when the English merchant ship *Coquette* arrived in Guaymas. He used this occasion to demonstrate his superiority over the collector, who represented the federal authorities. Knowing that the ship had a large cargo and that Almada would not allow him to legally appropriate the customs, he relieved Almada of his duties, replacing him with one of his puppets. His officials then collected the customs, applying 40 percent of the revenues to the debts Sonora incurred during the war against the *Imperium* and applying the remainder to the campaigns against the Indians. After this show of strength, Pesqueira returned the customshouse to Almada.[11] This incident underlined Pesqueira's growing tendency to operate independently of México D.F.

RETURN TO CIVIL GOVERNMENT

Sonora returned to civil rule. On August 14, 1867, Juárez decreed that the states should hold elections. On September 27, 1867, Pesqueira scheduled Sonora's local elections and announced his decision not to be a candidate, indicating his desire to return to private life to manage his haciendas and mines. Friends, however, began a "draft Pesqueira" movement, leading him to announce:

I neither accept nor renounce the candidacy which you offer me, but if the different groups of the state draft me, I cannot but accept the mandate, even though I have resolved to withdraw myself from it as soon as possible.[12]

García Morales, Pesqueira's running mate, headed the draft movement. He unified support by establishing Pesqueira clubs throughout the state. The campaign theme: Sonora needs a man of Pesqueira's tried administrative ability to heal the ravages of war. During this time, Pesqueira prepared the state for civil rule. In November of 1867, he relinquished control of the state's military forces to his trusted aide, Jesús García Morales. On the first of the following month, Sonorans elected Governor Pesqueira to another term.

During the elections, complaints circulated about Pesqueira's desire for another term.[13] Most Sonorans, however, put aside their differences. Whether from a feeling of gratitude or from a desire for peace, they returned the caudillo to office.

After this election, Pesqueira's relationship with the legislature changed. When the Third Constitutional Legislature convened on November 28, the legislature was in no mood to rubber stamp his actions. From the start it was obvious that opposition to the governor would erupt from the assembly. Domingo Elías Gonzales, a lawyer and educator who had supported the liberal cause during the French intervention, led the dissidents: Francisco C. Aguilar, whose background is unknown; Ramón Martínez, a lawyer who married a Pesqueira and later joined the governor's supporters; and Francisco Moreno Buelna, active in politics for the district of Ures.[14]

Many citizens in the major towns supported the opposition because they were tired of Pesqueira, believing that he presented an obstacle to reform legislation. Almost immediately friction developed within the administration, erupting when García Morales resigned from the office of deputy governor to become the federal military commanding general of the state. The opposition bloc would not cooperate with the governor and they prevented the filling of the deputy-governorship until May 28, 1868. Finally, the legislature appointed the governor's friend, Manuel Monteverde.[15]

Another source of irritation was Pesqueira's opposition to the election of a magistrate of the state supreme court and several judges. He alleged that they had aided the imperial forces and, therefore, should not be allowed to hold office. The legislators disagreed and, in spite of the governor's opposition, approved their commissions. This annoyed Pesqueira especially since he was not accustomed to being opposed.[16]

Pesqueira, on the other hand, began to neglect his official duties and took frequent sojourns to his hacienda, Las Delicias.* The frequency of these leaves reminded Sonorans of Antonio López de Santa Anna's frequent retreats to Manga de Clavo.[17] Consequently, the burden of office devolved on Secretary of State Manuel Monteverde, who ruled through the grace of Pesqueira.

---

*Enriqueta de Parodi, *Sonora* p. 217. The following is the governor's record during his twenty years in office. His absenteeism is clearly illustrated:

Substitute Governor	8-9-56	to	5-6-57	I. Pesqueira
Constitutional Governor	5-7-57		8-27-57	J. de Aguilar
Constitutional Governor	8-28-57		4-7-61	I. Pesqueira
Interim Governor	4-8-61		6-7-61	J. Escalante Moreno
Constitutional Governor	6-8-61		8-10-65	I. Pesqueira
Governor and Commandant	8-11-65		3-17-66	García Morales
Constitutional Governor	3-18-66		6-10-68	I. Pesqueira
Substitute Governor	6-11-68		12-31-69	M. Monteverde
Constitutional Governor	1-10-69		7-27-69	I. Pesqueira
Substitute Governor	7-28-69		10-8-69	M. Monteverde
Constitutional Governor	10-9-69		12-12-69	I. Pesqueira
Substitute Governor	12-13-69		6-12-70	M. Monteverde
Constitutional Governor	6-13-70		1-23-72	I. Pesqueira
Interim Governor	1-27-72		2-28-72	J. Astiazaran
Constitutional Governor	2-10-72		2-28-72	I. Pesqueira
Interim Governor	3-10-72		9-23-72	J. Astiazaran
Constitutional Governor	9-16-73		8-31-75	I. Pesqueira
Constitutional Governor	9-10-75		4-2-76	J. Pesqueira

Legislative opposition increased and a running battle in the highly partisan state press raged. In an editorial dated February 7, 1868, *La Estrella de Occidente* lambasted the legislature as a "do-nothing legislature," charging that it frequently obstructed legal procedures for lack of a quorum. A week later this newspaper openly attacked *El Pueblo de Sonora* (another paper) for criticizing Pesqueira's failure to make headway with the legislature. In the next issue of the weekly newspaper, *La Estrella* responded to charges of *El Pueblo* that the former was Pesqueira's puppet. Both papers hurled charges and countercharges. This running battle, however, came to an abrupt halt about the end of the month, when *El Pueblo de Sonora* suspended publication, charging interference with freedom of the press.[18]

By May, rumors spread that another opposition newspaper had been planned. Reportedly, Domingo Elías Gonzales, leader of the anti-Pesqueiristas, headed this group. Upon learning of the project, *La Estrella* questioned the motives of Elías and his associates, asking whether it would be the paper's policy to oppose the governor and the liberal party.* On May 15 *La Estrella* again attacked Elías and his cohorts for daring to advance García Morales' candidacy for governor, accusing Elías of bad faith. It became apparent that opposition to Pesqueira would not be tolerated; the opposition suddenly subsided when the legislature named Monteverde deputy governor. This allowed Pesqueira to return to Las Delicias.[19]

INDIAN MENACE

Renewed Yaqui and Mayo outbreaks in the last days of 1867 ended Pesqueira's vacation. After the French intervention, encroachments in these regions by land-hungry Sonorans had multiplied, angering the Indians. The Yaqui rebels were the first to revolt when, in the latter part of 1867, a group of Indians killed soldiers led by Ramón Talamantes, the Commanding General of the Yaqui Valley at Bacum. In December the Yaqui crossed the Mayo River to join their brothers of that valley. There they attacked the garrison at Santa Cruz, killing an Indian cacique named Matías and fourteen of his followers who opposed the rebellion. Next, the rebels attacked the pueblos of Etchojoa and San Pedro. Sonora officials responded by sending Alejo Toledo, Commandant of the Sonora national guard, and José S. Prado, the prefect of Alamos, against the rebellious Indians.[20]

These operations had little success; therefore, Colonel Prospero Salazar Bustamante with a contingent of five hundred men left Guaymas for the embattled area. Upon reaching the Yaqui River, Colonel Bustamante established his general headquarters at Medano, which he chose because it stood adjacent to a river's mouth. From that location he sent expeditions into the Yaqui and Mayo valleys, engaging in frequent successful skirmishes.[21]

La Estrella de Occidente, March 8, 1868. By this time, opposition to the liberal party was tantamount to treason.

The savage war continued into the year 1868, with government forces constantly pursuing the Indians, who usually confined their activities to the outer edges of the rivers. While they limited their encounters to skirmishes, they were fierce, and neither side showed mercy nor offered quarter. The Sonorans treated the Indians cruelly, mistreating the women and children who were taken prisoners and profitably confiscating the Indians' personal property, such as livestock and food, in addition to their lands.[22]

On February 12, 1868, Colonel Salazar Bustamante routed a party of Indians near Cocorit, on the south side of the Yaqui River and deep in Yaqui country. Republican government forces killed thirty-three Indians, taking an equal number of prisoners. Three days later, six hundred more Indians arrived in Cocorit, requesting peace. Colonel Bustamante took them into custody, ordering them to deliver their arms. When he collected only forty-eight weapons, he insisted that the number should be at least three hundred.

The angry colonel then released a proportionate number of Indians, marching the prisoners to the town of Bacum where Salazar Bustamante ordered the Indians herded into the local church which he used as a stockade. The troops then separated ten chiefs selected to be shot if the Indians made a false move. A disaster took place the night of the eighteenth: the official state newspaper reported that the ten chiefs attempted to escape under the cover of darkness and were shot by the state militia.[23] The firing, according to the newspaper account, caused a chain reaction with the soldiers blasting into the church. The soldiers ignored the facts that the Indians occupied a church which offered the traditional right of asylum and that they were unarmed.

Panic gripped the Indians as the Sonora soldiers fired artillery into the church. Defenseless, they stampeded, but the Sonorans continued their determined shooting. By 2:00 A.M. only fifty-nine Indians remained alive in the church; about one hundred and twenty lay dead. In the confusion, however, the rest had miraculously escaped. In contrast, the Sonorans lost only four in this inhuman massacre.[24]

This action at Bacum broke the Indian resistance, and by May, 1868, the Yaqui and Mayo revolt had ended. Military Commander Jesús García Morales then ordered the evacuation of his troops. But on July 5, 1868, the Mayo rebels revolted again, this time attacking the town of Etchojoa, killing eighteen people, among whom numbered the local judge. Then four hundred Mayo directed their force against the town of Santa Cruz.

Upon hearing of this uprising, Lieutenant Colonel José T. Otero, with a national guard contingent, left to pursue the rebels. The campaign continued until October. Sonora troops again overwhelmed the Indians, who had few firearms or supplies. When these ran out, the Mayo surrendered.[25]

Meanwhile, the Apache continued their war of extermination without cease. From November, 1866, until the beginning of February, 1869, these Indians murdered seventy-eight men, eleven women, and seventeen children.

The total number of deaths reached one hundred and sixteen. In contrast, the Sonorans killed no more than thirty-five Apache Indians. The state lost more than sixty thousand pesos as the result of thefts, burnings, and lost cattle. Early in 1868, the governor asked the federal government to help finance an effective expedition against the Apache. It was impossible for the Sonorans to fight two wars at the same time; they could not fight both the Apache and the Cahita.* In 1869, the United States Consul in Sonora pointed out that stepped-up North American operations in Arizona had worsened conditions in Sonora, with many of the Apache shifting their operations into Sonora, and recommended joint action.[26]

In the 1870s, the campaigns against the Apache reached a new intensity. Up to this time, many called Sonora the "great Apache Rancho." Observers wrote that white settlers existed in Sonora only because of Apache benevolence, for the Indians permitted the settlers to raise and care for the cattle and to farm grain for Indian plunder. The Sonora government had to take drastic measures against the marauders. During the 1870s, in the district of Altar, the government employed Papagos to hunt down the Apache, thus taking advantage of the historical enmity between these two Indian tribes. In addition, the government paid the Papagos three hundred pesos for each Apache scalp. In 1871, the Papagos hunted down the Apache, defeating them near the town of Arivaipa, Arizona, taking twenty-odd prisoners and slaying over one hundred Apache.[27]

These measures, however, merely served as stopgaps, as the Apache continued their raiding throughout the sixties and the seventies; in 1870 alone, they killed one hundred and twenty-three Sonorans, wounded forty-four others, and captured seven more. Pesqueira failed to control the Apache, and once more he appealed to the federal government for its assistance. Conditions worsened to the point that it appeared as if the Apache had depopulated Sonora's northern frontier. The federal government attempted to help, and passed a law granting Sonora six thousand pesos per month to assist it in its campaigns against the Apache; soon afterwards it raised the sum to ten thousand.[28]

Relations between the U.S. and Sonora worsened, especially between the authorities and citizens of Arizona and those of Sonora. Again, many Sonorans blamed the U.S. for their plight, pointing to the policies of General O.O. Howard, the U.S. military commander in charge of herding the Apache into reservations. They accused him of arming the Apache and encouraging Apache leaders Eskiminzin and Cochise to raid Sonora.[29] Friction between the North Americans and Sonorans continued throughout Ignacio Pesqueira's

---

*Fernando Pesqueira, ed., "Documentos para la Historia de Sonora," Segunda Serie, Tomo IV, typewritten copy in the Biblioteca y Museo de Sonora, Hermosillo, Archivo General de la Nación, Secretaría de Gobernación, Archivos Viejos, Legajo 1833-1854, February 26, 1868. Pesqueira used his influence to encourage Sonorans to join the U.S. Army in order to fight the Apache.

era and lessened only as the northern frontier became more tame. A conspiracy of events helped end the Apache threat. The railroad extended into southern Arizona, bringing more settlers and soldiers to protect them.*

DOMESTIC CONFLICTS

Throughout the French intervention and the U.S. Civil War, United States-Sonora relations had been cordial. Once at peace, however, old grievances reemerged. Border tensions increased and Anglo-Americans again urged the annexation of Sonora.[30]

Sonora officials responded by raising taxes on goods transported through Sonora to Arizona, which in turn intensified the Arizona press campaign calling for the purchase of Sonora. An article dated November 16, 1867, appeared in the *Southern Arizonian*; it protested the high duties charged. The article reminded the readers of the North Americans' aid to Sonorans during the French intervention, righteously contending that North Americans had not charged Sonorans duties for supplies needed in their struggle against the French.[31]

North Americans in Sonora also actively worked for secession. Although their number did not exceed two hundred, they began to dominate the commerce of the state. According to United States consular records toward the end of the 1860s, six North Americans were merchants, three owned hotels, four engaged in agriculture, and the overwhelming majority were miners. By the later 1860s, the latter complained chiefly about the high taxes imposed upon the mining industry, asserting that these taxes were almost confiscatory, and also protesting the 21 percent export tax on silver. Although many miners remained, the Americanos alleged that many had been "ruined in fortune and broken in spirit."[32] Although the duties were federally imposed, most of the foreign investors blamed the Sonora government for their calamities.

The tax problem was especially acute in Sonora, for the Indian wars drained large sums of money.[33] Moreover, Pesqueira appeared unable to ameliorate the state's economic plight as his only solution was to impose taxes on top of federal taxes.

In March of 1869, United States Consul Willard criticized a state import tax, documenting general dissatisfaction with Pesqueira:

Politically this part of Mexico is quiet. Commercially, everything is at a standstill and the Custom House is enforcing full duties on all imported goods on arrival which is causing general dissatisfaction to all our merchants.[34]

---

*It was not until the 1880s that a railroad linking Guaymas and Nogales was finally built – the Southern Pacific Line, which passed through Hermosillo, making the latter the Chicago of Sonora.

Consul Willard referred to a new state tax that the governor had sponsored. State officials collected this import tax upon arrival, refusing to release goods before payment. It placed a burden on merchants who had to spend capital before they had earned a profit. It prevented cheating on taxes; nonetheless, merchants looked upon the measure as another burden. This taxation issue caused a breach not only between the governor and foreigners, but between the governor and the state's merchants.

In 1868, Sonora suffered a catastrophe when, on October 15, the rains continued to pour for seventy-two consecutive hours. The rains pounded and the sea became turbulent, with the surf devastating Sonora's coast. Inland the rains also fell in torrents, damaging much property. The storm raged from Mazatlán to Guaymas, flooding the Mayo and Yaqui valleys and washing out towns, such as Navojoa on the Mayo River. The banks of the Yaqui River allegedly rose fifty-six feet. The storm caused an estimated one and a half million dollars of damage.

The rains struck Alamos, eroding many of the adobe buildings which crumbled under the pounding of the waters. On the seventeenth the arroyo broke its banks, forcing the evacuation of many of the best neighborhoods of Alamos.[35] Many people perished while attempting to escape; the fortunate escaped with no more than the shirts on their backs.

These fortunate Alameños took refuge on the hill of Guadalupe where they stayed for a day before moving to the church, the only remaining safe building in the city. Nature had reduced this once beautiful city into a desert. Pesqueira sympathetically exempted Alameños from taxes. Unfortunately, the aid amounted to tokenism, for impoverished Sonora could not give tangible support.[36]

INTERNAL DISORDERS

Fortunately the last of the 1860s saw relatively few major civil wars; the ones that did erupt were quickly subdued. Nevertheless, these wars are significant as they underscored the growing dissatisfaction with Pesqueira and the Juaristas.

Salvador Vásquez was an imperialist officer who had fought against Pesqueira during the French intervention and a bitter enemy of the governor who had ordered the execution of Vásquez' father for political reasons. Vásquez, a full-blooded Indian, charged that Pesqueira discriminated against him because of his Indian ancestry. After the defeat of the imperialist forces, Vásquez fled to Casas Grandes, Chihuahua, to await the opportunity to return. In June of 1868, the opportunity arrived and he invaded Sonora. On June 8, 1868, he occupied the town of Granados, but almost immediately the state militia hunted him down, routing him at the town of Oputo. Soon afterwards, Pesqueira captured Vásquez and his followers. Again, the Vásquez incident underscores the alienation between Pesqueira and the Indian population of the state, which apparently viewed the caudillo as an enemy. [37]

On March 13, 1869, Colonel Adolfo Palacio rebelled at Culiacán, proclaiming Plácido Vega governor of Sinaloa. The garrison at Fuerte, Sinaloa, immediately seconded Palacio, who in turn transferred his operations to Fuerte, which bordered Sonora. These actions alarmed Sonorans, who fully expected to be invaded. Pesqueira took defensive measures, alerting troops on the Mayo River and mobilizing them in the event Alameños supported Vega. Pesqueira also went to Guaymas where he planned his campaign with federal commander General Jesús García Morales. Meanwhile, a Sinaloa militia of five hundred men under General Eulogio Parra marched against Palacio's army, which retreated into Chihuahua; Parra followed Palacio and defeated the rebels on March 18. [38]

Sonora remained quiet as military opposition did not materialize in the state. Although discontent with Pesqueira, Sonora's dissidents believed that it would be futile to challenge the governor at this time.

On April 27, 1869, another disagreement between the governor and the legislature erupted. Pesqueira asked permission for another three-month leave, desiring to return to Las Delicias, and retain full executive powers. The legislature granted the leave only with the condition that Pesqueira invest his vice-governor with executive powers. [39]

On May 30, legislators issued their first salvo when scrutinizing the accounts of the general treasurer, Félix Rodríguez. Some deputies insinuated that Rodríquez had engaged in illegal activites; however, the deputies never brought the matter before the legislature in spite of the fact that Rodríguez requested it. The vice-governor asked for an extraordinary session, but the assembly refused to entertain the case. [40] Moreover, Rodríguez continued in office until 1870.

Pesqueira entered into his fourth term in office on December 1, 1869. He had been opposed by Ricardo Johnson who was, in fact, favored in the districts of Alamos and Moctezuma. Johnson's candidacy had not been properly organized, and even though Pesqueira had lost considerable public confidence, he still had enough dedicated friends who could rally support. [41]

At the national level, signs of discontent toward Benito Juárez also appeared. Many Mexicans had tired of their old leader who, like Pesqueira, seemed to consider the presidency his personal property. As a result of Juárez' victory, dissidents rebelled. This anti-Juárez activity crystallized in the Plan of Zacatecas, which declared the Juárez government illegal. On February 8, 1870, at Villa Concepción, Sinaloa, Plácido Vega declared support for the plan and Trinidad García de la Cadena, Governor of Zacatecas, as president of Mexico. [42]

Sonorans viewed this revolt with interest, although not immediately supporting it. According to the North American Consul at Guaymas, anti-Pesqueira elements wanted to see if Vega could mount a successful revolt before joining him. To do so, Vega had to gain support in Sinaloa and demonstrate his ability to win. Meanwhile, some anticipated that the rebels might invade Guaymas to seize its custom receipts. This threat ended when the customs collector left for México D.F., taking all the money with him.[43]

Changes were taking place in Mexico during this period. The government slowly began to consolidate the nation and control many of the regional caudillos. One of the last of the strongmen – Manuel Lozada – operated in Nayarit, openly defying the Juárez government for many years. Lozada, an Indian chieftain, had supported the conservatives during the wars of reform and French intervention. After these wars, he continued to defy Juárez, who found it convenient to ignore Lozada. While Lozada did not take an active role in Vega's revolt, he is said to have sponsored Vega, giving him aid and comfort. In the opinion of U.S. consular agents, both Lozada and Vega had ambitions to establish a western republic.[44]

Vega sought to raise money for his conspiracy by ordering the frigate *Forward*, under the flag of San Salvador and the command of Fortino Vizcaíno, to sail from Tepic to Guaymas and La Paz to force contributions. On the morning of May 28, Vizcaíno landed in Guaymas and, without firing a shot, surprised the authorities and easily subdued the guards at the jail, after which he imprisoned the customs officials and removed 42,300 pesos and goods from the merchants of the port.[45]

García Morales learned of the invasion and returned to the vicinity of Guaymas, immediately preparing to repel the invaders. He organized a small force and drove the rebels out of Guaymas. García Morales sent word to Hermosillo, Ures and Mazatlán, informing authorities there of what had taken place.[46]

At Mazatlán, at the request of the German consul and local merchants, authorities sent the North American ship *Mohican* to overtake the *Forward*. The *Mohican* caught the *Forward* and set it on fire. Vega's revolt dissipated, thus ending the threat to Sonora. Vega's piratical actions, however, had humiliated Sonorans, and residents of the port of Guaymas demanded that the federal government station permanent forces at the port. Meanwhile, Pesqueira sojourned at his hacienda at Las Delicias.[47]

And Vega returned to Tepic where he sought sanctuary with Lozada.[48] This incident would not be the last involving Pesqueira's one-time friend.

The end of the revolt of Zacatecas ushered in the 1870s. The chaos of the 1860s had taken its toll and conditions in Sonora remained critical. Census estimates note that none of Sonora's major cities showed an increase in population.[49] Disunity among Sonorans increased and the affairs of state became more chaotic. Pesqueira in turn became more indifferent, governing the state as if it were his personal fief.

CHAPTER 9

Decline of Ignacio Pesqueira

In 1870 Pesqueira was fifty years old and, although relatively young, it probably appeared to many Sonorans that the caudillo had ruled forever. It was obvious that his popularity had dwindled and that his promises to bring order to Sonora had never materialized; Sonorans still could not safely travel the state's roads, especially the caminos north of Magdalena which the Apache made hazardous.[1] The Indians continued their rebellion, depopulating the northern frontier and rendering development, by Sonoran or foreign entrepreneurs, impossible in this section of the state.

Pesqueira had attempted to cope with the problem but his efforts rendered meager results. Aware of his decline, Pesqueira attempted to regain the image of the man on horseback by personally leading campaigns against the Apache;[2] however, his attempts proved pathetic. How could Sonorans forgive the defeat of La Pasión, his abandonment of Sonora during the French occupation, and his arbitrary attacks on the legislature?

Moreover, federal authorities attempted to gain control of Sonora during the 1870s. The federal government began sending troops to Sonora to combat the Apache. State officials resented these efforts, interpreting them as possible infringements upon the state's sovereignty, and openly criticized the central government for not sending enough men to safeguard Guaymas, let alone fight the Apache. Sonorans wanted money, not troops, and local control.

Merchants throughout Sonora continued to complain about taxes. The Guaymas merchants protested the state tax on incoming goods, in 1870 threatening not to comply. Again, the government averted a crisis by compromising and not collecting the tax.[3]

Other affairs of state remained in chaos. Industry — especially mining of gold, silver, and copper — remained unproductive, having been abandoned from the time of the French intervention. This exacerbated the state's already complicated and unsettled economic problem.[4]

Discord between Sonora and Arizona continued. On December 24, 1870, an incident occurred which intensified existing friction. At Mission Camp, Arizona, North Americans were killed by Mexicans. The facts of the case are vague, largely due to the embroiled correspondence between Ignacio Pesqueira and Arizona Governor A.P.K. Safford, who demanded the extradition of Pedro Pino, Tomás Sánchez, and Román N. (name unknown), and to the sensationalism created by the press on both sides of the border.

Emotions rose when reprisals occurred on both sides. North Americans alleged that three Mexicans who had stolen furniture and five horses had killed Charles Reed, Santiago Little, and Tomás Oliver, and wounded Reed's wife. The Mexican version differed, contending that when the Mexican workers wanted to quit and demanded their wages, the North American employer refused, severely beating one of the Mexicans. A friend of the employer shot into the group, wounding one Mexican; and then the Mexicans defended themselves, resulting in the killing.[5]

North Americans in Arizona sought revenge and Francisco Gándara, the brother of the former governor, Manuel Gándara, was among the Mexicans who would perish. In February of 1872, a group of North Americans rode to Gándara's ranch close to La Agua Negra on the Gila River, where they accused Francisco of stealing a mule; an altercation ensued during which a North American, James Bodel, and Francisco shot each other. Bodel's companions abandoned the ranch, searching for a Mexican who had vowed to avenge Gándara and murder him. Soon the two camps polarized – Mexicano versus gringo. The Sonora press, not immune to the hatred, recorded violent reactions, and the pejorative term "greaser" was used by Arizona writers.[6]

Throughout Pesqueira's administration tension had been present between the two frontier folk, and in fact part of Pesqueira's success during his first years was his ability to unify Sonorans against the Yanqui threat. In the 1870s, the danger was not as clear as it had been during the days of Henry Crabb. Neither could the memory of Manuel María Gándara unite Sonorans behind Pesqueira, for the injustices of Don Manuel had been muted by time. Finally, in the 1870s, many had become disillusioned with the liberal cause; they no longer believed the slogans which the liberals had failed to implement.

Conditions had remained unsettled since the French intervention and, while Pesqueira remained in almost complete control of Sonora, he was helpless to improve matters. Federal aid was meager during this period, affording Sonora little support.

Sonora felt the effects of neglect. The U.S. Consul at Guaymas documented the gravity of the situation, reporting that the population of the state declined from 150,000 in 1840 to 133,300 in 1861, and to 108,211 in 1870.[7] The majority of the emigrants had gone to California and Arizona, depopulating the state's northern sections especially. According to *El Eco de Sonora*, April 17, 1871, this emigration aggravated affairs, making Sonora's roads more insecure and allowing the Apache to penetrate further into the state. Sonora's depopulation operated on the cycle of futility because a lack of safe roads made it impossible to export and develop the state's mines, contributing to economic instability.

Other major causes of Sonora's depression were her isolation – lack of communication and trade – and her burden of excessive federal export and import taxes. Part of the solution would have been to encourage immigration; Pesqueira had attempted to do this. Embroiled internal politics, however, thwarted his efforts, which generally proved ineffective. The U.S. Consul at Guaymas evaluated the Sonora situation:

In this age of rapid communication and changes, and great development, when the rest of the civilized world is moving onward, we find this people going backward. The ignorance of the masses and the bigotry of the higher classes reject all progress.[8]

In his report, Garrison reiterated Sonora's many problems, among which loomed the instability caused by its many wars.

PLAN OF LA NORIA

A major threat appeared from the outside, triggered when Benito Juárez was again a candidate for president of Mexico. Many Sonorans had tired of the old caudillo; even his trusted aide Sebastián Lerdo de Tejada had decided to oppose his chief by running for president himself. General Porfirio Díaz also chose to run. Both candidates had considerable following.[9] Many of the citizenry had grown disenchanted with Juárez, who acted more and more arbitrarily, shattering his former image of a constitutional, disinterested statesman.

The 1871 campaign was vigorous; none of the three candidates received a majority. The matter was referred to the Mexican congress, which declared Juárez President of Mexico since he had a plurality.[10] This action immediately touched off a wave of protests.

On November 8, 1871, at La Noria (approximately thirteen miles from the city of Oaxaca), Porfirio Díaz revolted against Juárez. Díaz supported the Constitution of 1857 and the principle of no reelections. An impressive array of generals declared for the Plan of La Noria.[11]

By the spring of 1872, federal forces under the command of General Sostenses Rocha defeated Díaz in his own home state of Oaxaca. In this battle, federal troops killed Félix Díaz, brother of Porfirio and the latter fled to Nayarit. In the mountains of Nayarit he received the protection of Manuel Lozada, the Indian chieftain who still ruled Nayarit independently of the national government.[12]

Many Sonorans openly criticized Juárez and considered his reelection an assurance that Pesqueira's rule would continue. Juárez, therefore, added Pesqueira's enemies to his own.*

---

*El Eco de Sonora February 13, 1871, promoted the candidacy of Pesqueira for president of Mexico before Juárez announced his candidacy for reelection. It reasoned that the northern frontier had been ignored by the other presidents of Mexico because they knew nothing of the problem. Pesqueira, therefore, would be the ideal candidate.

Pesqueira, clearly lacking interest in administrative detail, ran for reelection. Intense pride and a belief that only he could save Sonora encouraged the caudillo to remain in office and the flattery of friends reinforced his determination.[13]

Opposition to the caudillo was formidable. Even the governor's old and trusted aide and relative by marriage, Jesús García Morales, had decided to challenge him. Many Sonorans considered García Morales the foremost defender of the Constitution of 1857 and Sonora. Since the French intervention, there seemed to be a gradual alienation between García Morales and Pesqueira, with no outward manifestation that would serve as absolute proof because the latter did not publicly criticize his old friend. Yet, since García Morales had become federal military commanding officer of the state, his loyalty was to national sovereignty and, therefore, he could not freely heed the desires of his old mentor as before. Pesqueira, in turn, believed that García Morales still served in the national guard and thus the caudillo was resentful when the latter did not accept his ideas.[14] Perhaps the death of Pesqueira's first wife, García Morales' sister, contributed to the break.

García Morales, now an independent leader, received considerable press support. *El Voto Libre*, for example, supported García Morales on the basis of "no reelection," a point that enhanced García Morales' candidacy. A bitter campaign raged; however, conservative opposition to Pesqueira did not develop. Gándara, who was in Sonora at the time, refrained from participating in the election campaign. On July 22, 1871, when the results were known, the "voters" again reelected Pesqueira, although García Morales carried Alamos and part of Moctezuma (as in the case of Johnson) and ran a close second in the other districts. Many attributed Pesqueira's victory to illegal control of the ballot boxes. On September 15, 1871, the Sonora legislature formally installed Pesqueira as governor and Joaquín M. Astiazarán as deputy-governor.[15]

In Guaymas on October 29, the twelfth battalion commanded by Jesús Leyva declared itself for Porfirio Díaz and the Plan of La Noria. Leyva, born in Guaymas in 1837, formerly a member of the national guard, serving with distinction during the French intervention and as suppressor of the Romo-Ballesteros revolt of 1870, created a schism in the liberal party of the state and highlighted internal animosities.[16]

The Guaymas detachment's commandant Miguel Vega attempted to extinguish the rebellion, but his own men murdered him and joined Leyva. Vega had fought valiantly and many of his officers joined in his defense. He killed one of the rebels with his own hands before finally being overwhelmed. Flushed with victory from a successful coup in Guaymas, the rebels then attacked and defeated the local guard.[17]

In the confusion, Jesús García Morales managed to escape from the port city to the ranch of Noche Buena. From this ranch, he sounded the alarm, alerting the rest of Sonora. At this point, García Morales apprised Alamos' prefect Vicente Ortiz of the danger. Meanwhile, Leyva controlled Guaymas for four days, imposing forty-five thousand pesos in forced loans, before departing by sea for Alamos.[18]

Leyva's revolt had popular backing and statewide support, as anti-Pesqueira dissidents seized the opportunity to register their complaint. The opposition centered around Alamos. The rebels, however, lacked coordination, and they allowed prefect Ortiz to fortify the city and request assistance from government troops located in the Yaqui and Mayo river valleys and from La Villa del Fuerte in Sinaloa.

On November 1, Pesqueira requested and received from the legislature extraordinary powers. On the following day, he marched from Ures to Hermosillo where he activated additional national guard troops, preparing to ride to the "sound of the guns." On November 4, Pesqueira and his army arrived in Guaymas, and from the port he dispatched fifty men to seek out the enemy.[19]

Also active were the revolutionists, who had landed in Agiabampo on November 6 and proceeded to Alamos, occupying it and forcing prefect Ortiz to retreat to Minas Nuevas, where the rebels pursued him. In Alamos the revolutionaries obtained thirty-five thousand pesos from the merchants.[20]

Governor Pesqueira countered this threat by recruiting one thousand men from throughout the state; five hundred were from Alamos alone. On November 10, Pesqueira began his march through the Yaqui region where six days later his army arrived at Navojoa on the Mayo River. When Leyva heard of Pesqueira's strength, he — with an army of about seven hundred — hurriedly departed from Alamos toward the center of Sonora. Prefect Ortiz reentered Alamos with a small force.[21]

Pesqueira in turn sought out the enemy and sent a contingent of militia led by José J. Pesqueira to chase Leyva. Pesqueira moved to reinforce José, and, on November 23, 1871, he surprised Leyva at Potrerito Seco, between the pueblos of Bacanora and Arivechi. Pesqueira defeated the rebels, killing seventeen and taking about one hundred prisoners. In Soyopa, Pesqueira ordered immediate execution for Jesús Leyva and many of his officers. He sent another twenty-four officers to Fort Fronteras to fight against the Apache. This move proved ill advised as, on May 6, 1872, the rebel officers deserted the fort. Pesqueira then incorporated rank and file into his regular army.[22]

On November 27, 1871, the Sonora legislature commended Pesqueira for his quick persecution of the rebels. Three days later he received the applause and felicitations of friends at Ures, and it appeared as if his prestige had regained some of its former luster. Nevertheless, the results proved negative, for subsequent events further disrupted already confused affairs, halting commerce within Sonora and worsening the already critical economy of the state.[23]

Adding to the chaos, Colonel José Palacios and his garrison seconded Díaz' Plan of La Noria on November 17 at Mazatlán. This move forced Governor Eustaquio Buelna to escape to Sonora and leave Sinaloa in the hands of Porfiristas. In Sonora, Buelna petitioned Pesqueira's support. Pesqueira recognized Sinaloa's plight and prepared to assist her sister state, dispatching Colonel Salazar Bustamante with four hundred men and two pieces of artillery to support state troopers.[24]

The advisability of Pesqueira's action and others that followed can be seriously questioned. Sonora's economic situation was deplorable and funds spent in Sinaloa could have been better spent on the northern frontier attempting to subdue the Apache and reconstruct the state. Fiscal chaos semiparalyzed the state's economy and hence Sonora was in extreme need of immediate recuperation. But again, Pesqueira rode to the "sound of the guns," perhaps in a last desperate effort to recapture the glory of his 1859 triumphant march into Mazatlán.

On December 7, the legislature granted Pesqueira extraordinary powers to deal with the rebellion in Sinaloa. One week later, Pesqueira marched from Ures to Alamos, arriving on January 8, 1872. From there he prepared to enter Sinaloa, where General Ramón Corona from Guadalajara had arrived on December 14, 1871, to lead in the struggle. The minister of war recommended that Corona and Pesqueira cooperate with each other in Sinaloa's reconquest. Corona's arrival, however, is further reason why Pesqueira should have limited his participation to sending supplies and money. The federal government authorized Corona to arm a ship to blockade the port of Mazatlán, because it was a ready and lucrative source of income. Corona wanted Pesqueira's support and, as an inducement, offered Pesqueira command of the Fourth Division, which Corona commanded.[25]

Meanwhile, the rebel leader, General Márquez de Leon, marched from Culiacán to the villa of Sinaloa and occupied the town. On January 15, Pesqueira sent troops to Sinaloa, and the next day he personally entered the state at the head of an army of one thousand Sonorans. A week later Pesqueira directed his forces to the villa of Sinaloa. There General Márquez readied his troops, preparing to defend the villa against the northerners. The next day when the two armies met, Pesqueira took the initiative and captured the Plaza de Armas, occupying half of the villa. Márquez, an excellent general, defended the villa from the rooftops of the adobe houses. It iş alleged that the Sonorans had almost won when the prisoners whom Pesqueira had permitted to join his army at Potrerito Seco deserted him, firing upon their fellow Sonorans. This created mass confusion among the Sonorans and dispersed them in all directions. Only Pesqueira and his officers remained united and returned to Alamos. The humiliating experience, however, did not break Pesqueira, who prepared to return to Sinaloa.[26]

In Alamos, with prefect Ortiz' assistance, Pesqueira arbitrarily recruited men for another expedition and soon the caudillo's ranks swelled to about one thousand "volunteers."* Meanwhile, Colonel José Pesqueira, the governor's cousin, continued to fight in Sinaloa meeting with limited success. With a force of about two hundred men, José took the plaza at Villa Fuerte, and shortly afterwards at Culiacán, whereupon Ignacio Pesqueira rewarded his cousin by promoting him to the rank of full colonel. On March 1, 1872, at the head of a large army, Ignacio Pesqueira returned to Sinaloa.[†] His immediate destination was Culiacán, upon which he descended with a force of about one thousand men and six pieces of artillery. Márquez also neared Culiacán with almost two thousand men. On the evening of the twenty-sixth, Pesqueira approached the city; the next morning Márquez arrived and was harassed by Pesqueira's cavalry. The city immediately split in half, Pesqueira controlling one section and Márquez the other. A long bitter battle ensued, destroying much of the city.[27]

General Márquez established his headquarters in a thread factory, preparing to engage the Sonorans. For over a month both sides fired cannons at each other, engaging in only minor skirmishes as both generals appeared reluctant to carry the fight, not wanting to commit themselves. Culiacán's inhabitants suffered greatly during this time and the stalemate continued until General Sóstenses Rocha, the victor at Oaxaca, arrived in Mazatlán with two thousand federal troops. Márquez, fearing that he would be outflanked and caught in the middle between Rocha and Pesqueira, bombarded Pesqueira's sector on the evening of May 7 and, under the cover of fire, retreated to Durango, closely pursued by the Sonorans.[28]

Since Pesqueira could not capture Márquez, the governor abandoned his chase, returning to meet Rocha. The two generals then discussed Sinaloa's fate. The Sonora caudillo must have been incensed when Rocha did not automatically carry out his wishes and instead appointed General Domingo Rubí, an enemy of Pesqueira, Sinaloa's interim governor. The Sonoran then withdrew from the scene, protesting Rocha's usurpation of authority. On June 28, 1872, Pesqueira arrived in Guaymas and immediately retired to his

---

*La Estrella de Occidente, February 23, 1872, stated that Pesqueira was in Alamos with fifteen hundred men.

[†]Donato Guerra to Manuel Márquez, Durango, March 18, 1872, in Alberto María Garreño, Archivo del general Porfirio Díaz, X, 52-53. This letter stated that in the event General Márquez would defeat Pesqueira again, an invasion of Sonora was projected — another factor making Pesqueira's sojourn to Sinaloa extremely risky.

hacienda at Las Delicias, entrusting his deputy-governor, Joaquín Aztiazarán with the government.

As the crisis passed, anti-Pesqueira deputies renewed their opposition. On July 1, the legislature curtailed the extraordinary gubernatorial powers. The deputy-governor protested this action, emphasizing that hostilities had not formally ended and open warfare still raged in Sinaloa, endangering the safety of Guaymas and Alamos. The legislature, however, ignored Aztiazarán.[29]

Meanwhile, the Sinaloa rebels retook Mazatlán. Pesqueira reluctantly returned to office, arriving in Ures on October 5. By this time, federal reinforcements had arrived in Sinaloa, ending the resistance and the need for Pesqueira's presence. Furthermore, Lerdo de Tejada, who had become president after the death of Juárez, granted a general amnesty to all the dissidents. A tenuous peace prevailed throughout Sonora.[30]

The rebellion also highlighted the growing struggle for control of Sonora between Pesqueira and the federal government. Ignacio Pesqueira had arbitrarily used funds from the customs at Guaymas during the hostilities. His friend Mauro F. Díaz, the collector of internal revenue at Guaymas, had acceded to all the governor's requests; hence, federal officials replaced Díaz with Gerónimo V. Sándoval. Pesqueira interpreted this act as a challenge to his authority and a hindrance to the war effort. He therefore ordered Díaz to remain the collector, suspending the order of the Minister of the Treasury. Federal employees at Guaymas immediately protested this action; Pesqueira's old adversary, District Judge Domingo Elías González, questioned the legality of the governor's action.[31]

The governor, nevertheless, ignored critics. When events in Sinaloa again threatened Sonora, he demanded that federal officials at Guaymas advance him funds, sending Governor Buelna to the port to collect them. In Guaymas Buelna acted arbitrarily, forcing the collector of customs, Adolfo Carsi, to clear a ship's cargo at an illegally import-discounted rate. Pesqueira encouraged this action to prevent Porfiristas from collecting the revenues at Mazatlán. Of course federal employees protested and were imprisoned by Buelna. The Sonora press severely criticized the federal officials for unpatriotic hindrance of the war effort.[32]

Pesqueira then sent Manuel Escalante to the nation's capital to justify his actions. The federal government for the moment did nothing, waiting until peace could be restored; thereupon, the Minister of War sent Colonel José María Rángel with two hundred men to restore the federal employees to the customshouse in October of 1872.[33] A conflict between the two authorities could have easily erupted; Pesqueira, in fact, vigorously protested Rángel's action to the federal officials in Sinaloa, for the caudillo considered this action arbitrary. Pesqueira stated that he wanted to preserve the public peace and that he did not overtly oppose Rángel. This did not prevent him, however, from publicly criticizing the Minister of War, General Mejía; in addition, Pesqueira had the legislature send a protest to the federal congress, asking that no more federal troops be sent to Sonora.*

TATO LEGACY

Rumors about favoritism and public corruption frequently circulated in Sonora. Other than the accusations of anti-Pesqueira forces, it becomes almost impossible to document any malfeasance during the Pesqueira years. The Tato affair, however, clearly casts a shadow upon Governor Pesqueira, and, although no positive proof incriminates him personally, considerable circumstantial evidence points to his malfeasance. The Tato scandal would haunt the Sonora caudillo to his dying day.

On January 26, 1868, Lieutenant Colonel José Ignacio Tato, a native of the pueblo of Bacoachi, Sonora, died in Cannes, France. His will would later have widespread repercussions in Sonora. Under its terms, dated December 21, 1867, Tato bequeathed a small sum of money to his brother and to a friend, José Gregorio Martínez del Río, resident of México D.F. and member of a prominent family. Tato also bequeathed money to the physician who attended him during his last illness. The deceased also left one hundred thousand francs for a school to be built in his native town. The remainder of the fortune he earmarked for the construction of charitable hospitals in Sonora. The fortune of this philanthropist amounted to more than a million francs, consisting of loans owed by French railroads. The will designated José Gregorio Martínez del Río, a Mexican, and Espíritu Francisco Eugenio Gazagnaire, a notary public in France, executors.†

In 1869, the Sonora legislature received notice of the Tato will and made immediate plans to redeem the small fortune. Pursuant to this, the deputies appointed Pedro G. Tato to represent the town of Bacoachi and the Sonora hospitals. Almost immediately lack of funds presented problems, whereupon Hilario Gabilondo offered to lend the state five thousand pesos. With this sum in hand, Tato traveled to France, where French officials did not recognize him as the emissary had failed to take the proper identifying credentials.[34]

---

*A.F. Garrison to Fish, Guaymas, September 30, 1873, "Despatches from U.S. Consuls in Guaymas," reports that there were no federal troops in Sonora at that time. A consular report of December 31, 1873, however, reports that there were then four hundred federal soldiers in Sonora, mostly in Guaymas.

†Corral, p. 108. Ignacio Pesqueira to the Legislature, Las Delicias, July 21, 1869, Archivo del Congreso del Estado de Sonora, 1869, Box 31, Exp. 1072, in Fernando Pesqueira, "Documentos para la Historia de Sonora," Cuarta Serie, Tomo III, tells of the importance of the Tato legacy to Sonora.

Commissioner Tato returned to Sonora without a single centavo. In 1870, after acquiring the proper documents, he again returned to Paris. There he encountered additional difficulties, which he overcame only with the assistance of one Jules Favre. Officials recognized his credentials, but fate again conspired against him: The Franco-Prussian War made it impossible to do business in France. Tato therefore returned to Sonora, again without a settlement. This time he left Bertrand Cazaet power of attorney to continue negotiations.[35]

The legislature fully expected Commissioner Tato to return with the inheritance and, consequently, they appropriated funds for the construction of hospitals. Hilario Gabilondo meanwhile had grown restless and demanded payment of his loan. Moreover, the legislature imprudently had loaned the school at Bacoachi twenty thousand pesos.[36]

The scandal then deteriorated to pathetic depths. State officials eventually collected 738,000 francs, of which they only received 225,560 francs in hand. It is still a mystery as to what happened to the remaining 512,440 francs. Moreover, documents pertaining to the Tato Affair conveniently disappeared. Evidence either indicates that the banking houses charged exorbitant rates or that state officials absconded with the monies. The culprits, however, were never officially uncovered.

The losers — the hospitals and the Sonorans — were victimized by unscrupulous public officials and an absentee governor, for eventually the institutions lost all of the legacy.[37] It is therefore understandable that the Tato scandal further shook public confidence in the integrity of the governor.

The Tato Affair finally climaxed in 1873 when Pesqueira's enemies made him personally responsible for the fiasco, blaming the loss of this fortune on Governor Pesqueira's personal dishonesty. They charged that Pesqueira cooperated in this fraud. It is noted, however, that Ramón Corral, Pesqueira's political enemy, who later wrote the governor's biography, exonerated him of any direct involvement. Corral does, however, blame Pesqueira for neglect: Stating that if the governor had overseen the collection and administration of the legacy, this lamentable incident might not have occurred; Pesqueira could have prevented the malfeasance, if such did exist; instead of sojourning at Las Delicias, he could have deterred his friends from plundering the Tato estate.[38]

UNREST IN SONORA INCREASES

As many of the citizens felt more oppressed by the governor, opposition to Pesqueira increased. The state legislature reflected this mood, and on November 1, 1872, it again embarked on a collision course with the governor. The Third Sonoran Constitutional Legislature in May, 1869, passed many constitutional reforms, postponing their adoption for a later date. The Fifth Constitutional Legislature ratified the reforms. The governor, however, refused to accept the changes because he considered them a direct affront to his authority, especially the clause calling for "no reelection."[39]

This opposition immediately divided the legislature into two factions: pro- and anti-Pesqueira. Some assemblymen, partisans of the governor, by walking out of the chambers, prevented the legislature from conducting business for lack of quorum. Discussions over the reelection issue spread throughout the state. The government-controlled press lauded Pesqueira as the founder of republicanism in Sonora, questioning how a republican and liberal state such as Sonora could ever pass such an anti-liberal act as Article 19 of the state constitution, which provided for "no reelection." The press argued that the power to elect should be vested in the people and not in the legislature.[40]

The press personally attacked the reformers, comparing them to conservatives and monarchists. Editorials labeled their arguments sophisms: a constitution as a social contract was a fallacy. The press editorialized that Article 19 states that the sovereignty rests with the people. The press further observed that the reformers, in passing Article 19, acted arbitrarily, and concluded that it was the natural right of the people to choose their own leaders and that the legislature could not abridge this right.[41]

Pesqueira, in the days that followed, violated the constitution by preventing the seating of his opponents. His actions grew increasingly arbitrary; on April 22, 1873, Pesqueira replaced the unseated deputies with his own puppets. He then ordered his deputies to ratify another constitution with all the suggested reforms of the previous constitution, excluding only the "no reelection" clause.[42]

Both sides aired their views to the public. The reformers – centered in Alamos, Hermosillo, and Guaymas – through newspapers such as *El Pueblo Sonorense* and *La Voz de Alamos*, defended the reforms and condemned Pesqueira's actions. The leaders of the reformed constitution solicited the opinion of a famous jurist in México D.F. to bolster their case. The judge supported the constitutionality of the reforms, stating that Pesqueira had acted in an unconstitutional manner, and the dissidents circulated the dictum throughout Sonora.[43]

Pesqueira countered by airing his side and pressuring the town councils to protest the reform measures. The newspaper, *La Estrella* (June 13, 1873) responded to Pesqueira's critics, praising him: " *¡Pesqueira es la paz, es el progreso, es él la libertad; Pesqueira, el patriota, el valiente y caballero, es el idolo y el salvador del pueblo Sonorense!* " (Pesqueira means peace, progress, liberty; Pesqueira the patriot, brave and a gentleman, is the idol and savior of the Sonoran people!) These "impartial" sources, naturally approving the governor's actions, are indicative of the caudillo's vehement campaign.[44]

However, many Sonorans who had become increasingly disenchanted with Pesqueira sided with the reformers. In 1873, Pesqueira again stood for reelection. Although many people openly disapproved, no overt opposition took place, since most believed that it would be useless to run a candidate against him. The public had lost confidence in the state's institutions and in so-called "free elections."[45]

Opposition to Pesqueira unexpectedly came from the elected deputy from Hermosillo to the federal congress, Hilario S. Gabilondo Jr., who wrote a series of articles criticizing Pesqueira in one of the capital's newspapers. He questioned Pesqueira's Indian defenses and his negotiations with James Eldredge to construct a railroad in Sonora. In addition, the writer questioned Pesqueira's constitutional interpretations. Pesqueiristas labeled Gabilondo an ingrate who had turned against his benefactor, charging that Gabilondo was too young to question a statesman like Pesqueira or to judge constitutional questions. The press ridiculed him with the label, " ¡Pobre niño! " (Poor child!). Gabilondo's criticism, nevertheless, did force an investigation of the railroad contracts, which indeed could be questioned: a group of Arizona capitalists had received terms described as extremely onerous. For example, the railroad entrepreneurs would receive sixteen thousand acres of land for each mile of rail laid. To raise operating capital, the grantees would issue fifty-year bonds; the state would also award the company fifty thousand pesos for each mile laid. Sonora would guarantee payment of the capital and interest accrued on the bonds. When it completed the line, the company could float another issue of bonds at the rate of five thousand pesos for each mile laid. In return, Eldredge and associates were not even bound to secure the contract with a bond of completion. Slowly, as facts came to light, Pesqueira's image became more jaded, but he again managed to obtain reelection.[46]

This election, while it had not been contested, did trigger an abortive revolt, again pitting Alamos against the governor. The rebels charged that the caudillo had ignored reforms, held illegal elections, and arbitrarily ruled Sonora. In this milieu, on September 19, 1873, Carlos Conant announced his plan at the mining town of Promontorios, near Alamos, rejecting Pesqueira's reelection and proclaiming the constitution of November 1, 1872. On September 20, Conant and his partisans occupied Alamos, where he had many followers. There he borrowed thirty-six thousand pesos, while at the same time sending Patricio Robles to the Yaqui to enlist their expected support.[47]

Pesqueira moved against the rebels, preparing to lead an expedition against these traitors. He appeared before the state legislature, petitioning for extraordinary powers, which the deputies granted along with an authorization of thirty-five thousand pesos. He appealed for the support of the people, mobilized the national guard, and called for peace. On October 20, Pesqueira left for Alamos, taking personal charge of the operations.[48]

The divergent state forces converged on Alamos to suppress Conant's rebellion. At Buenavista, various units of the state militia incorporated and placed themselves under Colonel Salazar Bustamante. On October 5, Bustamante, with one hundred seventy infantrymen and one hundred cavalrymen, marched on Alamos. One week later, Pesqueira departed for that same city.[49]

Conant, learning the strength of approaching state militia, realized the uselessness of resisting and left for Chihuahua. Once across the Sierra Madre, he dispersed his troops, and at the villa of Chinipas, the rebels surrendered their arms.

Salazar followed the rebels into Chihuahua, not respecting the state borders. On September 24, 1873, the Sonora troops entered the villa of Chinipas, brandishing weapons and firing indiscriminately. They demanded that the authorities surrender the rebels and the arms. Townspeople, however, reported that the rebels had left, and gave Sonorans only the arms. Salazar's men captured only one unfortunate rebel, Cayetano Monzán, whom they hanged, thus ending the Conant revolt.[50]

Pesqueira had not actively participated in the action; since he was robbed of the opportunity to play the strong man, the short-lived revolt cost him dearly.* Pesqueira resorted to additional forced loans, and extraordinary taxes. "The Revolution in Sonora," *Arizona Sentinel*, October 25, 1873, wrote that Pesqueira in Alamos decreed thirty-two thousand pesos in forced loans and fifty thousand in extraordinary taxes. Once more Alamos paid the lion's share, for Pesqueira punished the city for its "disloyalty." The revolt had failed because Conant was unknown in Sonora and without statewide support. The revolution, in fact, proved to be counter-productive, allowing Pesqueira another opportunity to "ride a white horse" and plunge the state further into debt.[51]

LAST MONTHS OF 1873

Revolts such as Conant's worsened conditions, accelerating the exodus of many Sonorans. Toward the end of 1873, the *Arizona Citizen* observed the large numbers of Sonorans migrating during that year to Arizona:

---

*Willard to Hunter, Guaymas, June 30, 1873, "Despatches from U.S. Consuls in Guaymas," states that the era of the independent caudillo began to disappear as the national government consolidated the provinces.

The cause of this sudden influx is the poverty of the people and the stagnation in business, and some may fear that the Alamos revolt will spread all over Sonora. It is said thousands unemployed have nothing to subsist on [which is] quite unnecessary in a country as rich as Sonora. (October 11, 1873)

Sonora mirrored the rest of the nation in this poverty. The causes included the continuing stagnation of mining within the state, with less than one million pesos minted that year. Much of the agricultural land of Sonora laid fallow, and production was limited to about one-fourth of arable land. Pesqueira's attempts to reform the economy proved inept, causing more discontent among the commercial houses of Alamos, Hermosillo, and Guaymas.[52]

During 1873, the *Arizona Sentinel* published a serialized account of Sonora affairs. The articles painted the vicious cycle of poverty that entrapped Sonora. The article recommended: (1) the need to develop the Guaymas trade; (2) effective exploitation of mining; and (3) the necessity for a railroad to assist in the effective control of the Apache. These papers also described the factionalism within the state, indicating the difficulty in preparing such a report on Sonora because Sonorans either decidedly supported or vehemently denounced the governor.[53]

An account of 1873 would not be complete without a comment on the Apache. As noted, Sonorans had criticized the U.S.'s handling of the Apache menace: General O.O. Howard, charged with the Apache containment in Arizona, was especially criticized. In *Cycles of Conquest*, Edward Spicer wrote of Howard's approach to the Indians:

. . .a distinct bias in favor of the Indians. . . .[He]took the view that Indian leaders were good men who would respond with cooperative spirit and integrity to fair offers of rights to certain territory and protection from settlers. . . . [Howard was] often ignorant of the absence of real tribal organization among Indians and of the bitterness of settler-Indian conflict and its background. (pp. 436-37)

Sonorans would have disagreed with this appraisal of Howard's policies. They accused him of complicity with the Apache in their raids into Sonora and said that he had entered into a treaty with Cochise, allowing him to raid and kill in Sonora in return for peace in Arizona.[54]

Pesqueira gave credence to the Howard-Cochise understanding and blamed Howard for past Apache problems, but U.S. officials denied such an arrangement. Relationships between Sonora and the U.S. improved toward the end of 1872, when General George Crook took charge of relocating the Apache to reservations.[55]

In 1871, Crook had been assigned the task of subduing the Apache by the War Department. Crook immediately won favor among Mexican officials by visiting Sonora and Chihuahua, and conferring personally with civil and military authorities. Crook also improved relations with Arizona officials, for as a veteran Indian fighter, he understood the biased settler's viewpoint of the Apache. Crook fought relentlessly to subjugate the Indians, remaining constantly in the field.[56]

Communication between Pesqueira and Arizona's Safford also improved during this period. Pesqueira appreciated the opportunity to coordinate the Apache campaigns with Crook. Crook wanted to concentrate the Apache in a reservation in the southeastern section of Arizona and wanted Pesqueira to build forts along this section to prevent the Apache from escaping into Sonora. Federal authorities, however, thwarted these plans and Crook could not obtain the proper authorization. The unwillingness of United States officials to press the war against the Apache blunted Crook's effectiveness.[57]

Nevertheless, control of the Indians improved after this period. The growth of settlements and the coming of the railroad to Arizona would help to subdue them.[58] Yet, the year of 1873 indicated an increasing dissatisfaction with Pesqueira. A stillness before the storm followed the Conant revolt.

CHAPTER 10

Fall of the Caudillo

As Pesqueira's base grew less secure, he became increasingly arbitrary, hoarding the governor's office as though it belonged to him by virtue of divine right. At the same time he ignored the duties of that office and appeared bored with the daily routine. Pesqueira more and more resembled the late President Santa Anna, ruling through puppets and taking frequent sojourns to his hacienda at Las Delicias.[1]

In 1874 this pattern of neglect continued; he took repeated leaves from office, with the first lasting from January to May, 1874. Immediately after, Pesqueira extended his leave to September 15, when the legislature gave him a leave of absence for another six months until April 26, 1875.[2] Pesqueira's inability to cope with domestic problems had become increasingly apparent. There is no doubt that he should have resigned at this time, allowing someone more willing to devote time and energy to administering the state to take charge. Even his most enthusiastic admirers found it difficult to condone the governor's actions.

Personal tragedies plagued Pesqueira during this period, undoubtedly influencing his behavior: on June 14, 1874, his twenty-two year old son Ramón passed away; previously, within a period of two years, three sons and a sister had died.[3] These sad events took their toll; nevertheless, Pesqueira was the governor and his duty was to run the state.

Sonora drifted dangerously during 1874. The Conant Revolt created a milieu of tensions in Alamos. The heavy hand of José María Loaiza, prefect of that district, worsened conditions, for his oppressive measures increased the resentments of the inhabitants of that city; from Alamos new protests would emanate.[4]

On June 26, 1874, citizens of Alamos petitioned the Sonora legislature, complaining about the taxes imposed on May 29. The increased taxation, they contended, stifled industry and small businesses within their city and the state. There is little doubt that the Alameños' contention was true. Taxes fell unjustly on the state's commercial centers; for example, of five million pesos assessed on Sonorans in direct taxes, one million pesos were assessed against Alamos alone. The state also collected three and one-half million pesos from the cities of Guaymas, Hermosillo, Ures, and Alamos. Therefore, the remaining one and one-half million pesos would come from the hacendados, rancheros, and miners, whom it will be recalled, were the former supporters of Gándara. Ironically, the Pesqueira administration was taxing those who had one time been his benefactors, while indirectly supporting former enemies.[5]

Alameños were not the only ones to protest government taxes. The Guaymas merchants, also unhappy about these assessments, made their feelings known. They protested the right of the state to tax foreign trade and to collect an 8 percent state import tax.[6]

The Apache, Sonora's perennial problem, continued to raid the state. Pesqueira's inability to effectively control them deepened the dilemma. The state offered scalp bounties to the Papago, a measure that did not prove effective; the efforts of local authorities to neutralize the Apache also failed. By 1874, national authorities finally became convinced that official state efforts had failed and, therefore, México D.F. moved to take a more active role in the Indian campaigns.

The central government first established a system of military colonies in various pueblos on the frontier. Federal authorities then placed military federal commander General Jesús García Morales in charge of operations. The federal troops proved handicapped as were the state forces. This event, nevertheless, was important because it brought to the surface continuing alienation between state and federal authorities. Sonora state officials habitually acted independently, resenting what they considered the national government's intrusions upon their sovereignty.* In spite of the federal encroachments and the critical Apache problem, Pesqueira remained at Las Delicias, leading many Sonorans to question whether their governor wanted to govern or cared about the state.

THE BEGINNING OF THE END

In April of 1875, the Yaqui and Mayo uprisings began again, now led by the legendary Yaqui cacique, José María Leyva, popularly known as Cajeme.[7] The Cajeme years marked the last concentrated resistance of the Yaqui and Mayo against the *yori*. This resistance weakened the Pesqueira government's efforts to eradicate the anti-Pesqueira insurrection in the summer of 1875.

Cajeme was born in Hermosillo in 1837 to Francisco Leyva, from the town of Huirivis, and Juana Pérez, from Potam, both Yaqui Indians. They raised Cajeme in Rahum, the center of Yaqui conservatism and nationalism.[8] He spent much of his childhood among the Mexican people, from whom he

---

*La Estrella de Occidente, October 30, 1874; La Estrella de Occidente, November 6, 1874. This was also an indication that the federal government, recovering from the effects of the War of Reform and the French intervention, was extending control over Sonora. During this time, federal authorities also extended mail service to Sonora.

José María Leyva,
popularly known as Cajeme

Laureano Calvo Berber,
Nociones de Historia de Sonora
Rendered from photo

learned the Spanish language and Mexican ways. In 1849, he migrated to California with his father, prospecting for gold; later he returned to Sonora and lived in Guaymas during the 1850s.

While in Guaymas, Cajeme learned how to read and write and enlisted in the army, serving with the Urbans against Raousset de Boulbon. During the War of Reform, he went to Tepic, Nayarit, and then drifted north again in 1859. In Sinaloa he met the Sonora troops who then fought to free Sinaloa from the forces opposing the Constitution of 1857.[9]

During his early military career in the 1850s and 1860s, Cajeme remained loyal to Ignacio Pesqueira, fighting against his own people who generally backed the conservative forces. In 1868, the army promoted Cajeme to the rank of captain for his role in subduing the Yaqui revolt of 1867. Again in 1873, he demonstrated his loyalty to Pesqueira by helping to smother the Conant rebellion. In 1874 Pesqueira rewarded Cajeme, naming him Alcalde Mayor of the Yaqui and Mayo, in addition to the title of Captain General of the Yaqui.

Cajeme took advantage of the opportunity by consolidating the Yaqui forces, reorganizing both civil and military administrations. Before the time of Cajeme, the leader in peacetime did not necessarily lead the tribe in war. Cajeme centralized his control and, although he strengthened the tribe, many of his people opposed him.[10]

In 1875, state authorities were preparing for the coming election. The opposition realized that its past efforts had been dissipated through lack of organization. Led by José Quijada, Adolfo Almada, and others, they initiated efforts to run a candidate against Pesqueira. Delegates from various anti-Pesqueira clubs met at Guaymas, where they promoted General Jesús García Morales as candidate.[11] The opposition adopted the name Independent Party, limiting their early tactics to attacking Pesqueira. The governor remained at his hacienda, taking no action to placate his foes. By May, 1875, it became evident that Pesqueira would face serious opposition in the reelection; therefore, instead of running for governor, Pesqueira supported the candidacy of his cousin, José J. Pesqueira.

Pesqueira partisans then moved to establish clubs of their own to support José Pesqueira's candidacy. Ramón Corral led the anti-Pesqueiristas in Alamos, conducting a heated journalistic battle. He edited several newssheets, among them El Fantasma. Corral, who would be vice-president of the Mexican Republic twenty years later, was hounded by government authorities. Most accounts paint Corral a hero, but A.F. Pradeau contends that Corral had been charged with absconding with four hundred dollars belonging to Miguel and Joaquín Urrea, and set free only on the condition he leave the state. Most sources, however, claim Corral left the state because of political persecution.[12]

The independent party described Pesqueira as a man who once had had liberal ideas but no longer. The independent press criticized Pesqueira's handling of the electoral question and declared the issue of "no reelection" essential to Sonora liberty. Newspapers likened Pesqueira's naming his cousin to succeed him to Emperor Charles V's retiring to the monastery – Las Delicias as Pesqueira's sanctum – and handing down the crown to Philip II.[13]

In turn, the old general's partisans actively organized clubs such as El Club del Pueblo. Much fanfare surrounded Ignacio Pesqueira's campaigning for his cousin. An honor guard and a band greeted him in Guaymas.[14]

While some popular sentiment for the governor still flickered, widespread discontent existed. The popular vote overwhelmingly favored Jesús García Morales. José Pesqueira, however, won the election when Pesqueira's puppets in the state legislature nullified the votes of Altar, Alamos, and Arizpe. This action underscored Pesqueira's ingratitude, for García Morales had been a loyal friend, partisan, and relative by marriage. The governor's behavior robbed García Morales of a much desired honor and proved too much for Sonorans to accept, creating inevitable conflict. Immediately rumors spread that a revolt led by attorney Domingo Elías Gonzalez and Alfonso Mejía, collector of customs, would be launched. This conspiracy did not immediately materialize; however, the Yaqui and Mayo had taken to the warpath. The legislature granted Pesqueira extraordinary powers to deal with

Francisco Serna

Laureano Calvo Berber,
Nociones de Historia de Sonora

the Indian rebellion. In the last days of June, Pesqueira heightened tensions by imposing forced loans of thirty-five thousand pesos and, on July 27, Pesqueira mobilized the national guard.[15]

On August 11, 1875, twenty days before José Pesqueira assumed the governorship, simultaneously from the villa of Altar and the pueblo of San Ignacio in the district of Magdalena, dissidents proclaimed the Plan of Altar. Under the leadership of Francisco Serna, the framers of the plan listed Pesqueira's abuses and petitioned the president of Mexico to nullify the elections and appoint an interim governor until new elections could be held.[16]

Francisco Serna — native Sonoran and scion of prominent ancestors, customs chief at the port of Libertad, and well-respected throughout Sonora — led the rebels. In 1875 he had been the candidate for vice-governor and García Morales' running mate. After the fraudulent elections, Serna took the initiative in opposing Pesqueira. During the early stages the state forces overwhelmed the rebels, and the military commander of Altar and Magdalena, Francisco Altamirano, defeated them on August 23, 1875, at Altar.[17]

This setback forced Serna and many of Altar rebels to flee across the border into Arizona. Serna retreated to Tubac where he recovered from wounds and Francisco Del Río, a Serna partisan and former administrator of the customshouse at Altar, went to Tucson to buy arms. During this time, it became evident that the revolt had gained momentum. An editorial in the

Estrella de Occidente expressed the belief that Elías Gonzalez led the conspiracy and stated that he should come into the open. Vicente Ortiz, a wealthy Alamos miner, reportedly financed the venture.[18]

José Pesqueira charged that Serna was being allowed to prepare for an invasion from that sanctuary. Safford, governor of Arizona, denied the charge, although he admitted that many refugees resided in the state and that rumors of a mounting revolution were circulating.[19] Complicating matters, many of the Tucson residents had fled from Sonora and favored Serna because they opposed Pesqueira.

On November 8, 1875, Serna crossed the border from Arizona into Sonora at the head of a cavalry unit. The next day at La Calera, he routed state troops led by Francisco Redondo, and occupied the villa of Altar. Fourteen days later, Altamirano surprised Serna's chief, Agustín García, with two hundred fifty men and retook the plaza of Altar.[20]

This defeat did not end the resistance, and in Arizpe, Juan Escalante seconded Serna with frontier troops. Escalante routed the Pesqueiristas under Cayetano Silva at Santa Cruz. Rumblings from Alamos saw Luis and Lorenzo Torres reject José Pesqueira's government. In the meantime, the Yaqui raids increased and, accompanied by the Mayo under Cajeme's leadership, they burned numerous ranches, as well as the pueblos of Cocorit in the Yaqui Valley and Santa Cruz, the seaport at the mouth of the Mayo River.

By September, the revolt reached alarming proportions and José Pesqueira took more active measures against the rebels. He considered the Indian insurrection to be instigated by his political enemies. On October 4, 1875, José Pesqueira had decreed another extraordinary contribution of thirty thousand pesos to combat the Apache. This levy increased the irritation of the masses, and gave impetus to Serna's cause. At the same time, José Pesqueira attempted to emulate his cousin by taking personal charge of the campaign against the Yaqui while Ignacio, who had been appointed vice-governor by the legislature, handled the affairs of state.[21]

The intensity of the Yaqui-Mayo revolt dismayed many Sonorans, especially since they had been at peace throughout 1874. In retrospect, however, it is clear that encroachments on their lands had increased during recent years and that state authorities were determined to exploit the valleys of the Mayo and Yaqui. The Constitution of 1873, Article IV, states:

> To deprive the Yaqui and Mayo tribes of the rights of citizenship while they maintain the anomalous organization that they have in their towns and rancherías, but allow the enjoyment [of those rights] to individuals of the same tribes who reside in the organized pueblos of the state.[22]

Under Cajeme the Yaqui and Mayo took advantage of the civil war to claim and defend their land and to expel the *yoris*.[23]

The Yaqui chose an opportune time to make their demands, because Governor José Pesqueira was having difficulty. On November 11, the governor marched to Guaymas, where eight days later he imposed another contribution of forty thousand pesos. Again, this action added fuel to the Sernista revolt. On December 1, José Pesqueira, with state militia, encountered the Yaqui under Cajeme near Pitahaya. Before the battle the governor sent a message to Cajeme, making certain overtures; Cajeme turned them down, sending word that he would meet Pesqueira on the battlefield. At 3:00 p.m. the fighting began, but the better equipped Sonora militiamen won the battle, killing over sixty Indians and wounding twenty others.[24]

The battle did not break the Yaqui-Mayo resistance. Many Indians escaped to the hills, carrying on their fight from there. José Pesqueira confined his campaign to the edges of the rivers, pillaging the Indian villages and treating the captured Indians cruelly. Ironically, many miners and hacendados cared for the refugee Yaqui, protecting them from the army.[25]

The Battle of Pitaya had forced José Pesqueira to ignore the Serna revolt. Encouraged by the revolt of the Yaqui and Mayo, the Sernistas gained support. On December 28, Francisco E. González attacked and took the plaza at Ures, and although Pesqueiristas soon forced him to abandon the capital, González transferred his hostilities to the district of Arizpe. As 1876 began, González again shifted his operations to the district of Ures. On January 21, 1876, the Pesqueiristas again defeated him near the Noria of Borquez, mortally wounding him.[26]

By this time the Yaqui had recovered from their Pitahaya defeat and were in full strength, pressing the Pesqueiristas. The latter also had to contend with the forces of Luis and Lorenzo Torres in Alamos, and those of Escalante and Serna in the north. Yet, while the state militia could not quell the rebellions, the Altar rebels along with the Yaqui and Mayo Indians never really threatened Pesqueira's power.[27]

Meanwhile, support for the Plan of Altar, which was previously underground, surfaced. In Hermosillo, on January 1, 1876, Colonel Antonio Palacio denounced Pesqueira and seconded Serna. Many of the residents of Hermosillo supported Palacio's action. These residents had for many years opposed Ignacio Pesqueira.[28] Palacio enlisted five hundred well-armed partisans and gradually the revolt spread.

During this period, Ignacio Pesqueira abandoned the comfort of Las Delicias and participated personally in the military campaigns. Desperation turned him into a despot who marched on Hermosillo to begin a reign of terror. He persecuted and suppressed his enemies, filling the jails with innocent people, whose only sin had been guilt by association — friends of Serna or his partisans. He levied forced loans and confiscated property. Ignacio Pesqueira's treatment of Hermosillo grew so despotic that a mass exodus took place. Citizens of that city took refuge in Guaymas, where they received the protection of federal troops stationed there.

Hostilities continued, and José Pesqueira abandoned the Yaqui Valley to aid in the prosecution of the civil war. He turned his attention to Guaymas, where General Jesús García Morales had brought federal troops after the fraudulent elections. There José Pesqueira demanded that the Hermosillo refugees be delivered to him. District Judge Antonio Morán protected these refugees and placed them under his own jurisdiction. In turn, Colonel José María Rángel, prefect and military commander of Guaymas, enforced the judge's order, not allowing the refugees to be removed from the port. García Morales himself backed Rángel.[29]

Matters worsened when one of Pesqueira's partisans, Fernando M. Astiazarán, a district judge, countermanded Morán's order. Despite this, Rángel continued to aid and comfort the refugees, many of whom he moved out of Pesqueira's reach while enlisting others into his federal forces.

In the vicinity of Alamos, Lorenzo Torres led the resistance to the Pesqueiristas; these forces operated independently of Serna. Furthermore, prefect José T. Otero actively challenged Torres in this district. The rebels and the Sonora militia frequently skirmished during the month of January, 1876; finally, on the seventeenth, the rebels occupied the plaza of Alamos and routed Otero at Minas Nuevas. This encouraged Torres, and two days later he formally joined Serna, considerably strengthening the Sernista revolt and consolidating opposition to Pesqueira.[30]

These events encouraged many Alameños to support Serna openly and their support proved to be a turning point, for the resources of the city would be as essential to the success of the movement to overthrow Pesqueira as they had been in Gándara's defeat. During this time, the Alamos press attacked Pesqueira, calling for an end to his tyranny, nicknaming him *"Tata Pesqueira"* (Grandpa Pesqueira). The press charged that the general began his career as a liberal, but that he had become intoxicated with power. It is interesting to note, that while the Pesqueiristas and Sernistas considered themselves liberals, the latter's main grievance against Ignacio Pesqueira was that he erred when he separated himself from the "best citizens" and catered to those who followed him blindly. In reality, neither faction championed the so-called "little man."[31]

STALEMATE

After Lorenzo Torres' endorsement of the Plan of Altar, Antonio Palacio from Hermosillo transferred his activities to Alamos. There Palacio actively pursued a small Pesqueirista group led by José T. Otero, who attempted to gain control of the district. A number of skirmishes around Alamos ensued.[32]

Palacio's arrival encouraged many to support the revolt more actively, and soon his army swelled to about seven hundred men. At Alamos he met the Torres forces, and the two armies joined, marching to the interior of the state to challenge the "Tyrant." Many partisans considered this move premature, for the Pesqueiristas dominated the interior.[33]

Meanwhile, new recruits reinforced Otero when he retreated to Baroyeca to meet the governor and apprise him of the Alamos events. At Baroyeca, Otero received arms and added troopers to combat the dissidents. Torres learned of Otero's Baroyeca rendezvous with the governor and thereupon attempted to surprise them. On February 4, 1874, Torres met Otero, who with his strengthened army defeated Torres. The rebel army, ripped apart, retired to Alamos.[34] Otero, accompanied by José Pesqueira, also marched south, where four days later they occupied Alamos.

Many Alameños panicked with the arrival of the Pesqueiristas, for they remembered the suppression of Hermosillo, and therefore, many fled from the city. Otero in turn took strong measures, decreeing that citizens who had fled must return within four days or have their property confiscated. He declared them disturbers of the public peace,[35] and ruled the city by martial law.

Governor José Pesqueira then began a reign of terror, levying heavy forced loans on Alameños. The Pesqueiristas used extortionist methods on those who hesitated, taking the reluctant contributors to the summit of a mountain and exposing them to the rays of the sun until they complied. José Pesqueira used such violent measures that he alienated even the most sympathetic of his partisans. On February 16, 1876, he decreed an extraordinary contribution from Sonorans of seventy-two thousand pesos, and then he restricted travel within the state.[36]

The state militia successively carried on an active campaign against the Sernistas, routing the enemy many times. The rebels, in spite of tremendous odds, bravely continued their struggle. Serna and Lizárraga operated in Altar, Francisco Moraga and Lorenzo Torres in the outskirts of Alamos, and Colonel Juan Escalante in the northern sector of the state. The rebels limited their warfare to a guerrilla type, since they numbered only about five to six hundred throughout the state. The Pesqueiristas, although numerically greater and possessing superior resources, could not quell the revolt, for many Sonorans abetted and shielded the rebels.[37]

Moreover, the Yaqui and the Mayo were sapping the strength of the state militia. Otero divided his force, and sent a contingent against the Yaqui. Rumors persisted that Cajeme had joined the Sernistas and that in February of 1876 he had placed the Yaqui under Torres. The situation worsened with almost the entire populations of Alamos, Guaymas, Hermosillo, and Ures opposing the government. Finally, Colonel José Pesqueira, much concerned, appealed to the federal government for assistance to put down the rebellion and break the stalemate.[38]

ARRIVAL OF GENERAL VICENTE MARISCAL

Hence President Lerdo de Tejada issued General Vicente Mariscal a commission to remedy the situation in Sonora and the latter left México D.F. for Sonora on January 27, 1876. He landed in Guaymas on March 1, and, on the same day, he pleaded with the belligerents to suspend hostilities, wanting time to arbitrate the conflict.[39]

Mariscal immediately left for Alamos with a force of one hundred men of the Fifteenth Battalion. On the way rebel partisans told Mariscal their grievances against Pesqueira. When Mariscal arrived at Alamos he received an enthusiastic ovation.[40] There he met with José Pesqueira.

An immediate controversy arose as to the purpose of the federal mission. Pesqueira believed that the federal army had been sent there to support his "legitimate" government. Mariscal, on the other hand, interpreted his role as that of a mediator. Pesqueira, in a huff, abandoned Alamos, marching to the capital. On March 14, Mariscal declared the state under martial law, assuming political and military control of Sonora.[41]

Governor Pesqueira protested Mariscal's actions, further alienating the federal general. Fearing Pesqueira's perfidy, Mariscal requested Torres to become an auxiliary to his army. Upon returning to Alamos, Torres received a memorable reception, with people lining the flower-strewn streets. Mariscal personally witnessed the popularity of the rebels in Alamos, which, like the other centers of commerce within Sonora, vehemently opposed Pesqueira. [42]

Mariscal requested that Serna meet him in Hermosillo; the latter complied, proceeding to Hermosillo, where he received a tumultuous accolade. Mariscal had marched from Alamos to Guaymas, where residents warmly demonstrated their approval. Mariscal strengthened his forces by recruiting volunteers during this period.

The Pesqueiristas watched the events from Ures, submitting quietly to the federal government's authority. Instead of staging a counterrevolution, the old caudillo retired to Las Delicias, for his popularity reached a low ebb with many of the leading citizens petitioning Mariscal to remain in control until new elections could be held.[43]

About the time of Mariscal's arrival, a letter dated March 5, 1876, was written to Mariscal by Francisco Serna in Tucson. In it Serna denounced Pesqueira, whom Serna accused of ruling Sonora through criminal and violent means. He wrote that there were many refugees in Arizona who had fled from Pesqueira's regime. It is interesting that Serna accused Pesqueira of suppressing independent thought by persecuting opponents through use of the mob, shouting, "¡Viva Pesqueira, mueran los ricos! " (Long live Pesqueira, death to the rich!) — the same charges that were levelled at Gándara about the time he was overthrown. The letter also indicated that these revolutions were by no means sponsored by the masses, but by special interests within the state. The Yaqui and the Mayo revolted because of encroachments on their land, but the Sernistas revolt emanated from discontent over Pesqueira's disregard for the constitution and his failure to bring economic stability to Sonora. There is no indication that in the Pesqueira years the masses had any other role than being pawns in the over-all struggle.[44]

LAST DAYS OF IGNACIO PESQUEIRA

Sonora affairs deteriorated to utter chaos. The federal constitution had been defunct since the last years of the Ignacio Pesqueira dictatorship. Mariscal moved to reactivate the document by proclaiming a general amnesty, attempting to conciliate all sides. The Sernistas agreed to Mariscal's terms, but the Pesqueira partisans refused to accept them, protesting the federal commander's authority. The Pesqueiristas, however, did not cause any trouble, and peace for the time ensued.[45]

On April 3, 1876, Mariscal appointed Jesús Quijada — who belonged to Pesqueira's opposition and was a member of the 1872 Sonora legislature which ratified the reform constitution of that year — to the post of secretary of government. Mariscal also named new district prefects for the express purpose of reorganizing the public treasury.[46]

During this period, the Apache problem took an interesting turn. On April 15, as part of increasing raids, the Apache routed a government force, killing several soldiers. Changes, however, had taken place on the Arizona side of the border. North American authorities seriously attempted to stop the Apache, moving them from their reservation at Chiricahua, close to the Sonora border, to a more distant reservation at San Carlos. They hoped that distance would discourage the Apache from crossing the border. But the move proved futile, for the Apache continued to raid Sonora.

In October of 1876, the Apache chiefs Juh and Gerónimo approached Mariscal and unexpectedly asked that the Apache be allowed to live in peace in Sonora. Sonora authorities granted this request on the condition that the Apache live within the military colonies and accept doles. This would eliminate the Apache's necessity to plunder and raid. State officials undertook this experiment which proved unsuccessful as the Indians soon returned to the warpath.[47]

Meanwhile, the Plan of Tuxtepec embroiled conditions in Sonora. This plan, issued on January 1, 1876, denounced Sebastian Lerdo de Tejada's intention to run again for president, listing the usual list of grievances and announcing its adherence to the principles of "effective suffrage and no reelection." Again Porfirio Díaz led the revolution, recruiting men and raising money freely in the United States and enjoying considerable support in Mexico.[48]

The revolt's indecisiveness contributed to considerable confusion in the several states of the Republic. At first Lerdistas drove Díaz back into the United States, but he soon returned to continue the fight. While the rebellion raged in many states, Lerdo held elections in October, 1876, declaring himself reelected. Immediately, José María Iglesias, President of the Supreme Court, denied the legality of the elections, declaring himself president of the Republic. This split the Lerdistas, since a number of them favored Iglesias.

In Sonora during the first days of the revolt, Mariscal as well as the Pesqueiristas remained loyal to Lerdo. In fact, Sonora numbered among the minority of states that did not take part in the general insurrection. However, events in Sinaloa threatened Sonora. Mariscal, reacting to the threat, sent Prospero Salazar Bustamante, with troops from the military colonies, to occupy the Villa Fuerte in Sinaloa.

In Sonora the situation became confused. When Iglesias separated from Lerdo, Mariscal denounced him. The fortunes of the war soon changed however. In that same October, Díaz and his supporters had been victorious over Alatorre at Tecoac, preparing his way to México D.F. On November 21, Lerdo fled to the United States, abandoning the struggle, making Iglesias the de jure president of Mexico under the national constitution. Mariscal had no choice but to recognize him as president.[49]

Lerdo's defection numbered the days of La Reforma. In December, Porfirio Díaz' forces took Mexico and this presidential switch immediately affected Sonora. Upon learning the turn of events, José J. Pesqueira rushed to Las Delicias. After conferring with Ignacio Pesqueira, José sent a communiqué to Mariscal, stating that due to the change in government Mariscal's commission had become ineffective and, therefore, executive power reverted to Pesqueira. He also demanded that Mariscal recognize José Pesqueira's legitimacy. On December 19, José Pesqueira denounced Mariscal publicly and the former claimed his own legitimacy.[50]

Mariscal answered that his commission had not terminated and that it became incumbent upon him to resist Pesqueira's treachery. Mariscal also issued a circular apprising Sonora of the turn of events, estimating that the revolt would be short lived. By this time the Pesqueiristas had left Las Delicias, attempting to recruit followers. The times had passed by the caudillo and many of his old friends refused even to see him.[51]

During this period the Sonora press took on comic overtones. Mariscal, who had refused to recognize Díaz until his revolt succeeded, now accused José and Ignacio Pesqueira of hypocrisy, asserting that the latter had supported Lerdo and Iglesias and in fact had been an enemy of the suddenly respectable Díaz.* Mariscal condemned the Pesqueiras for doing what most

*F. Tolentino to a friend, February 19, 1877, *El Democrata*, March 5, 1877; *La Prensa*, January 11, 1877; Mariscal to Luis Torres, January 13, 1877, in Cârreno, XVII, 22-23. Mariscal wrote that Pesqueira was retreating but would surely return to Las Delicias or La Cananea.

people in Sonora had done — recognizing Lerdo and later switching to the Plan of Palo Blanco (a revised version of the Plan of Tuxtepec, modified on March 21, 1876).[52]

On January 25, 1877, Mariscal repelled a vigorous attack on Ures, forcing the Pesqueiristas to retreat. This attack defeated the attackers, and Florencio Ruiz, the commandant of the military colonies of Huasabas in the district of Moctezuma, forced Pesqueira to retreat to Janos, Chihuahua.[53]

With the Pesqueira threat removed, Mariscal had a clear field. On February 5, 1877, he formally recognized Díaz, who in turn acknowledged Mariscal, who now had the problem of Sonora's civil administration. Which constitution would the state operate under: that of 1861, 1872, or 1873? A circular dated June 15, 1877, ended martial law, stating that Sonora would be governed under the Constitution of 1873.[54] Shortly afterwards, Sonorans prepared for new elections.

Immediately the state divided into two factions — one supporting Vicente Mariscal and the other for Francisco Serna — and again a bitter struggle for the governorship erupted. Much of the Sonora press sided with El Club de la Reforma, attacking Mariscal as an outsider of unknown ancestry. However, the term "liberal" must be qualified. Both the Pesqueiristas and the anti-Pesqueiristas claimed to be liberal and both sides were equally class conscious. This was demonstrated by the attack in the Sonora press on Mariscal. The pro-Serna press also charged that Ignacio Pesqueira's former supporters had switched to Mariscal. The pro-Mariscal press lauded him as the only man able to insure order in Sonora, claiming that Ignacio Pesqueira might return.[55]

Tensions rose, and again the adversaries traded charges that the elections would be fraudulent. Sonorans elected Mariscal governor, and the situation neared civil war. But again Francisco Serna proved unselfish and accepted the results of the election. On July 3, 1877, the Sonora legislature declared Mariscal governor and Serna deputy-governor. On the following day, Mariscal published an optimistic report, highlighting Sonora's economic and educational improvements from the time he had entered the state.[56]

In the meantime, Ignacio Pesqueira actively politicked in Chihuahua. From Janos, he marched to Rancho San Antonio in Durango, where he conferred with General Francisco Naranjo. Pesqueira asked for support for his cousin José, but Naranjo advised Ignacio Pesqueira to personally lobby Díaz. Ignacio Pesqueira thus marched to México D.F.,* where Pesqueira charmed Díaz into believing that he had supported the president's Plan of Palo Blanco. This set the stage for Ignacio Pesqueira's return to Sonora.[57]

---

*La Prensa, May 6, 1877, alleged that Pesqueira was a tyrant like Terrazas of Chihuahua, Romero Vargas of Puebla, and Alvarez of Guerrero, who were other strong men during Pesqueira's reign.

RETURN OF IGNACIO PESQUEIRA

Díaz appointed General Epitacio Huerta Sonora's military commander. In the middle of July, Huerta's party — three federal generals and Ignacio Pesqueira[58] — landed in Guaymas on the warship *México*. News of Pesqueira's arrival immediately spread throughout Sonora and many citizens speculated that Ignacio Pesqueira had returned to seize control with Huerta's backing. Matters worsened because the federal commander tacitly contributed to ambivalence.

In Guaymas, Pesqueira partisans received their old leader with open arms. While Ignacio Pesqueira had lost favor since 1872, there could be no doubt that he still enjoyed substantial support. Huerta's party went to Hermosillo, where the residents had received notice of Pesqueira's approach. The city divided itself into two camps — Mariscalistas versus Pesqueiristas. Pesqueira's foes, far outnumbering his friends, booed their old leader and hurled verbal insults at him. The city commissioned a youth, Fernando Méndez, to intercept Huerta. Fernando told the federal commander that, "inspired by sincerity and patriotism," Hermosillo's youth would not "vacillate in opposing Pesqueira's return."[59]

This day probably represented Pesqueira's darkest day, since the insults of the mob probably brought back old memories of his defeat at La Pasión and being called the assassin of Potrerito Seco. One press account stated: " *¡Malditos sean los hombres que como D. Ignacio Pesqueira son los vampiros del pueblo!* " (Damned be men like Ignacio Pesqueira who are vampires of the people!) Huerta witnessed this vehement reaction toward Ignacio Pesqueira, leaving no doubt as to pervasive public attitudes.[60]

Afterwards, Mariscal and Serna met with Huerta and the meeting established that both Mariscal and Serna would resist Huerta if he attempted to reinstate Pesqueira. Therefore, the party left for Ures, arriving on July 29. Again the people of that city turned out to renounce their former governor. An atmosphere of violence prevailed in the capital that forced Huerta to take precautions to protect Pesqueira's life. Many people feared that Pesqueira would attempt a comeback.

To counter this threat, Mariscal took a leave of six months and prepared to go to México D.F. to lobby his cause, leaving Francisco Serna in charge. On August 11, 1877, the Sonora legislature permitted the executive branch the power to seize the conspirators or to take any measures necessary to prevent a rebellion.[61]

Meanwhile, Huerta realized that conditions were not what he expected and prudently withdrew his sponsorship of Ignacio Pesqueira. Huerta gave the old caudillo a military escort to his hacienda at Las Delicias, where he spent his last days.[62]

DEATH OF IGNACIO PESQUEIRA

Ignacio Pesqueira, at the age of fifty-seven years, retired from public life, but unlike many of the other regional Mexican strong men, he made no further attempts to regain control of his lost empire. He retired to his hacienda at Las Delicias, one of the richest men in Sonora, dedicating himself to his numerous business ventures. The hacienda, located twenty miles southwest of Arizpe, consisted of about thirty thousand acres of fertile land. On the section west of the Sonora River, grew wheat, corn, and other cereals. The balance of the hacienda consisted of good grazing land for Pesqueira's thousands of head of cattle and about four and a half miles from the hacienda stood his Santa Elena Mine.

During his retirement, Pesqueira traveled to the United States where he sold his Santa Elena Mine to North American interests for three hundred fifty thousand dollars, after which he moved his residence to another hacienda at Bacanuchi on the outskirts of Arizpe. There he engaged in mining, lumbering, and cattle raising.[63]

To the end, a group of faithful admirers surrounded Ignacio Pesqueira. Many Sonorans remained Pesqueiristas, anxiously awaiting their hero to bring them back to power. There is no evidence that the caudillo planned a return. Finally, Ignacio Pesqueira suffered a stroke that left him paralyzed and on January 4, 1886, he died.

Ramiro de Garza, in a recent article, writes that Pesqueira died without the benefit of clergy. His death certificate reads:

No. 14. — Don Ignacio Pesqueira — In the Parish of Arizpe, on the fifth day of the month of February of one thousand eight hundred and eighty sixth year: I, Father JUAN URÍAS performed the service with CRUZ ALTA to the corpse of the old Governor of Sonora, Ignacio Pesqueira who was some sixty years old who died of paralysis and did not confess to me. I give faith. — Pbro. Juan Urías. (Free translation.)

This document, according to Garza, conclusively proved the general's dedication to the liberal cause, for in refusing the last rites, his anti-clericalism was underscored. This may well be true and the old caudillo may have believed that he was a liberal, for anti-clericalism in the nineteenth century represented the principal requisite of liberalism. But the times had changed and the interests controlling the "times" wanted more than mere slogans. Pesqueira's burial in the pantheon of Arizpe marked the passing of an age.

Conclusion

An evaluation of Ignacio Pesqueira is difficult, since he belonged to an age in which only the most fit and ruthless survived as regional leaders. The fact that he was better prepared than most men of his time to govern justly is perhaps the most lamentable aspect of his career. Pesqueira was not an illiterate cacique; having pursued his education in Spain and in Paris, he had what in his day was considered a superior education. His early inclinations were liberal, having been exposed to the ideas of the Enlightenment and the French Revolution. Yet he evolved into a despot, a fact that even an admirer attested: "Pesqueira executed the most absolute power; he became a true dictator and even his enemies could not demolish him in the twenty years that he reigned."[1] Pesqueira dictated rather than governed, and while defending the Constitution of 1857, he ended in subverting his own state constitution in 1873.

Pesqueira failed to promote the expectations of Sonora's merchants and miners, as he never fully coped with the main problems that plagued Sonora and, consequently, during the years of Pesqueira commerce declined. Mining could not be exploited without controlling the Apache. The best farm lands in Sonora lay fallow without the cooperation of the Yaqui and Mayo and attempts to encroach the Yaqui and Mayo lands drove these Indians to the warpath. Pesqueira alienated large segments of the Sonora populace by running Sonora for the benefit of a small clique. The indiscriminate use of taxation powers climaxed Pesqueira's long list of failures, contributing to the paralysis of Sonora's commerce, aggravating the ever-present cycle of poverty, and thus encouraging revolutions.[2] In turn, these conditions discouraged immigration to the state and in fact caused an alarming exodus, worsening the situation.*

A more prudent man might have consolidated Sonora rather than further factionalizing the state. Pesqueira betrayed the promise of his first inaugural speech to put Sonora above self-interest, and, in fact, many of his acts seem to have been performed merely to augment personal glory. The excessive taxation to finance his ventures increased discontent and further discouraged business. Finally, in the last half of his rule, he became increasingly capricious, as the infirmities of age and personal tragedies contributed to his fall.

La Prensa, February 5, 1877. This article contends that when Pesqueira took over in 1856, property within Sonora was worth more than twenty-five million pesos, and in 1877, it was worth half that amount. The article also charges that the state had not progressed during Pesqueira's rule as he had merely conserved power to exploit the state for the benefit of his close friends.

Despite these shortcomings, Pesqueira must be ranked as one of Sonora's foremost leaders. He paved the road to the eventual rise of commerce within Sonora by crushing the power of Gándara and his feudal farmers. After the War of Reform and the French intervention, Pesqueira subdued all remnants of conservatism within Sonora. And it was the opposition to Pesqueira, personal rather than philosophical, that in fact contributed to the legislature gaining respectability through its resistance to the governor.

It is doubtful whether a weaker man could have controlled the executive branch for such an extended period. In fact, during the era of Ignacio Pesqueira, Sonora's factionalism made it impossible to have impartial representation. Too many factions and potential caciques rendered Sonora ungovernable. Without Pesqueira the state might have been subjected to a blood bath, resulting in chaos; for this reason the Pesqueira era may have been a necessary evil in the evolution of Sonora.

To Pesqueira's credit, he refused to be a partner to secessionist schemes. He always supported the de jure government in México D.F., although until the end he retained de facto control. He can be commended for his support of the Constitution of 1857 and his refusal to accede to French demands. He can be criticized, however, for abandoning Sonora in its hour of need when he fled into Arizona during the French intervention. Also, Pesqueira draws criticism both for his alleged complicity with Crabb which, if it took place, was limited to allowing the latter to colonize the northern frontier of Sonora (see chapter 3), and for allegedly arranging with Lieutenant Coult to hoist the U.S. flag in case the French invaded Sonora (see chapter 7).

In addition to internal threats, Pesqueira's Sonora had the disadvantage of bordering the U.S. during a period in which North Americans had designs on the state's territory. Pesqueira resisted North American encroachments, although at times overexploiting the Sonorans' Yanqui-phobia to hide his lack of programs. To his credit, he kept North American immigration to Sonora to a minimum, a master stroke considering the fate of Texas and California. It is perhaps unfair to evaluate Pesqueira's contribution to Sonora in the perspective of the years that followed his public career. The capitalists, during the Díaz regime which followed, developed the state's natural resources and established peace, however, Díaz was not forced to contend with many of the problems that plagued Ignacio Pesqueira.

During the time of Pesqueira, Sonorans could not psychologically accept the foreign aid necessary to exploit their natural resources. In the first half of the Pesqueira regime, it would have been impossible to accept large-scale foreign assistance, for memories of the Mexican-American War, the Treaty of Guadalupe-Hidalgo, the Gadsden Purchase, and the filibusters were still fresh in Sonorans' minds. The opposition would have capitalized on any cooperation with the North Americans to overthrow Pesqueira, whose position during his first years had been tenuous.

Pesqueira represented the times. They dominated him: he did very little to change them and, in fact, they consumed him. Pesqueira's importance lies in the fact that he held the state together. He prevented Sonora from disintegrating into the total chaos that would have either forfeited this territory to the North Americans or which would have at least drastically retarded the growth that began in the 1880s.

Pesqueira's era set the stage for Sonora's economic advancement, for even before his death Pesqueira began to witness many changes and possible future solutions to the problems that had confronted him as governor. The isolation of the land lessened in 1879 with construction commencing on the first telegraph in Sonora. On May 27, 1880, contractors completed a short line between Guaymas and Hermosillo. By the time of Pesqueira's death, the telegraph lines criss-crossed the state. Meanwhile, in 1881, construction of the first railroad actually began, and by 1884 the railroad linked the Sonora interior with the North American lines of Arizona.[3]

The advent of the railroad ended the state's isolation. The simultaneous linking of Arizona with the rest of the United States facilitated both settler migration to that territory and the transportation of sufficient troops to herd the Apache into the reservation. The discovery of new deposits of copper, silver, and gold, which attracted even more settlers, finished the struggle of the valiant Apache. Arizona's population doubled during the 1880s, and large-scale cattle ranching resumed in southern Arizona, with many Apache from the adjoining reservations working for wages on these ranches.[4] These factors combined to neutralize the Apache both in Sonora and in Arizona, bringing peace and order in which the resources of these states could be exploited.

The Yaqui and the Mayo were another matter. Even after Pesqueira's death, they continued to defend their lands from encroachments by the Mexican settlers. After the Pesqueira era, these encroachments became more concerted. In the early 1880s, Governor Carlos R. Ortíz of Alamos began an all-out assault on the Indians of the valleys. The Indians resisted, and incessant guerrilla warfare raged from 1882 until 1885. This Indian effort was cut short, however, when the national government sent twelve hundred federal soldiers into the Yaqui Valley. After 1885 the government troops hammered away at the Yaqui and the Mayo, literally clubbing them into submission. In the spring of 1887, Mexican troops captured and executed the great Yaqui leader, Cajeme. After Cajeme, the Yaqui and the Mayo were at the mercy of Sonora businessmen-politicians, who with the aid of the national government and foreign capital, poured into these valleys.[5]

In the 1890s, the Richardson Construction Company entered Sonora, promoting irrigation and surveys in the Yaqui and Mayo valleys. Under Porfirio Díaz, Mexican and North American capitalists exploited the state's resources; the Díaz government freely dispensed mining, land, and railroad concessions to the president's friends and foreigners. Business within Sonora prospered through adequate capital, modern machinery, and railroad transportation. Meanwhile, the army permanently quieted the Mayo, although their cousins, the Yaqui, continued to defend their lands. In 1901, to rid themselves of the Yaqui, government interests sold more than five thousand Yaqui to the haciendas of Yucatán and Oaxaca. Many others fled to escape the savage war of extermination launched by Sonora and federal officials between the years of 1890 and 1910.[6]

Nevertheless, many Yaqui continued to resist, although they never again really became a threat. In 1926 they made their last futile gesture to protest the confiscation of their land, and as a consequence the Mexican army hunted them down.[7] The Yaqui continue to preserve their ways, although Cárdenas made the Yaqui a government within a government in 1939. They are fighting a losing battle, for the tide of modernization is permanently ending their isolation.

With the advent of Díaz, relations with the North Americans improved making it no longer necessary to annex Sonora. Foreigners had more freedom to exploit the state economically,[8] and after Pesqueira the imperialism of the Yanqui changed from territorial to economic.

The factionalism that had existed in Sonora when Pesqueira came to power became a thing of the past. The different special interests that had united to unseat Pesqueira continued to function in the legislature, opposing the continuance of anything that resembled Pesqueira's "strong man" rule. These factions opposed his successor, Vicente Mariscal, when he began to emulate the old caudillo. The only thing they wanted was an ambiance to exploit in peace; they had it under Díaz. The passing of Pesqueira has been summed up by Joseph Park, an Anglo-American Sonora historian:

The overthrow of Ignacio Pesqueira marked the end of the age of iron men in Sonoran politics, and the state entered a long period of tranquility under the governorship of businessmen controlled from Mexico by Porfirio Díaz.[9]

Notes

CHAPTER 1
PAGES 1–14

1. "Los Acontecimientos del Río Yaqui," *La Voz de Sonora*, August 15, 1857.
2. Eduardo W. Villa, *Galería de Sonorenses ilustres*, p. 137.
3. *La Voz de Sonora*, September 15, 1857.
4. Francisco P. Troncoso, *Las Guerras*, p. 20.
5. Charles Lempriere, *Notes in Mexico*, pp. 148-149.
6. *Railroad Record Supplement* (Cincinnati), February 25, 1856.
7. "Mexico's Forgotten Frontier," p. 247.
8. Quoted in Sylvester Mowry, *Arizona and Sonora*, p. 41.
9. Eduardo W. Villa, *Historia del Estado de Sonora*, pp. 209-210.
10. Stevens, "Mexico's Forgotten Frontier," pp. 94-95.
11. Hubert Howe Bancroft, *Northern Mexican States*, II, 743-5.
12. See Edward H. Spicer, *Cycles of Conquest*. Part I, chapter 2, pp. 46-85, deals with the Yaqui and Mayo.
13. Patricio Nicoli, *El Estado de Sonora*, p. 88.
14. Ibid., p. 93.
15. José Francisco Velasco, *Sonora: Its Extent*, trans. William F. Nye, p. 51.
16. Spicer, *Cycles of Conquest*, pp. 86-91.
17. Velasco, *Sonora*, pp. 91-104.
18. Spicer, p. 112.
19. Archivo General de la Nación, Secretaría de Gobernación, Archivos Viejos, Legajo 1833-54; *Indios bárbaros*, No. 2, Ministerio de Relaciones, Internales y Externales, 1850, Expediente No. 33, found in Fernando Pesqueira, ed., "Documentos Para la Historia de Sonora," Tercera Serie, Tomo VII, typewritten copy in the Biblioteca y Museo de Sonora, Hermosillo.
20. Rufus Kay Wyllys, *The French in Sonora*, pp. 20-33.
21. *Historia de Sonora*, p. 183.
22. Joseph F. Park, "The History of Mexican Labor," pp. 5-6.
23. Velasco, *Sonora*, p. 23.
24. Stevens, "Mexico's Forgotten Frontier," pp. 165-6.
25. Ibid., pp. 144-64.
26. James Morton Callahan, *American Foreign Policy*, pp. 230-1.
27. William R. Manning, ed., *Diplomatic Correspondence*, Documents 3772-4476, IX, 188; J. Fred Rippy, *The U.S. and Mexico*, pp. 126-9.
28. Paul Neff Garber, *The Gadsden Treaty*, p. 32.
29. Park, *The History of Mexican Labor*, p. 91; Fernando Pesqueira, "Documentos Para la Historia de Sonora," Segunda Serie, Tomo III. (Park's translation is edited by the author.)
30. Wyllys, *The French in Sonora*, p. 7.
31. *Nociones de Historia de Sonora*, p. 50.
32. Laurence Greene, *The Filibusterer*, p. 29.
33. Wyllys, *The French in Sonora*, pp. 52-5.
34. Ibid., pp. 162-4.
35. Ibid.; Maurice Soulie, *The Wolf Cub*.
36. *Diplomatic Negotiations*, pp. 7-8.
37. Lempriére, *Notes in Mexico*, p. 150.

CHAPTER 2

1. Sylvester Mowry, *Arizona and Sonora*; p. 50.
2. John Russell Bartlett, *Personal Narrative of Explorations and Incidents in Texas, New Mexico, California, Sonora and Chihuahua*, I, pp. 282-83; José Francisco Velasco, *Sonora*, p. 27.
3. John C. Cremony, *Life Among the Apaches*, p. 39.
4. Robert Conway Stevens, "Mexico's Forgotten Frontier," p. 173.
5. Interview with Fernando Pesqueira, the University of Sonora, Hermosillo, August 22, 1966.

6. Ibid; Ramón Corral, *Obras históricas*, p. 25; Eduardo W. Villa, *Galería de Sonorenses*, pp. 137-38; Hector Pesqueira, "Rectificando Datos de la Vida del Gral"; Ramiro de Garza, "Don Ignacio Pesqueira," pp. 19-21.
7. Villa, *Galería de Sonorenses*, p. 138; Garza, p. 20.
8. Francisco R. Almada, *Diccionario de historia, geografía y biografía Sonorenses*, p. 574.
9. Interview with Fernando Pesqueira, August 22, 1966.
10. Corral, p. 26; Villa, *Galería de Sonorenses*, p. 138.
11. Francisco R. Almada, *Diccionario de historia, geografía y biografía Sonorenses*, p. 574.
12. Hector Pesqueira, "Rectificando"; Villa, *Galería de Sonorenses*, p. 138; Francisco Sosa, *Las estatutas de la reforma*, p. 7; Almada, p. 574; Eduardo W. Villa, *Historia de Sonora*, p. 212.
13. Villa, *Historia de Sonora*, p. 212; Almada, p. 574.
14. Almada, pp. 574-75.
15. Villa, *Galería de Sonorenses*, pp. 138-39.
16. Stevens, "Mexico's Forgotten Frontier," p. 150; Villa, *Galería de Sonorenses*, pp. 61-64; Alberto Caldiaz Barrera, *Dos gigantes, Sonora y Chihuahua*, I, p. 22.
17. Almada, pp. 288-89; Stevens, "Mexico's Forgotten Frontier," p. 149; Villa, *Historia de Sonora*, p. 223.
18. Almada, p. 289; Carlota Miles, *Almada of Alamos*, pp. 16-17.
19. James Box, *Captain James Box's Adventures and Explorations in New and Old Mexico*, pp. 240-41.
20. Ernesto de la Torre Villar, "Las Notas Sobre Sonora, del Capitán Guillet (1864-1866)," p. 57.
21. Charles D. Poston, "Building a State in Apache Land," pp. 204-205, 211.
22. Henry Bamford Parkes, *A History of Mexico*, pp. 227-29.
23. Manuel María Gándara, *Manifestación que hace al gefe supremo de la republica el ciudadano Manuel María Gándara*, p. 6; Laureano Calvo Berber, *Nociones de historia de Sonora*, p. 187; *La Voz de Sonora*, September 28, 1855.
24. *La Voz de Sonora*, October 19, 1855; Villa, *Historia de Sonora*, p. 239; Manuel María Gándara, "Estatuto Orgánico," *Plan Politico Proclamado* (Ures), October 22, 1855.
25. Resolution of the Council of State, signed by Ramón Encinas, L. Morales, I.M. Loaiza, Ures, February 19, 1856, in *La Voz de Sonora*, February 22, 1856.
26. *Historia de Sonora*, p. 241; José de Aguilar to the citizens of Sonora, March 18, 1856, *La Voz de Sonora*, March 21, 1856.
27. *Historia de Sonora*, p. 241.
28. Ignacio Pesqueira and others to the governor of Sonora, Ures, April 2, 1856, *La Voz de Sonora*, April 4, 1856.
29. Col. D. Juan Espíndola to Ignacio Pesqueira, April 6, 1856, *La Voz de Sonora*, April 11, 1856; Ignacio Pesqueira to Espíndola and José de Aguilar, Ures, April 7, 1856, *La Voz de Sonora*, April 11, 1856.
30. Laureano Calvo Berber, *Nociones de historia de Sonora*, p. 189.
31. *La Voz de Sonora*, April 24, 1856; Villa, *Historia de Sonora*, pp. 241-42.
32. Aguilar to Gándara, April 23, 1856, *La Voz de Sonora*, April 24, 1856; Gándara to Aguilar, Santa Rita, April 25, 1856, *La Voz de Sonora*, April 27, 1856; Aguilar to Gándara, Ures, April 26, 1856, *La Voz de Sonora*, April 27, 1856; Gándara to Aguilar, April 27, 1856, *La Voz de Sonora*, April 28, 1856; Aguilar to Gándara, Ures, April 27, 1856, *La Voz de Sonora*, April 28, 1856.
33. *La Voz de Sonora*, April 30 and May 23, 1856; "El Lic. José de Aguilar Gobernador del Estado de Sonora, a Sus Habitantes," Ures, April 30, 1856, *La Voz de Sonora*, May 9, 1856.
34. "Gacetilla de la Capital," *La Voz de Sonora*, May 16, 1856; Cirilo Ramírez, "Abandona de la Frontera," *La Voz de Sonora*, June 27, 1856; Villa, *Historia de Sonora*, p. 242; *La Voz de Sonora*, May 30, 1856.
35. Villa, *Historia de Sonora*, p. 242.
36. Pesqueira to Gándara, Arizpe, May 26, 1856, in Villa, *Historia de Sonora*, pp. 242, 244.
37. *Historia de Sonora*, p. 244.
38. José de Aguilar to District Prefects, Topahui, July 25, 1856, *La Voz de Sonora*, August 9, 1856; Villa, *Historia de Sonora*, p. 246; Corral, *Obras históricas*, pp. 26, 27.

39. Villa, *Historia de Sonora*, p. 246; José de Aguilar to the State Prefects (sheriffs of a county), Topahui, July 25, 1856, *La Voz de Sonora*, August 9, 1856.
40. "La Ciudad de Alamos," *La Voz de Sonora*, October 3, 1856; Villa, *Historia de Sonora*, p. 246.
41. Corral, p. 27; Villa, *Historia de Sonora*, p. 246.

CHAPTER 3

1. Ramón Corral, *Obras historicas*, p. 28; Hubert Howe Bancroft, *Northern Mexican States and Texas*, II, p. 695.
2. John R. Bartlett, *Personal Narrative of Explorations and Incidents in Texas, New Mexico, California, Sonora and Chihuahua, During the Years 1850, '51, '52, and '53*, II, pp. 439-42.
3. Robert H. Forbes, *Crabb's Filibustering Expedition into Sonora, 1857*, p. 5.
4. Rufus Kay Wyllys, *The French in Sonora, 1850-1854*, p. 49.
5. Horace Bell, *Reminiscences of a Ranger*, pp. 213-14.
6. Ibid., pp. 214-15.
7. William O. Scroggs, *Filibusters and Financiers*, p. 6.
8. Ibid., p. 308.
9. Rufus Kay Wyllys, "Henry A. Crabb," p. 184; Theodore H. Hittell, *History of California*, p. 806; *San Francisco Bulletin*, May 18, 1857.
10. Scroggs, p. 17.
11. Ibid., p. 309.
12. James Morton Callahan, *American Foreign Policy in Mexican Relations*, p. 231; Scroggs, p. 308; Wyllys, "Henry A. Crabb," p. 184.
13. Bell, p. 220.
14. Juan A. Robinson, *Statement of Juan A. Robinson.*
15. José de Aguilar to Military Commandant of Sinaloa, Ures, July 12, 1856, Archivo Historico del Estado de Sonora, Hermosillo, Gaveta 3-2, 233.3/6.
16. Robinson, pp. 17-20; *La Voz de Sonora*, May 9 and July 4, 1856.
17. *La Voz de Sonora*, September 5, 1856.
18. Laureano Calvo Berber, *Nociones de historia de Sonora*, pp. 192-96.
19. México, Secretaría de Guerra y Marina, Archivo General, Fracción Primera, Operaciones Militares, 1857, Legajo 13 (Crabb Expedition), No. 5; Crabb to T.J. Oxley, San Francisco, December 1856, in Wyllys, "Henry A. Crabb," p. 183.
20. Archivo Historico del Estado de Sonora, Hermosillo, Gaveta 3-2, 233.3/6.
21. Calvo Berber, p. 198.
22. Crabb to Redondo, March 26, 1857, Sonoita, in Villa, *Historia de Sonora*, pp. 249, 251.
23. Eduardo W. Villa, *Historia de Sonora*, p. 251.
24. Translation in Forbes, p. 15. See also Villa, *Historia de Sonora*, p. 251.
25. Forbes, p. 16.
26. Bancroft, *Northern Mexican States*, II, p. 695.
27. *San Francisco Bulletin*, May 13, 1857; William R. Manning, *Early Diplomatic Correspondence of the United States* (Documents 4309, 4311, and 4313), IX, pp. 917, 918-19, and 919-923; Forbes, p. 58; Sylvester Mowry, *Memoir of the Proposed Territory of Arizona*, p. 22.
28. Charles D. Poston, "Building a State in Apache Land," p. 291; Bancroft, *Northern Mexican States*, II, p. 695.
29. Forbes, pp. 48-49.

CHAPTER 4

1. Ramón Corral, *Obras históricas*, pp. 28-29; Eduardo W. Villa, *Galería de Sonorenses*, p. 138 and *Historia de Sonora*, p. 267; Francisco R. Almada, *Diccionario de historia, geografía y biografía Sonorenses*, pp. 19-20.
2. Francisco Troncoso, *Las guerras con las tribus Yaqui y Mayo del estado de Sonora*, p. 52; Corral, p. 29; Villa, *Historia de Sonora*, p. 269.
3. *La Voz de Sonora*, October 21 and November 4, 1857; Corral, p. 30; Laureano Calvo Berber, *Nociones de historia de Sonora*, p. 206.
4. *La Voz de Sonora*, January 1, 1858.
5. Yáñez to the military commander of Guaymas, October 20, 1857, Ibid., December 2, 1857; *Plan of Tacubaya*, December, 1857.
6. Corral, p. 30; Villa, *Historia de Sonora*, p. 269.
7. Calvo Berber, pp. 206-207; Corral, p. 30; *La Voz de Sonora*, March 5, 1858.

8. Troncoso, p. 52; Corral, p. 31.
9. *La Voz de Sonora*, June 11, 1858.
10. Corral, p. 29; Villa, *Historia de Sonora*, p. 269; Ibid., October 16, 1857.
11. *La Voz de Sonora*, July 30, 1858.
12. Wilfred Hardy Callcott, *Liberalism in Mexico*, pp. 1-42; Henry Bamford Parkes, *A History of Mexico*, pp. 233-50.
13. Villa, *Historia de Sonora*, p. 270.
14. *La Voz de Sonora*, July 16, 1858.
15. Pesqueira to the Prefects, Alamos, December 19, 1858, *La Voz de Sonora*, January 7, 1859.
16. Villa, *Historia de Sonora*, p. 153.
17. Lewis Dent to the consul of Guaymas, San Francisco, February 9, 1860, "Despatches from U.S. Consuls in Guaymas, Mexico, 1832-96," Vols. I-IV, The National Archives.
18. Vicente de Paula Andrade, *Noticias biográficas*, p. 66.
19. Calvo Berber, p. 209; Corral, p. 31.
20. Corral, p. 32.
21. *La Voz de Sonora*, November 2, 1858; Corral, p. 32.
22. Calvo Berber, p. 211.
23. Carlota Miles, *Almada of Alamos*, p. ix.
24. José María Pérez Hernández, *Comprendido de la geografía del estado de Sonora*, p. 89.
25. Miles, pp. 20-21; Corral, p. 32.
26. Miles, p. 21.
27. Ibid., pp. 21-22.
28. Ignacio Pesqueira, "Circular to the People," Alamos, October 30, 1858, *La Voz de Sonora*, November 25 and 26, 1858.
29. Corral, p. 33.
30. Hubert Howe Bancroft, *Northern Mexican States and Texas*, II, p. 649.
31. Ibid., p. 691.
32. Ibid., pp. 695, 650.
33. Almada, pp. 835-42 and 251-52.
34. Miles, pp. 28, 66-67.
35. Corral, p. 33; Ibid., p. 22; circular dated February 2, 1859, appearing in *La Voz de Sonora*, February 11, 1859.
36. Corral, p. 33.
37. James D. Richardson, *A Compilation of the Messages and Papers of the Confederacy*, V, 512-14; Ibid., pp. 33-34; *La Voz de Sonora*, February 11, 1859; Eustaquio Buelna, *Apuntes para la historia de Sinaloa 1821-1882*, p. 53.
38. Corral, pp. 33-34; *La Estrella de Occidente*, July 8, 1859.
39. *La Estrella de Occidente*, July 15, 1859; Buelna, p. 54; Almada, p. 576.
40. Corral, p. 35.

CHAPTER 5

1. "Despatches from U.S. Consuls in Guaymas, Mexico, 1832-96," Vols. I-IV, The National Archives.
2. Laureano Calvo Berber, *Nociones de Historia de Sonora*, pp. 163-67.
3. Ibid., pp. 163-64.
4. Fernando Pesqueira, ed., "Documentos Para la Historia de Sonora"; Manuel Monteverde, Hermosillo, August 30, 1859, *La Estrella de Occidente*, September 9, 1859.
5. *Diccionario porrua*, p. 836.
6. L.W. Inge to Robert McLane, August 15, 1859, "Despatches from U.S. Ministers to Mexico, 1823-1906," Vol. XXIV, The National Archives.
7. *Arizona and Sonora* (1864), p. 35.
8. Caleb Cushing, *Contract*, pp. 2, 3, and 5; Francisco F. de la Maza, *Código*, I, 641.
9. J.E. Calhoun and Associates, San Francisco, to J.B. Jecker, April 5, 1859, "Despatches from U.S. Ministers to Mexico."
10. Stone to Pesqueira, and Pesqueira to Stone, Guaymas, *La Voz de Sonora*, April 15 and 30, and May 7, 1858.
11. *La Estrella de Occidente*, June 22, 1860; *La Voz de Sonora*, July 30, 1858.

12. Stone to Lewis Cass, Guaymas, December 23, 1858, "Despatches from U.S. Consuls in Guaymas, Mexico, 1832-96," Vols. I-IV, The National Archives.
13. Joseph Park, "The History of Mexican Labor," p. 32; Stone to Cass, Guaymas, December 23, 1858, "Despatches from U.S. Consuls in Guaymas."
14. Robert Rose to Cass, Guaymas, January 19, and February 4 and 28, 1859, "Despatches from U.S. Consuls in Guaymas."
15. L.W. Inge to Robert McLane, San Francisco, April 20, 1859, "Despatches from U.S. Ministers in Mexico."
16. Stone to J.B. Jecker and Company, May 27, 1859, "Despatches from U.S. Ministers to Mexico"; Rose to Stone, Guaymas, May 27, 1859, "Despatches from U.S. Consuls in Guaymas."
17. Conner to Cass, Mazatlan, May 26, 1859, "Despatches from U.S. Consuls in Mazatlan, Mexico," Vols. II-IV, The National Archives.
18. Doris W. Bents, "The History of Tubac," pp. 160-63.
19. Quoted in Park, "History of Mexican Labor," p. 31.
20. Robert McLane to L.W. Inge, Veracruz, June 9, 1859, "Despatches from U.S. Ministers to Mexico."
21. Inge to McLane, August 15, 1859, "Despatches from U.S. Ministers to Mexico"; Veracruz, October 1, 1859, "Despatches from U.S. Ministers to Mexico; Juan Antonio de la Fuente to Henry R. de la Reintrie, Veracruz, September 28, 1859, "Despatches from U.S. Ministers to Mexico."
22. Samuel Flagg Bemis, *Diplomatic History*, p. 39.
23. *La Estrella de Occidente*, September 9, 1859.
24. Park, "History of Mexican Labor," p. 36; *La Estrella de Occidente*, November 18, 1859.
25. *La Estrella de Occidente*, November 18, 1859.
26. Villa, *Historia de Sonora*, p. 273; Allden to Porter, Guaymas, October 25, 1859, "Despatches from U. S. Consuls in Guaymas."
27. Porter to Pesqueira, Guaymas, *La Estrella de Occidente*, November 18, 1859.
28. Corral, pp. 37-38; Allden to Porter, Guaymas, November 18, 1859, "Despatches from U.S. Consuls in Guaymas."
29. Allden to Porter, Guaymas, November 21, 1859, "Despatches from U.S. Consuls in Guaymas."
30. Thomas Robinson to Farrelly Allden, Guaymas, November 20, 1859, "Despatches from U.S. Consuls in Guaymas."
31. Allden to Cass, Guaymas, November 18, 1859, "Despatches from U.S. Consuls in Guaymas"; Corral, pp. 37-38.
32. Allden to Cass, Guaymas, October 31, 1859, "Despatches from U.S. Consuls in Guaymas"; *La Estrella de Occidente*, December 21, 1859.
33. Park, *History of Mexican Labor*, p. 34.
34. "El Tratado," *La Estrella de Occidente*, February 17, 1860.

CHAPTER 6

1. "Building a State in Apache Land," p. 296.
2. Ramón Corral, *Obras Históricas*, p. 38; Laureano Calvo Berber, *Nociones de historia de Sonora*, p. 215; *La Estrella de Occidente*, July 6, 1860.
3. Carlota Miles, *Almada of Alamos*, pp. 40-41; Eduardo W. Villa, *Historia de Sonora*, p. 274; Calvo Berber, p. 215.
4. Villa, *Historia de Sonora*, p. 274.
5. *Arizona and Sonora* (1864), p. 36.
6. Browne, p. 144.
7. Ibid., p. 168.
8. Calvo Berber, p. 215.
9. Henry F. Dobyns Collection; José María Pérez Hernández, *Compendio de la geografía del estado de Sonora*, p. 105.
10. John R. Bartlett, *Personal Narrative*, I, p. 432; Edward H. Spicer, *Cycles of Conquest*, pp. 513-14.
11. Calvo Berber, p. 216.
12. Ibid.
13. Ibid.
14. Ibid.
15. Ibid., p. 217.

16. Bartlett, *Personal Narrative*, pp. 468-69; Browne, pp. 248-49.
17. Captain James Box, *Captain James Box's Adventures*, p. 243; José Francisco Velasco, *Sonora*, pp. 25-26.
18. *La Estrella de Occidente*, October 26, 1860.
19. Calvo Berber, pp. 216-17.
20. Eduardo W. Villa, *Galería de Sonorenses ilustres*, p. 141.
21. Calvo Berber, p. 219.
22. Villa, *Historia de Sonora*, p. 275; Miles, p. 20.
23. Villa, *Historia de Sonora*, p. 275.
24. Francisco R. Almada, *Diccionario de historia, geografía y biografía Sonorenses*, pp. 202 and 577; F. Allden to Secretary of State, Guaymas, October 31, 1861, "Despatches from U.S. Consuls in Guaymas, Mexico, 1832-1896"; Ernesto de la Torre Villar, "Las Notas Sobre Sonora," I (1953), pp. 56-57.
25. Miles, p. 26.
26. Corral, p. 41.
27. Miles, p. 27.
28. Corral, p. 41.
29. Miles, p. 27.
30. Ibid.
31. Ibid., pp. 13-14, 27-30.
32. Villa, *Historia de Sonora*, p. 278.
33. Corral, pp. 41-42.
34. Ibid.
35. Miles, pp. 26, 29-30.
36. Ibid., pp. 30-31, 55.
37. Ibid., pp. 29, 61-62.
38. Ibid., p. 56.
39. Mary Williams, *The People and Politics of Latin America*, pp. 472-73.
40. William Baker to William Seward, Guaymas, May 15 and June 30, 1862, "Despatches from U.S. Consuls in Guaymas."
41. Corral, p. 43; Graham to Pesqueira, Guaymas, March 28, 1862, *La Estrella de Occidente*, April 25, 1862.
42. Graham to Pesqueira, Guaymas, March 31, 1862, found in the Archivo Histórico del Estado de Sonora, Hermosillo, Gaveta 16-1, p. 383.
43. Pesqueira to Graham, Ures, April 10, 1862, *La Estrella de Occidente*, April 25, 1862; Corral, p. 43.
44. Villa, *Historia de Sonora*, pp. 278-79; Calvo Berber, p. 223; Corral, p. 44.
45. Baker to Seward, Guaymas, May 15, 1862, "Despatches from U.S. Consuls in Guaymas"; Torre Villar, "Las Notas Sobre Sonora," pp. 56-57.
46. Baker to Seward, Guaymas, May 15, 1862, "Despatches from U.S. Consuls in Guaymas"; Corral, p. 44.
47. Nuño to Baker, Guaymas, April 30, 1862, *La Estrella de Occidente*, May 9, 1862; Calvo Berber, p. 223; Corral, p. 44.
48. Hays to Pesqueira, Guaymas, July 29, 1862, Archivo Histórico del Estado de Sonora, Hermosillo, Gaveta 16-1, p. 384; Baker to Seward, Guaymas, July 25, 1862, "Despatches from U.S. Consuls in Guaymas."
49. Baker to Pesqueira, Guaymas, July 26, 1862, Archivo Histórico del Estado de Sonora, Hermosillo, Gaveta 16-1, p. 384.
50. Calvo Berber, p. 223.

CHAPTER 7

1. Eduardo W. Villa, *Historia de Sonora*, p. 282; Ramón Corral, *Obras Históricas*, p. 47.
2. Laureano Calvo Berber, *Nociones de historia de Sonora*, p. 223-24; Juárez to Pesqueira, México, July 23, 1862, Archivo Histórico del Estado de Sonora, Hermosillo, Gaveta 15-4.
3. Toombs, Secretary of the Department of State, Montgomery, May 1861, to John F. Pickett, in James D. Richardson, *Messages and Papers of the Confederacy*, II, p. 21; J. Fred Rippy, *The United States and Mexico*, pp. 233-36.
4. Rippy, *U.S. and Mexico*, pp. 233-36.

5. *San Francisco Bulletin*, January 4, February 6, and April 10, 1861.
6. H.H. Sibley to Pesqueira, Fort Bliss, Texas, December 16, 1861, "Despatches from U.S. Consuls in Guaymas, Mexico, 1832-1896," Vols. I-IV, The National Archives; Villa, *Historia de Sonora*, p. 280; Corral, p. 45; Calvo Berber, p. 222.
7. Carleton to Pesqueira, Fort Yuma, May 2, 1862, Archivo Histórico del Estado de Sonora, Hermosillo, Gaveta 16-1, p. 384; *Volunteer Troops to Guard Mails*, pp. 84-85, Pesqueira to Carleton, Hermosillo, June 2, 1862.
8. Archivo del Congreso de Sonora, September 26, 1863, Box 27, Expediente 860, found in Fernando Pesqueira, ed., "Documentos Para la Historia de Sonora," Cuarta Serie, Tomo III, typewritten copy in the Biblioteca y Museo de Sonora, Hermosillo; Francisco R. Almada, *Diccionario de historia, geografía y biografía Sonorenses*, p. 577.
9. Villa, *Historia de Sonora*, p. 282; Corral, p. 47.
10. Genaro García, ed., *Colección de documentos inéditos o muy raros para la historia de México*, Segunda Parte, Tomo XVI, doc. ix, pp. 34-36, and XVII, doc. xxi, p. 75; Juan Manuel Valencia, "Diplomacia Imperialista en Sonora, 1864," in Pesqueira, "Documentos," Tercera Serie, Tomo IX.
11. Zeltner to Arroyo, Panama, January 20, 1864, C-I, in Pesqueira, "Documentos," Tercera Serie, Tomo IX.
12. Ibid., Arroyo to Zeltner, Palacio Imperial, March 5, 1864, C-III and Zeltner to Arroyo, Panama, April 28, 1864, C-VI, and Fourniel to Zeltner, Panama, April 28, 1864, C-VII, and Zeltner to Arroyo, Panamá, May 4, 1864, C-XI, and Fourniel to Arroyo, San Blas, June 29, 1864, C-XIV.
13. Ibid., Fourniel to Arroyo, La Paz, July 3, 1864, C-XVII, and Fourniel to Pesqueira, Guaymas, July 9, 1864, C-XIX.
14. Ibid., Pesqueira to Fourniel, Ures, July 11, 1864, C-XX.
15. Ibid., Fourniel to Arroyo, D'Assas, July 20, 1864, C-XXII.
16. James Morton Callahan, *American Foreign Policy in Mexican Relations*, p. 298; Mariano Cuevas, *Historia de la iglesia en México*, V, p. 341; Carlota Miles, *Almada of Alamos*, p. 173; Percy F. Martin, *Maximilian in Mexico*, pp. 197-98; Justo Sierra, *Evolución política*, pp. 376-395; García, XVII, pp. 125-26, doc. xxviii, and XVIII, pp. 131-48.
17. Hubert Howe Bancroft, *Northern Mexican States and Texas*, II, p. 696; Calvo Berber, p. 226.
18. Calvo Berber, p. 226; Pesqueira to the People of Sonora, Ures, November 30, 1864, in Pesqueira, "Documentos," Tercera Serie, Tomo IX; Jack Autry Dabbs, *The French Army in Mexico, 1861-1867*, p. 99; Martin, p. 206.
19. Charles Allen Smart, *Viva Juárez*, pp. 298, 300.
20. Evans Coleman, Jr., "Senator Gwinn's Plan for the Colonization of Sonora," p. 498; Charles D. Poston, "Building a State in Apache Land," p. 297.
21. Jay Mann Collection; Carleton to Pesqueira, Santa Fe, April 20, 1864, and Pesqueira to Carleton, Guaymas, May 29, 1864, Archivo Historico del Estado de Sonora, Hermosillo, Gaveta 16-1, p. 384.
22. Jay Mann Collection.
23. Dabbs, pp. 99-100; Castagny to Bazaine, Mazatlán, February 16, 1865, García, XXIV, pp. 228-35, doc. liii.
24. Calvo Berber, p. 227; Bancroft, *Northern Mexican States*, II, p. 696; Corral, p. 49.
25. Villa, *Historia de Sonora*, p. 285.
26. Corral, pp. 50-51.
27. Edward Conner to Seward, Guaymas, April 29, 1865, "Despatches from U.S. Consuls in Guaymas"; Castagny to Sonorans, Ures, April 14, 1865, in Ignacio Ramirez, *Obras de Ignacio Ramírez*, pp. 281-84.
28. Calvo Berber, p. 228; Villa, *Historia de Sonora*, p. 285; Corral, p. 52; Dabbs, p. 100.
29. Dabbs, p. 100.
30. Calvo Berber, p. 228; Almada, p. 578.
31. Interview with Fernando Pesqueira, Hermosillo, Sonora, August 22, 1966; Thomas Edwin Farnish, *History of Arizona*, IV, pp. 190-91; Charles Lewis Collection.

32. Almada, p. 578.
33. Villa, *Historia de Sonora*, p. 286.
34. Sierra, *Evolución*, pp. 399-400.
35. Ernesto de la Torre Villar, "Las Notas Sobre Sonora del Capitan Guillet (1864-1866)," p. 59; Fernando Pesqueira, "Documentos," Primera Serie, Tomo VII, *Alcance al número 5 del periódico oficial al departamento de Sonora*, October 23, 1865.
36. Torre Villar, "Las Notas Sobre Sonora," pp. 54, 56.
37. Ibid., p. 55.
38. Miles, p. 175; Villa, *Historia de Sonora*, p. 287.
39. Miles, p. 175-76; Fernando Pesqueira, "Documentos," Primera Serie, Tomo VII, *Alcance al numero 2 del periodico oficial del departmento de Sonora*, October 3, 1865.
40. Miles, p. 176.
41. Dabbs, p. 100.
42. Miles, p. 177.
43. Ibid., p. 178.
44. Ibid.
45. Almada, p. 579; Calvo Berber, p. 230.
46. Miles, p. 179.
47. Corral, p. 55.
48. Ibid.
49. Ibid., p. 57.
50. Ibid., p. 58.
51. Dabbs, p. 176; Corral, pp. 58-59.
52. Bancroft, *Northern Mexican States*, II, p. 697; Ibid.
53. *La Estrella de Occidente*, September 14, 1866; Martin, pp. 273, 283; Calvo Berber, p. 233; Eduardo Villa, *Galería de Sonorenses ilustres*, p. 143; Bancroft, Northern Mexican States, II, p. 697.
54. Ibid.
55. Villa, *Historia de Sonora*, p. 302.
56. Castagny to Sonorans, Ures, April 14, 1865, in Ramirez, pp. 281-84; Villa, *Historia de Sonora*, p. 286; Ramiro de Garza, "Don Ignacio Pesqueira," pp. 28-30.

CHAPTER 8

1. Jack Autry Dabbs, *The French Army in Mexico*, 1861-1867, p. 213; *La Estrella de Occidente*, March 22, 1867.
2. Dabbs, pp. 214, 216.
3. *Diccionario porrúa de historia*, p. 971.
4. Ibid.
5. Ibid., pp. 982, 1021-22.
6. Laureano Calvo Berber, *Nociones de historia de Sonora*, pp. 234-35.
7. *La Estrella de Occidente*, June 7 and 28, and May 24, 1867; Ignacio Ramírez, *Obras de Ignacio Ramírez*, p. 28.
8. A.F. Pradeau, *The Mexican Mints of Alamos and Hermosillo*, p. 39; Ramón Corral, *Obras históricas*, p. 69; *La Estrella de Occidente*, June 7, and July 12, 1867.
9. Ignacio Ramírez, p. 28.
10. *La Estrella de Occidente*, August 30, 1867.
11. Corral, pp. 70-71.
12. *El Imparcial*, quoted in Alphonse Pinart, *Prints*, Document No. 1172; Hubert Howe Bancroft, *Northern Mexican States and Texas*, II, p. 701; *La Estrella de Occidente*, October 4, 1867.
13. *La Estrella de Occidente*, October 4, 1867.
14. Villa, *Historia de Sonora*, p. 305; Corral, pp. 74-75; Francisco R. Almada, *Diccionario de historia, geografía y biografía Sonorenses*, pp. 240-241, 454-55, and 489.
15. Corral, pp. 74-75; Calvo Berber, p. 235.
16. Villa, *Historia de Sonora*, p. 306.
17. Ramiro de Garza, "Don Ignacio Pesqueira," pp. 19-21.
18. *La Estrella de Occidente*, February 21 and 28, 1868.

19. Ibid., June 12, 1868.
20. Bancroft, *Northern Mexican States*, II, p. 701; Corral, p. 71.
21. Corral, pp. 71-72.
22. Ibid.; Francisco P. Troncoso, *Las guerras con las tribus Yaqui y Mayo de estado de Sonora*, pp. 57-58.
23. *La Estrella de Occidente*, February 28, 1868.
24. Ibid., García Morales to Pesqueira, Guaymas, February 24, 1868.
25. Corral, pp. 72-73.
26. *La Estrella de Occidente*, March 28, 1868; Willard to Fish, Guaymas, Quarterly Report, December 21, 1869, "Despatches from U.S. Consuls in Guaymas."
27. Clara Manson, "Indian Uprisings in Sonora, Mexico," p. 65; Corral, p. 85.
28. Corral, p. 85.
29. Ibid., p. 107.
30. J. Fred Rippy, *The U.S. and Mexico*, p. 282.
31. "Purchase of Sonora," *Southern Arizonian*, November 16, 1867.
32. Annual Consular Report by Willard, Guaymas, October 1, 1868, "Despatches from U.S. Consuls in Guaymas."
33. I. Pesqueira, February 26, 1868, in Fernando Pesqueira, "Documentos," Segunda Serie, Tomo IV.
34. March 2, 1869, "Despatches from U.S. Consuls in Guaymas."
35. Villa, *Historia de Sonora*, p. 306; Calvo Berber, p. 236.
36. Corral, pp. 76-78.
37. Almada, p. 821; Ernesto de la Torre Villar, "Las Notas Sobre Sonora del Capitan Guillet (1864-1866)," p. 59; Corral, p. 74; Fernando Pesqueira, "Documentos," Cuarta Serie, Tomo III, No. 30, Exp. 1055 del Archivo Histórico, Congreso del Estado de Sonora, Ano 1869, Pesqueira, Ures, April, 1869.
38. Willard to Seward, Guaymas, April 1, 1869, "Despatches from U.S. Consuls in Guaymas"; Corral, pp. 78-79.
39. Corral, p. 79.
40. Ibid.
41. Ibid., p. 80.
42. Calvo Berber, pp. 236-37; *La Estrella de Occidente*, March 11, 1870.
43. Willard to J.C.B. Davis, Guaymas, March 25, 1870, "Despatches from U.S. Consuls in Guaymas."
44. Ibid., March 31, 1870.
45. Ibid., June 3, 1870.
46. *La Estrella de Occidente*, June 3, 1870.
47. Ibid., September 2, 1870; Corral, p. 83.
48. Willard to Hunter, Guaymas, December 31, 1870, "Despatches from U.S. Consuls in Guaymas."
49. Pinart Documents, Document 1175.

CHAPTER 9

1. Willard to Davis, Guaymas, March 3 and 26, 1870, "Despatches from U.S. Consuls in Guaymas, Mexico, 1832-1896," Vols. I-IV, The National Archives.
2. Ibid., Willard to Hunter, Guaymas, Quarterly Report, Supplement to No. 95, December 31, 1870.
3. *La Estrella de Occidente*, February 25, 1870; Ibid., Willard to Davis, Guaymas, March 30, 1870, and Willard to Fish, Annual Report, Guaymas, October 1, 1870.
4. Willard to Davis, Guaymas, Quarterly Report, March 31, 1870, "Despatches from U.S. Consuls in Guaymas"; *La Estrella de Occidente*, September 30, 1870.
5. Safford to Fish, Tucson, December 29, 1871, *La Estrella de Occidente*, April 12, 1872; Safford to Pesqueira, Tucson, January 2, 1871, *La Balanza*, February 21, 1871; editorial, *La Estrella de Occidente*, April 12, 1872.
6. "La Prensa de Arizona y los Horrores Perpetrados en el Río Gila," and "Asesinatos en el Gila," *La Estrella de Occidente*, March 15, 22, and April 12, 1872.

7. A. Willard to State Department, Guaymas, September 30, 1871, "Despatches from U.S. Consuls in Guaymas,"
8. "La Guerra de Bárbaros en Sonora," *La Estrella de Occidente*, October 20, 1871; Garrison to Fish, Guaymas, September 30, 1872, "Despatches from U.S. Consuls in Guaymas."
9. Henry Bamford Parkes, *A History of Mexico*, pp. 281-82.
10. Lesley Byrd Simpson, *Many Mexicos*, p. 258.
11. *Diccionario porrus de historia*, p. 1106.
12. Parkes, p. 282.
13. Ramón Corral, *Obras históricas*, p. 83.
14. Archivo Histórico del Estado de Sonora, Hermosillo, Gaveta 17-4, p. 438; interview with Fernando Pesqueira, Hermosillo, Sonora, August 26, 1966.
15. *El Eco de Sonora*, April 10, 1871; *El Voto Libre*, May 19, 1871; *Arizona Citizen*, May 6, 1871; Corral, pp. 85-86; Archivo Histórico del Estado de Sonora, Hermosillo, Gaveta 17-4, p. 438.
16. Eduardo W. Villa, *Historia de Sonora*, p. 313; Hubert Howe Bancroft, *Northern Mexican States and Texas*, II, p. 701; *La Estrella de Occidente*, November 10, 1871.
17. Corral, pp. 86-87; Willard to Hunter, Guaymas, November 6, 1871, "Despatches from U.S. Consuls in Guaymas."
18. Villa, *Historia de Sonora*, p. 313; Corral, p. 87; Willard to Hunter, Guaymas, November 6, 1871, "Despatches from U.S. Consuls in Guaymas."
19. Corral, p. 87; *La Estrella de Occidente*, November 24, 1871.
20. Corral, pp. 87-88.
21. Ibid.
22. Ibid., pp. 88-89.
23. Laureano Calvo Berber, *Nociones de historia de Sonora*, p. 239; Willard to Hunter, Guaymas, December 29, 1871, "Despatches from U.S. Consuls in Guaymas."
24. Corral, p. 89; Calvo Berber, p. 239.
25. Corral, pp. 89-90.
26. Buelna, pp. 132-33; Calvo Berber, pp. 239-40; Pesqueira to the substitute governor of Sonora, Sinaloa, January 22, 1872, *La Estrella de Occidente*, January 26 and February 2, 1872; Bancroft, *Northern Mexican States*, II, p. 702.
27. Calvo Berber, pp. 239-40; Willard to Hunter, February 2, 1872, "Despatches from U.S. Consuls in Guaymas"; Corral, pp. 92-93; Buelna, p. 136.
28. Calvo Berber, p. 240.
29. Corral, pp. 99-100.
30. Ibid.
31. Ibid., p. 91.
32. *La Estrella de Occidente*, February 23 and March 1, 1872; Willard to Hunter, Guaymas, February 23, 1872, "Despatches from U.S. Consuls in Guaymas"; Corral, pp. 91-92.
33. Calvo Berber, pp. 240-41.
34. Corral, pp. 108-109.
35. Ibid.
36. Ibid., pp. 109-110.
37. Ibid., pp. 110-113.
38. Ibid., pp. 113-116.
39. Ignacio B. del Castillo, *Biografía de D. Ramón Corral*, p. 12; Calvo Berber, p. 241.
40. *La Estrella de Occidente*, June 7 and December 27, 1872.
41. Ibid., "La Questión Reforma," January 3, 1872.
42. Juan Atúnez to Pesqueira, Ures, November 27, 1872, Fernando Pesqueira, "Documentos," Primera Serie, Tomo IX; Calvo Berber, p. 242; Corral, pp. 101-102.
43. *La Estrella de Occidente*, June 20, 1873; Corral, p. 102.
44. *La Estrella de Occidente*, April 11, 1873; Corral, p. 102.
45. Corral, p. 104; Villa, *Historia de Sonora*, p. 319.
46. *El Mochuelo*, August 15, 1873; *La Estrella de Occidente*, July 11, 1873;

William S. Rosecrans Paper, Department of Special Collections, Collection 663, The Library of University of California, Los Angeles, Boxes 92 and 93; Corral, p. 96.

47. Manuel R. Urchurtu, *Apuntes biograficos del señor D. Ramon Corral,* p. 20; Calvo Berber,   p. 242; Archivo Historico del Estado de Sonora, Hermosillo, Gaveta 18-1, 453; Pesqueira to the People, Ures, September 28, 1873, *La Estrella de Occidente,* September 26 and October 3, 1873.

48. Pesqueira to the People, Ures, September 28, 1873, *La Estrella de Occidente,* October 3, 1873; Corral, p. 104.

49. *La Estrella de Occidente,* October 17 and 31, 1873.

50. Calvo Berber, p. 242; Corral, p. 105.

51. Urchurtu, pp. 16-17; Villa, *Historia de Sonora,* p. 320; Corral, pp. 105-106.

52. José María Pérez Hernández, *Compendio de la geografía del estado de Sonora,* pp. 58-59; Annual Report, Guaymas, September 30, 1873, "Despatches from U.S. Consuls in Guaymas"; Urchurtu, pp. 15-16, 18.

53. John C. Bacon, "Arizona and Sonora Papers," *Arizona Sentinel,* July 12 and the year of 1873.

54. "Los Apaches y Sus Atrocidades," *La Estrella de Occidente,* February 7 and June 20, 1873.

55. Ibid., Pesqueira to Safford, Las Delicias, March 14, 1873, and Pesqueira to John S. Hittel, Ures, March 14, 1873; Edward P. Smith to Pesqueira, Washington, September 16, 1873, *La Estrella de Occidente,* October 31, 1873; Spicer, *Cycles of Conquest,* p. 251.

56. John G. Bourke, *An Apache Campaign in the Sierra Madre,* pp. 19 and 29; Spicer, *Cycles of Conquest,* p. 437; Ross Santee, *Apache Land,* p. 38.

57. Crook to Pesqueira, Camp Grant, January 9, 1873, *La Estrella de Occidente,* July 4 and December 5, 1873.

58. Frank C. Lockwood, *The Apache Indians,* p. 40.

CHAPTER 10

1. Ramón Corral, *Obras históricas,* pp. 106, 116.

2. Ibid., pp. 116-17.

3. *La Estrella de Occidente,* June 19, 1874.

4. Manuel R. Urchurtu, *Apuntes biograficos del señor D. Ramón Corral,* p. 24; Corral, p. 116.

5. Archivo Histórico del Estado de Sonora, Hermosillo, Gaveta 18-2, p. 460; "Contribución Directa," *El Elector,* February 24, 1874.

6. *Golfo de Cortés* quoted in *La Estrella de Occidente,* March 6, 1874.

7. Corral, p. 118.

8. Edward H. Spicer, "Potam, a Yaqui Village in Sonora," Memoir No. 77.

9. Corral, pp. 149-52; Fortunato Hernández, *Las razas indígenas de Sonora y la guerra del Yaqui,* p. 123-24; Eduardo W. Villa, *Galería de Sonorenses ilustres,* p. 97, Francisco P. Troncoso, *Las guerras con las tribus Yaqui y Mayo del estado de Sonora,* p. 60.

10. Edward Spicer, ed., *Perspectives in American Indian Culture Change,* p. 56.

11. Corral, pp. 118-19.

12. Laureano Calvo Berber, *Nociones de historia de Sonora,* p. 243; *El Fantasma,* quoted in *El Amigo del Pueblo,* July 23, 1875.

13. *El Fantasma,* July 16, 1875; "Pesqueira I, Rey de Sonora," *El Convencional,* June 4, 1875.

14. *El Independiente,* May 13, 1875; *La Estrella de Occidente,* June 11, 1875.

15. Corral, pp. 119-20; Ramiro de Garza, "Don Ignacio Pesqueira"; *Arizona Citizen,* July 24, 1875.

16. *La Estrella de Occidente,* September 4, 1875.

17. Francisco R. Almada, *Diccionario de historia, geografía y biografía Sonorenses,* p. 741; Corral, p. 121; *La Estrella de Occidente,* August 27, 1875.

18. *La Estrella de Occidente,* September 3, 1875.

19. Safford to U.S. Consulate Office at Guaymas, October 16, 1875, "Despatches from U.S. Consuls in Guaymas."

20. Corral, p. 122.

21. Ibid.

22. Spicer, *Cycles of Conquest*, p. 67.
23. Troncoso, p. 59.
24. Corral, p. 122.
25. Ibid., p. 123; Manuel Balbás, *Recuerdos del Yaqui*, pp. 8-9.
26. Corral, p. 124.
27. U.S. Consul to Hunter, Guaymas, December 31, 1875, "Despatches from U.S. Consuls in Guaymas"; Spicer, *Cycles of Conquest*, p. 68; Calvo Berber, p. 243.
28. Corral, pp. 125-26.
29. *La Estrella de Occidente*, February 18, 1876; Corral, p. 129.
30. Corral, p. 130.
31. *Boletín Oficial*, February 26, 1876; *La Voz de Alamos*, April 8, 1876.
32. Corral, p. 130.
33. Ibid.
34. Ibid.
35. Ibid., pp. 130-31.
36. Ibid.
37. Ibid., p. 132.
38. *La Estrella de Occidente*, January 7, 1876; *Arizona Citizen*, February 19, 1876; Calvo Berber, p. 244.
39. Corral, pp. 132-33.
40. "Noticias de Alamos," *Garantías Individuales*, March 18, 1876.
41. Corral, p. 133.
42. Ibid.
43. Ibid., p. 134; "El Pueblo de la Ciudad de Ures, al Primer Magistrado de la Nación," *Boletín Oficial*, April 14, 1876.
44. Fernando Pesqueira, ed., "Documentos," Primera Serie, Tomo X.
45. Calvo Berber, p. 244.
46. Corral, p. 134.
47. Ibid., pp. 134-35.
48. *Diccionario porrúa de historia*, pp. 1634-35; Henry Bamford Parkes, *A History of Mexico*, p. 283.
49. Ibid., pp. 283-84; Corral, p. 136.
50. Patricio Nicoli, *El Estado de Sonora*, p. 7; Corral, pp. 136-137.
51. Mariscal to José Pesqueira, Las Delicias, December 31, 1876, *Boletín Oficial*, January 5, 1877.
52. *Diccionario porrúa de historia*, p. 1173; Boletin Oficial, January 5, 1877.
53. Calvo Berber, pp. 245-46.
54. Corral, p. 139; Calvo Berber, p. 247.
55. "El Independiente," *El Club de la Reforma*, April 29, 1877, and "Temores Infundados," May 6, 1877.
56. Ibid.; "Los Mariscalistas Se Quitan la Careta," May 13, 1877; Calvo Berber, p. 249.
57. *Alta California*, May 30, 1877; F. Tolentino to Mexico City, March 27, 1877, Telegram, F. Tolentino to F. Naranjo, April, 1877, in Carreño, XX, pp. 178, 264. *Boletín Oficial*, May 4, 1877; Corral, p. 140.
58. *La Prensa*, July 23, 1877.
59. *El Club de la Reforma*, April 29, 1877; "El Sr. General de Brigada D. Ignacio Pesqueira," *La Prensa*, July 23, 1877; *El Susurro*, July 28, 1877; *Boletín Oficial*, July 27, 1877.
60. *La Prensa*, August 11, 1877; Corral, p. 147.
61. Mariscal to Díaz, Hermosillo, August 28, 1877, in Alberto María Carreño, *Archivo del General Porfirio Díaz*; Corral, pp. 142-43.
62. *El Susurro*, September 28, 1877; Serna to Díaz, Ures, September 14, 1877, in Carreño, *Archivo del General Díaz*, XXVII, 103-104.
63. Corral, p. 144.

CONCLUSION

1. Francisco Sosa, *Las estatutas de la reforma*, p. 73.
2. Manuel R. Urchurtu, *Apuntes biográficos del señor D. Ramón Corral*, pp. 14-15.
3. Francisco R. Almada, *Diccionario de historia, geografía y biografía Sonorenses*, pp. 275-76, 779; Laureano Calvo Berber, *Nociones de historia de Sonora*, pp. 254-55.

4. Edward Spicer, *Cycles of Conquest*, pp. 253, 256.
5. Fortunato Hernández, *Las Razas Indigenas de Sonora y la Guerra del Yaqui*,
        p. 120; Claudio Dabdoub, *Historia de El Valle del Yaqui*, p. 293; Ramón
        Corral, *Obras históricas*, pp. 188-90.
6. Dabdoub, p. 293; Joseph F. Park, "The History of Mexican Labor," p. 149;
        Manuel Balbas, *Recuerdos del Yaqui*, p. 37; Ralph Beals, *The Contem-
        porary Culture of the Cahita Indians*, p. 211.
7. Edward Spicer, ed., *Perspectives in American Indian Culture Change*, p. 70.
8. Dabdoub, pp. 308-309.
9. Calvo Berber, p. 249; Park, *The History of Mexican Labor*, p. 148.

Bibliography

REFERENCE WORKS

Almada, Francisco R. *Diccionario de historia, geografía y biografía Sonorenses.* Chihuahua, Mexico: n.p., 1952.

Bemis, Samuel Flagg, and Grace C. Griffin. *Guide to the Diplomatic History of the United States, 1775-1921.* Washington: United States Government Printing Office, 1935.

Diccionario porrúa de historia, biografía y geografía de México. Segunda Edición. México: Editorial Porrúa, S.A., 1965.

Hale, Richard W. *Guide to Photocopied Historical Materials in the United States and Canada.* American Historical Society. New York: Cornell University Press, 1961.

Ker, Anita Melville. *Government Publications: A Guide to the more important publications of the national government of Mexico, 1821-1936.* Washington: United States Government Printing Office, 1940.

López, E. Y. *Bibliografía de Sonora.* Hermosillo: Estado de Sonora, 1960.

Schwegmann, George A., Jr., Director. *Newspapers on Microfilm.* Third Edition. Washington: Library of Congress, 1957.

—— *Newspapers on Microfilm.* Supplement 1 to Third Edition. Washington: Library of Congress, 1959.

Torre Villar, Ernesto de la. *Las fuentes Francesas para la historia de México y la Guerra de Intervención.* México: Sociedad Mexicana de Geografía y Estadística, 1962.

PRIMARY SOURCES

Documents

    1. *Manuscripts*

Archivo Histórico del Estado de Sonora, Hermosillo, Sonora, Mexico.

Charles W. Lewis Collection, Arizona Historical Society, Tucson, Arizona.

"Despatches from United States Consuls in Guaymas, Mexico, 1832-1896," Vols. I-IV. The National Archives. Washington: National Archives and Record Service, 1959-1961.

"Despatches from United States Consuls in Mazatlán, Mexico," Vols. II-IV. The National Archives. Washington: National Archives and Record Service, 1961.

"Despatches from United States Ministers to Mexico, 1823-1906," Vol. XXIV. The National Archives. Washington: The National Archives and Record Service, 1955.

"Detal y Algunos Documentos Relativos al Triunfo Alcanzado en el Puerto de Guaymas el 13 de Julio de 1854 Contra el Conde Gaston de Raousset Boulbon y Estrangeros Que Acaudillaba." Ures: Tipografía del Gobierno á Cargo de J. P. Siquerios, 1854.

Father Victor Stoner Collection, Arizona Historical Society, Tucson, Arizona.

Federico A. Ronstadt Collection, Arizona Historical Society, Tucson, Arizona.

Gándara, Manuel María. "Gándara's Original Autographed Letter to Bustamante on the State of Sonora, Urrea, Santa Anna . . . ," Guadalajara, November 18, 1845.

George Whitehall Parsons Collection, Arizona Historical Society, Tucson, Arizona.

Great Britain. Foreign Office. Consular Despatches from Mexico, 1822-1902. F. O. 50. Microfilm copies in the Bancroft Library, Berkeley, California.

_____ _____ Embassy and Consular Archives, Mexico. Correspondence, Ser. I, 1823-1902. F. O. 203. Microfilm copies in the Bancroft Library, Berkeley, California.

_____ _____ Embassy and Consular Archives, Mexico – Letterbooks, 1826-1899. F. O. 205. Microfilm copies in the Bancroft Library, Berkeley, California.

Henry F. Dobyns Collection, Arizona Historical Society, Tucson, Arizona.

Henry George Weiss Collection, Arizona Historical Society, Tucson, Arizona.

Jay Mann Collection, Arizona Historical Society, Tucson, Arizona.

Jesús García Collection, Arizona Historical Society, Tucson, Arizona.

Pesqueira, Fernando, ed. "Documentos para la Historia de Sonora," Primera Serie, Tomos V-XI. Typewritten copy in the Biblioteca y Museo de Sonora, Hermosillo, Sonora.

_____ "Documentos para la Historia de Sonora," Segunda Serie, Tomos III-IV. Typewritten copy in the Biblioteca y Museo de Sonora, Hermosillo, Sonora.

_____ "Documentos para la Historia de Sonora," Tercera Serie, Tomos VII-IX. Typewritten copy in the Biblioteca y Museo de Sonora, Hermosillo, Sonora.

_____ "Documentos para la Historia de Sonora," Cuarta Serie, Tomos II-III. Typewritten copy in the Biblioteca y Museo de Sonora, Hermosillo, Sonora.

Pesqueira, Ignacio. "A Sus Subordinados." Ures: Imprenta del Gobierno, 1857. "Circular." Ures: Imprenta del Gobierno, 1857. "¡Viva el Supremo Gobierno de la Nación!" "¡Viva Sonora Libre!" "¡Vivan los Valientes Defensores del Gobierno!" Ures: Imprenta del Gobierno, 1856. Bancroft Library, Berkeley, California.

_____ "Letter to His Excellency A. P. K. Safford, Governor of the Territory of Arizona, Tucson." Hermosillo, January 20, 1871, Cooler Collection, Arizona Historical Society, Tucson, Arizona.

Petra Etchells Collection, Arizona Historical Society, Tucson, Arizona. "Letter from Chittenden, July 1, 1876, and a Brave Woman, July 6, 1872." Read before the Arizona Historical Society. Copy from the Original Manuscripts, Tucson, Arizona.

Phoebe Bogan Collection, Arizona Historical Society, Tucson, Arizona.

Pinart, Alphonse. Prints: A collection of Mexican documents showing the history and development of the Northern Mexican states during the period 1824-1878.

P. R. Brady Collection, Arizona Historical Society, Tucson, Arizona. Letter from P. R. Brady, June 1, 1898.

Robinson, Juan A. "Statement of Don Juan A. Robinson." M-M375, Reel 97, Bancroft Library, Berkeley, California.

Sylvester Mowry Collection, Arizona Historical Society, Tucson, Arizona. "Volunteer Troops to Guard Mails." Letter from Ignacio Pesqueira to James Carleton, June 2, 1862, in Arizona Historical Society, Tucson, Arizona.

William S. Rosecrans Papers, Department of Special Collections, Collection 663. Library of the University of California, Los Angeles, Boxes 92 and 93.

2. *Published Materials*

Carreño, Alberto María. *Archivo del general Porfirio Díaz, memoria y documentos.* Tomos III-XXVIII. México: Editorial "Elede," S.A., 1947-1960.

Castañeda, Carlos E., ed. *Nuevos documentos Inéditos o muy raros para la historia de Mexico: La Guerra de Reforma según el archivo del gral. D. Manuel Doblado, 1857-1860.* San Antonio, Texas: Casa Editorial Lozano, 1930.

Corella, J., Antonio Escalante, y Ramón Corral, *La mayoría del estado al pueblo Sonorense.* Hermosillo: Imprenta de Roberto Bernal, 1878.

Cushing, Caleb. *Contract of the Mexican Government for the Survey of the Public Lands in the State of Sonora.* Washington: n.p., 1860.

Díaz, Lilia, trans. *Versión Francesa de México: Informes diplomáticos.* Vol. I, 1853-1858. Vol. II, 1858-1862. México: Colegio de México, 1963.

Gándara, Manuel María. "Estatuto Orgánico." *Plan Político Proclamado,* Ures, October 22, 1855.

—— *Manifestacíon que hace al gefe supremo de la República el ciudadano Manuel María Gándara, en la que espresa las causas que le obligaron a salir del estado de Sonora.* México: Imprenta de José A. Godoy, 1857.

García Cantú, Gastón. *El pensamiento de la reacción Mexicana, historia documental 1810-1962.* México: Empresas Editoriales, S.A., 1965.

García, Genaro, ed. *Colección de documentos inéditos o muy raros para la historia de México.* Tomos I-XXXVI. México: Librería de la Vda. de Ch. Bouret, 1905-1911.

Hamlin, Percy Gatling. *The Making of a Soldier: Letters of General R. S. Ewell.* Richmond, Va.: Whittet and Shepperson, 1935.

McDougall, J. A. "French Interference in Mexico." Speech in Senate. Baltimore: John Murphy and Co., 1863.

Manning, William R., ed. *Diplomatic Correspondence of the United States: Inter-American Affairs, 1831-1860, Mexico, 1848 (Mid-year)-1860.* Vol. IX. Washington: Carnegie Endowment for International Peace, 1937.

Memoria que la dirección de colonización e industria presentó al ministerio de relaciones en 7 de Enero de 1851, sobre el estado de estos ramos en el año anterior. México: Tipografía de G. Torres, 1851.

Miles, Carlota. *Almada of Alamos: The Diary of Don Bartolomé.* Tucson: Arizona Silhouettes, 1962.

Paredes, M. *Provectos de leyes sobre colonización y comercio en el estado de Sonora presentados a la cámara de disputados por el representante en la sesión del día 16 de Agosto de 1850.* México: Imprenta de Ignacio Cumplido, 1850.

Paullin, Charles O. *Diplomatic Negotiations of American Naval Officers, 1778-1883.* Baltimore: The Johns Hopkins Press, 1912.

Pereyra, Carlos. *Obras completas.* Tomos I-II. México: Libreros Mexicanos Unidos, S.A., 1959.

Plan Político Proclamado en Ayulta Modificado en Acapulco en Marzo de 1854, y Estatuto Orgánico del Estado de Sonora Espedido en 19 de Octubre de 1855. Ures: Tipografía del Gobierno, 1855.

Poston, Charles D. "Building a State in Apache Land," *Overland Monthly*, Second Series, July, 1894, pp. 87-93; August, 1894, pp. 203-213; September, 1894, pp. 291-297; October, 1894, pp. 403-408.

Purcell, Anita, ed. *Frontier Mexico 1875-1894: Letters of William L. Purcell.* San Antonio, Texas: The Naylor Co., 1963.

Railroad Record Supplement. Cincinnati, Monday, February 25, 1856.

Railway Company of Sonora: Contract Entered Into Between the Executive of the Republic of Mexico and David Boyle Blair, December 11, 1874. New York: Nathan Lane, Printer, 1875.

Ramírez, Ignacio. *Obras de Ignacio Ramírez.* Tomo II. México: Oficina Tipografía de la Secretaría de Fomento, 1889.

Report of the Trial of Luis Del Valle, Consul for the Republic of Mexico, at the Port of San Francisco, for a Breach of the Neutrality Laws of the United States in the District Court of the United States for the Northern District of California. San Francisco: Whitton, Towne and Co., Printer, 1854.

Richardson, James D. *A Compilation of the Messages and Papers of the Confederacy Including the Diplomatic Correspondence, 1861-1865.* Vols. I-II. Nashville: United States Publishing Co., 1905.

_____*A Compilation of the Messages and Papers of the Presidents, 1789-1897.* Vols. V-VII, X. Washington: Bureau of National Literature and Art, 1901.

Second Annual Report of the Santa Rita Silver Mining Company Made to the Stockholders, March 19, 1860. Cincinnati: Railroad Record Printers, 1860.

"Sonora – and the Value of Its Silver Mines," *Report of the Sonora Exploring and Mining Company Made to the Stockholders, December, 1856.* Cincinnati: Railroad Record Printers, 1856.

Sonora Exploring and Mining Company, Fourth Annual Report of the Sonora Exploring and Mining Company Made to the Stockholders, March, 1860. New York: Minns and Co., Stationers and Printers, 1860.

Torre Villar, Ernesto de la. "Las Notas Sobre Sonora, del Capitán Guillet (1864-1866)," *YAN* (Ciencias Antropológicas), I (1953), 46-59.

Torre Villar, Ernesto, Moises González Navarro, and Stanley Ross. *Historia Documental de México.* Tomo II. México: Universidad Nacional Autónoma de México, Instituto de Investigaciones Históricos, 1964.

Ulloa, Pedro. *Folleto comentorativo de la memorable jornada del 13 Julio de 1854 en su centenario 1854-1954.* Hermosillo: Imprenta Molleda Hnos., 1954.

United States of America, 37th Congress, Third Session, House of Representatives, Executive Document No. 34, Message from the President of the United States. "Present Condition of Mexico."

United States of America, 37th Congress, Second Session, House of Representatives, Executive Document, No. 100. "The Present Condition of Mexico," 1863.

United States of America, 39th Congress, First Session, House of Representatives, Executive Document No. 73, Message of the President of the United States of March 20, 1866, Relating to the Conditions of Affairs in Mexico, Parts 1 and 2. Washington: Government Printing Office, 1866.

Zaragosa, Ignacio. *Cartas y documentos.* Selección, introducción, y notas de Jorge L. Tamayo. México: Fondo de Cultura Económica, 1962.

Contemporary Accounts

Alvensleben, Baron Von. *With Maximilian in Mexico from the Notebook of a Mexican Officer.* London: Longmans, Green and Co., 1867.

Arizona Scrap Book of Azter Mining Company, Arizona Historical Society, Tucson, Arizona.

Bartlett, John R. *Charter and By-Laws of the Arizona Land and Mining Company.* Providence: Knowles, Anthony and Co., State Printers, 1859.

_____ *Personal Narrative of Explorations and Incidents in Texas, New Mexico, California, Sonora and Chihuahua, During the Years 1850, '51, '52, and '53.* Vols. I-II. New York: D. Appleton and Co., 1856.

Bell, Horace. *Reminiscences of a Ranger or Early Times in Southern California.* Santa Barbara: Wallace Hebberd Publishers, 1927.

Bell, James. "A Log of the Texas-California Cattle Trail, 1854," Part II, edited by J. Evetts Haley, *Southwestern Historical Quarterly,* XXXV (April, 1932), 290-316.

Bigelow, John. *Retrospections of an Active Life.* Vol. II. New York: The Baker and Taylor Co., 1909.

Bojórquez, J. de. "Introducción," *Sonora, Sinaloa, Nayarit: Estudio estadístico económico social elaborado por al estadística nacional.* México: Imprenta Mundial, 1928.

Bourke, John G. *An Apache Campaign in the Sierra Madre.* New York: Charles Scribner's Sons, 1958.

Box, Captain James. *Captain James Box's Adventures and Explorations in New and Old Mexico Being the Record of Ten Years of Travel and Research and a Guide to the Mineral Treasury of Durango, Chihuahua, the Sierra Nevada (East Side Sinaloa) and Sonora (Pacific Side) and the Southern Part of Arizona.* New York: James Miller, Publisher, 1869.

Browne, John Ross. *Adventures in the Apache Country: A Tour Through Arizona and Sonora, with Notes on the Silver Regions of Nevada.* New York: Harper and Brothers, Publishers, 1868.

Bullock, W. H. *Across Mexico in 1864-1865.* London and Cambridge: Macmillan and Co., 1866.

Calvin, Ross. *Introduction and Notes: Lieutenant Emory's Reports: A Reprint of Lieutenant W. H. Emory's Notes of a Military Reconnaissance.* Albuquerque: The University of New Mexico Press, 1951.

Carpenter, William W. *Travels and Adventures in Mexico.* New York: Harper and Brothers, 1851.

Carroll, H. Bailey, and J. Villasana Haggard. *Three New Mexico Chronicles: The Exposición of Don Pedro Bautista Pino, 1812; the Ojeada of Lic. Antonio Barreiro, 1832; and the Additions by Don José Agustín de Escudero, 1849.* Translated with Introduction and Notes. Albuquerque: The Quivira Society, 1942.

Clarke, A. B. *Travels in Mexico and California.* Boston: Wright and Hasty, Printers, 1852.

Cremony, John C. *Life Among the Apaches.* San Francisco: A. Roman and Co., 1868.

Eldredge, James. *A Short Description of the Frontier State of Sonora.* London: n.p., 1872.

Emory, Lt. Col. W. H. *Notes of a Military Reconnaissance, from Fort Leavenworth, in Missouri, to San Diego, in California, Including Part of Arkansas, Del Norte, and Gila Rivers.* Thirteenth Congress, First Session, Executive Document No. 41. Washington: Wendell and Von Benthuysen, Printers, 1848.

Emory, William H. *Report on the United States and Mexican Boundary Survey.* Vol. II. Thirty-Fourth Congress, First Session, House of Representatives, Executive Document, No. 135. Washington: Cornelius Wendell, Printer, 1859.

——— *Report on the United States and Mexican Boundary Survey.* Vol. I. Thirty-Fourth Congress, First Session, Senate, Executive Document No. 108. Washington: A. O. P. Nicholson, Printer, 1857.

——— *Report on the United States and Mexican Boundary Survey.* Vol. II. Thirty-Fourth Congress, First Session, Senate, Executive Document No. 108. Washington: A. O. P. Nicholson, Printer, 1859.

Escudero, José Agustín de. *Noticias estadísticas de Sonora y Sinaloa.* México: Tipografía de R. Rafael, 1839.

Foote, Henry S. *The Bench and Bar of the South and Southwest.* St. Louis: Soule, Thomas and Wentworth, 1876.

——*Casket of Reminiscences.* Washington: Chronicle Publishing Co., 1874.

Fremont, Col., and Maj. Emory. *Notes of Travel in California.* Dublin: James M. Glashon, 1849.

García Cubas, Antonio. *The Republic of Mexico in 1876.* Translated by George E. Henderson. Mexico: La Enseñanza Printing Office, 1876.

Gold and Silver Mining in Sonora, Mexico: Proposed Purchase of San Juan Del Río Mines and Lands Belonging to the Cincinnati and Sonora Mining Association. Cincinnati, Ohio: Wrightson and Co., 1867.

Gustafson, A. M., ed. *John Spring's Arizona.* Tucson: The University of Arizona Press, 1966.

Hamilton, Leonidas. *Border States of Mexico: Sonora, Sinaloa, Chihuahua, and Durango.* San Francisco: Bacon and Co., 1881.

Hardy, R. W. H. *Travels in the Interior of Mexico in 1825, 1826, 1827, and 1828.* London: Henry Colburn and Richard Bentley, 1829.

Johnston, Brevet, *et al. Reports of the Secretary of War with Reconnaissances of Routes from San Antonio to El Paso.* Washington: Union Office, 1850.

Lempriere, Charles. *Notes in Mexico in 1861 and 1862: Politically and Socially Considered.* London: Longman, Green, Longman, Roberts and Green, 1862.

Lyon, G. F. *Journal of a Residence and Tour in the Republic of Mexico in the Year 1826 with Some Account of Mines of That Country.* Vol. I. London: John Murray, 1826. Vol. II, 1828.

Malte Brun, Conrad. *La Sonora et ses Mines.* Paris: Arthur Bertrand, 1864.

Marryat, Frederick. *The Travels and Adventures of Monsieur Violet in California, Sonora and Western Texas.* London: Richard Bently, 1849.

Mason, R. H. *Pictures of Life in Mexico.* Vols. I-II. London: Smith, Elder and Co., 1852.

McCoy, Joseph. *Historical Sketches of the Cattle Trade of the West and Southwest.* Kansas City, Mo.: Ramsey, Millett and Hudson, 1874.

Morfras, Duflot de. *Travels on the Pacific Coast.* Translated, edited, and annotated by Marguerite Eyor Wilbur. Santa Ana, California: The Fine Arts Press, 1937.

Mowry, Sylvester. *Arizona and Sonora: The Geography, History, Resources of the Silver Region of North America.* Third edition. New York: Harper and Brothers, 1864.

——*Arizona and Sonora: The Geography, History and Resources of the Silver Region of North America.* New York: Harper and Brothers, 1871.

——*Memoir of the Proposed Territory of Arizona.* Washington: Henry Polkinhorn, 1857. Reprinted, Tucson: Territorial Press, 1964.

Nye, W. F. *La Sonora étendue, population, climat, produits du sol, mines, tribus Indiennes, etc.* Translated by A. De Zeltner. Paris: Au Bureau De La Revue Britannique, 1864.

Otero, Miguel Antonio. *My Life on the Frontier, 1864-1882*. New York: The Press of the Pioneers, 1935.

Pérez Hernández, José María. *Comprenido de la geografía del estado de Sonora*. México: Tipografía Comercio, a Cargo de Mariano Lara (Hijo), 1872.

Pfefferkorn, Ignaz. *Sonora: A Description of the Province*. Translated and annotated by Theodore E. Treutlein. Albuquerque: University of New Mexico Press, 1949.

Poston, Charles D. *Apache-land*. San Francisco: A. L. Bancroft and Co., 1878.

Prospectus of Sonora, Consolidated Mill and Mining Company, Altar District, State of Sonora, Mexico. New York: Thitchirer and Gloclacter, Printers, 1881.

Pumpley, Raphael. *Across America and Asia*. Fourth edition, revised. New York: Leypoldt and Holt, 1870.

Reid, John C. *Reid's Tramp: or a Journal of the Incidence of Ten Months Travel Through Texas, New Mexico, Arizona and California*. Selma, Alabama: John Hardy and Co., 1858.

Robertson, William Parish. *A Visit to Mexico*. Vol. II. London: Published for the Author, 1853.

Ruxton, George F. *Adventures in Mexico and the Rocky Mountains*. New York: Harper and Brothers, 1848.

Schuyler, Howard. *The Sonora Railway Resources and Revenue*. San Francisco: J. L. Rice and Co., 1878.

Scroggs, William O. *Filibusters and Financiers: The Story of William Walker and His Associates*. New York: Macmillan Co., 1916.

Senior, Nassau William. *Conversation with Distinguished Persons During the Second Empire from 1860 to 1863*. Vols. I-II. London: Hurst and Blochett, 1880.

_____*Conversation with M. Thiers, M. Guizot and Other Distinguished Persons During the Second Empire*. Vol. II. London: Hurst and Blochett, 1878.

Stone, Charles P. *Notes on the State of Sonora*. Washington: Henry Polkinghorn Printer, 1861.

Velasco, Aflonso Luis. *Geografía y estadística de la República Mexicana: XIV. geografía y estadística del estado de Sonora*. México: Oficina tipografía de la Secretaría de Fomento, 1893.

Velasco, José Francisco. *Noticias estadísticas del estado de Sonora acompañadas de ligeros reflecsiones*. México: Imprenta de Ignacio Cumplido, 1850.

_____*Sonora: Its Extent, Population, Natural Production, Indian Tribes, Mines, Mineral Lands, Etc*. Translated by William F. Nye. San Francisco: H. H. Bancroft and Co., 1861.

Walker, William. *The War in Nicaragua*. Mobile: S. H. Goetzel and Co., 1860.

Ward, Henry G. *Mexico in 1827*. Second edition. Revised and Enlarged. London: H. Colburn, 1829.

SECONDARY SOURCES

Books

Acosta, Roberto. *Apuntes históricos Sonorenses: La conquista temporal y espiritual del Yaqui y del Yaqo.* México: Apuntes Históricos Sonorenses, Imprenta Aldina, 1949.

Ainsa, J. Y. *History of the Crabb Expedition into Northern Sonora: Decapitation of the State Senator of California, Henry A. Crabb and Massacre of Ninety-Eight of His Friends at Caborca and Sonoita, Sonora, Mexico, 1857.* Phoenix, Arizona: n.p., 1951.

Andrade, Vicente de Paula. *Noticias biográficas sobre los ilustrísimos prelados de Sonora, de Sinaloa y de Durango.* Tercera edición. México: Imprenta del Museo Nacional, 1899.

Arrangoiz, Francisco de Paula. *Méjico desde 1808 hasta 1867.* Tomos I-II. Madrid: Imprenta á Cargo de A. Pérez Deball, 1872.

Baker, Nina Brown. *Juárez, Hero of Mexico.* New York: The Vanguard Press, 1942.

Balbás, Manuel. *Recuerdos del Yaqui: Principales episodios durante la campaña de 1899 á 1901.* México: Sociedad de Edición y Librería Franco Americana, S.A., 1927.

Bancroft, Hubert Howe. *History of Mexico.* San Francisco: A. L. Bancroft and Co., 1885.

_____*Native Races.* Vols. I, III, and V. San Francisco: The History Co., 1886.

_____*Northern Mexican States and Texas.* Vols. I-II. San Francisco: A. L. Bancroft and Co., 1884.

Bandelier, A. F. *Papers of the Archaeological Institute of America. Final Report of Investigations Among the Indians of the Southwestern United States, Carried on Mainly in the Years from 1880-1885.* Parts I-II. Cambridge University Press, 1890-92.

Bannon, John Francis. *The Mission Frontier in Sonora, 1620-1687.* New York: The United States Catholic Historical Society, 1955.

Beals, Ralph L. *The Comparative Ethnology of Northern Mexico Before 1750.* Berkeley: University of California Press, 1932.

_____*The Contemporary Culture of the Cáhita Indians.* Washington: Government Printing Office, 1945.

Bemis, Samuel Flagg. *A Diplomatic History of the United States.* Third edition. New York: Henry Holt and Co., 1950.

Bieber, Ralph D. *The Southwestern Trails to California in 1849.* Vol. XII, No. 3, Mississippi Valley Historical Society, December, 1925.

Bolton, Hubert Eugene. *Rim of Christendom: A Biography of Eusebio Francisco Kino: Pacific Coast Pioneer.* New York: The Macmillan Co., 1936.

Bosch García, Carlos. *Historia de las Relaciones Entre México y los Estados Unidos, 1819-1848.* México: Escuela Nacional de Ciencias Políticas y Sociales, 1961.

Brenner, Anita. *The Wind that Swept Mexico.* New York: Harper and Brothers, 1943.

Buelna, Eustaquio. *Apuntes para la historia de Sinaloa, 1821-1882.* México: Departamento Editorial de la Secretaría de Educación, 1924.

Caldíaz Barrera, Alberto. *Dos gigantes: Sonora y Chihuahua.* Tomo I. Hermosillo: Escritores Del Norte, 1964.

Callahan, James Morton. *American Foreign Policy in Mexican Relations.* New York: The Macmillan Co., 1932.

——*Diplomatic History of the Southern Confederacy.* New York: Frederick Unger Publishing Co., 1964.

——*Evolution of Seward's Mexican Policy.* Morgantown, West Virginia: West Virginia University, 1960.

Callcott, Wilfrid Hardy. *Church and State in Mexico, 1822-1857.* Durham: Duke University Press, 1926.

——*Liberalism in Mexico, 1857-1929.* Stanford: Stanford University Press, 1931.

Calvo Berber, Laureano. *Nociones de Historia de Sonora.* México: Librería de Manuel Porrúa, S.A., 1958.

Cárdenas, Leonard, Jr. *The Municipality in Northern Mexico.* El Paso: Texas Western College Press, 1963.

Castillo, Ignacio B. del. *Biografía de D. Ramón Corral.* México: Imprenta Dirigida por Juan Aguilar Vera, 1910.

Caughey, John Walton. *California.* Third edition. Englewood Cliffs, N.J.: Prentice-Hall, 1970.

Chapman, Charles Edward. *Colonial Hispanic American: A History.* New York: The Macmillan Co., 1933.

Cline, Howard F. *The United States and Mexico.* Cambridge: Harvard University Press, 1953.

Cooke, David C. *Apache Warrior.* New York: W. W. Norton and Co., 1963.

Coppey, Hypolite. *El conde Raousset-Boulbon en Sonora.* Translated by Alberto Cubillas. Hermosillo: Biblioteca Sonorense de Geografía e Historia, 1962.

Corral, Ramón. *Obras históricas, reseña histórica del estado de Sonora, 1856-1877: Biografía de José María Leyva Cajeme; Las razas Indígenas de Sonora.* Hermosillo: Biblioteca Sonorense de Geografía e Historia, 1959.

Crumrine, Lynne S. *The Phonology of Arizona Yaqui.* Anthropological Papers of the University of Arizona. Tucson: University of Arizona Press, 1961.

Cuevas, Mariano. *Historia de la iglesia en México: Libro tercero: De la Reforma al Centenario.* El Paso: Editorial "Revista Católica," 1928.

Cummings, Bryan. *First Inhabitants of Arizona and the Southwest.* Tucson: Cummings Publications, 1953.

Dabbs, Jack Autry. *The French Army in Mexico, 1861-1867.* The Hague: Mouton and Co., 1863.

Dabdoub, Claudio. *Historia de El Valle del Yaqui.* México: Librería de Manuel Porrúa, S.A., 1964.

Dale, Edward Everett. *The Indians of the Southwest: A Century Under the United States.* Norman: University of Oklahoma Press, 1949.

Datos Históricos Sobre Filibusteros de 1857 en Caborca, Sonora, Mexico. Caborca, Sonora: Publicados Por el Comité Organizado de las Fiestas del 6 de Abril, 1924.

Dawson, Daniel. *The Mexican Adventure.* London: G. Bell and Sons, 1935.

Decorme, Gerald. *La obra de los Jesuitas Mexicanos durante la epoca colonial: Tomo II. Las misiones.* México: Antigua Librería Robredo de José Porrúa e Hijos, 1941.

Dulles, John W. F. *Yesterday in Mexico: A Chronicle of the Revolution, 1919-1936.* Austin: University of Texas Press, 1961.

Encinas, Luis. *Sonora y Baja California.* México: n.p., 1944.

Engelhardt, Zephyrin. *The Franciscans in Arizona.* Harbor Springs, Michigan: Holy Childhood Indian School, 1899.

Farish, Thomas Edwin. *History of Arizona.* Vols. III-IV. Phoenix: The Filmer Brothers Electrotype Company, 1916.

Fergusson, Erna. *Mexico Revisited.* New York: Alfred Knopf, 1956.

_____*Our Southwest.* New York and London: Alfred A. Knopf, 1941.

Forbes, Robert A. *Crabb's Filibustering Expedition Into Sonora, 1857.* Tucson: Arizona Silhouettes, 1952.

Garber, Paul Neff. *The Gadsden Treaty.* Gloucester, Mass.: Peter Smith, 1959.

Gladwin, Winifred, and Harold S. Gladwin. *The Red-on-Buff Culture of the Papagueria.* Globe, Arizona: The Medallion, 1929.

_____*The Western Range of the Red-on-Buff Culture.* Globe, Arizona: The Medallion, 1930.

Gonzales Flores, Enrique. *Chihuahua de la independencia a la Revolución.* México: Imprenta León Sánchez, 1949.

Greene, Laurence. *The Filibuster: The Career of William Walker.* New York: The Bobbs-Merrill Co., 1937.

Hamlin, Percy Gatling. *"Old Bald Head" (General R. S. Ewell).* Strasburg, Virginia: Shenandoah Publishing House, Inc., 1940.

Hernández, Fortunato. *Las razas indígenas de Sonora y la guerra del Yaqui.* México: Talleres de la Casa Editorial "J. de Elizalde," 1902.

Hernández Sánchez-Barba, Mario. *La ultima expansión Española en América.* Madrid: Instituto de Estudios Políticos, 1957.

Hilton, John W. *Sonora Sketch Book.* New York: The Macmillan Co., 1947.

Hinton, Thomas B. *A Survey of Indian Assimilation in Eastern Sonora.* Anthropological Papers of the University of Arizona. Tucson: University of Arizona Press, 1959.

Hittell, Theodore H. *History of California.* Vol. III. San Francisco: N. J. Stone and Co., 1897.

Hornaday, William T. *Camp-Fires on Desert and Lava.* New York: Charles Scribner's Sons, 1909.

Ibarra, Alfred, Jr. *Sinaloa en la cultura de México.* México: Editorial Hidalgo, 1944.

Keratry, Count Emile de. *The Rise and Fall of the Emperor Maximilian.* Translated by G. H. Venables. London: Sampson Law, Son, and Marston, 1868.

Kroeber, A. L. *Uto-Aztecan Languages of Mexico.* Berkeley: University of California Press, 1934.

Laughlin, Edward Douglas. *The Yaqui Gold.* San Antonio: The Naylor Co., 1943.

León, N. *La imprenta en México.* México: Tipografía de "El Tiempo," 1900.

León Toral, Jesús de. *Historia militar: La intervención Francesa en México.* México: Sociedad Mexicana de Geografía y Estadística, 1962.

Lester, Robert. *Archaeological Excavations in the Northern Sierra Madre Occidental, Chihuahua and Sonora, Mexico.* Boulder: University of Colorado, May, 1958.

Lockwood, Frank C. *The Apache Indians.* New York: The Macmillan Co., 1938.

Manning, William R. *Early Diplomatic Relations Between the United States and Mexico.* Baltimore: The John Hopkins Press, 1916.

Martin, Percy F. *Maximilian in Mexico.* London: Constable and Co., 1914.

Maza, Francisco F. de la. *Código de colonización y terrenos baldíos de la República Mexicana, años de 1451 a 1892.* México: Oficina Tipografía de la Secretaría de Fomento, 1893.

McNeely, John H. *The Railways of Mexico: A Study in Nationalization.* Southwestern Studies, Vol. II, Spring, 1964, No. 1. El Paso: Texas Western College Press, 1964.

McWilliams, Carey. *North from Mexico: The Spanish-Speaking People of the United States.* Philadelphia and New York: J. B. Lippincott Co., 1949.

Medina, Francisco. *Monografía de Sonora.* México: Talleres Tipográficos Modelo, S.A., 1941.

Mendizabal, Miguel. *La evolución del Noroeste de México.* México: Publicaciones del Departamento de la Estadística Nacional, 1930.

Muzquiz Blanco, Manuel. *Sonora-Sinaloa: Visiones y sensaciones.* México: n.p., 1923.

Nicoli, Patricio. *El estado de Sonora: Yaquis y Mayos.* Segunda edición. México: Imprenta de Francisco Díaz de León, 1885.

Ocaranza, Fernando. *Los Franciscanos en las provincias internas de Sonora.* México: n.p., 1933.

Olea, Hector R. *La primera imprenta en las provincias Sonora y Sinaloa.* México: Imprenta y Fotograbado Aurelio Villegas, 1943.

Owen, Roger C. Marobavi. *A Study of an Assimilated Group in Northern Sonora.* Anthropological Papers of the University of Arizona. Tucson: University of Arizona Press, 1959.

Parkes, Henry Bamford. *A History of Mexico.* Boston: Houghton Mifflin Co., 1960.

Parodi, Enriqueta de. *Sonora: Hombres y paisajes.* México: Editorial Pafim, 1941.

Peck, Anne Merriman. *The March of Arizona History.* Tucson: Arizona Silhouettes, 1962.

Pitt, Leonard. *The Decline of the Californios.* Berkeley: University of California Press, 1966.

Powell, Fred Wilbur. *The Railroads of Mexico*. Boston: The Stratford Co., 1921.

Powell, Philip W. *Soldiers, Indians, and Silver*. Berkeley and Los Angeles: University of California Press, 1952.

Pradeau, A. F. *The Mexican Mints of Alamos and Hermosillo*. New York: The American Numismatic Society, 1934.

_____ *Numismatic History of Mexico from the Pre-Columbian Epoch to 1823*. Whittier: Western Printing Co., 1938.

Priestly, Herbert. *The Mexican Nation, a History*. New York: The Macmillan Co., 1923.

Ramírez, J. Fernando. *California y lenguas que se hablan en Sinaloa, Sonora y California*. México: Biblioteca de Historiadores Mexicanos, Editor Vargas Rea, 1950.

_____ *Exploraciones por Sonora y Nuevo México*. México: Biblioteca Histórica, 1949.

Rippy, J. Fred. *The United States and Mexico*. Revised edition. New York: F. S. Crofts and Co., 1931.

Rister, Carl Coke. *The Southwestern Frontier, 1865-1881*. Cleveland: The Arthur H. Clark Co., 1925.

Rives, George Lockhart. *The United States and Mexico, 1821-1848*. Vols. I-II. New York: Charles Scribner's Sons, 1913.

Robinson, Cecil. *With the Ears of Strangers: The Mexican in American Literature*. Tucson: The University of Arizona Press, 1963.

Sacks, B. *Be It Enacted: The Creation of the Territory of Arizona*. Phoenix: Arizona Historical Foundation, 1964.

Santee, Ross. *Apache Land*. New York: Charles Scribner's Sons, 1947.

Schefer, Christian. *Los orígenes de la Intervención Francesa en México, 1858-1862*. México: Editorial Porrúa, S.A., 1963.

Schlarman, Joseph H. L. *México tierra de volcanes*. Translated by Carlos de María y Campos. México: Editorial Porrúa, S.A., 1955.

_____ *Mexico, a Land of Volcanos*. Milwaukee: The Bruce Publishing Co., 1951.

Sierra, Justo. *Evolución política de pueblo Mexicano*. Segunda edición. México: Fondo de Cultura Económica, 1940.

_____ *Juárez: Sus obras y su tiempo*. México: J. Ballesca y Co., 1905-1906.

Simpson, Lesley Byrd. *Many Mexicos*. Berkeley and Los Angeles: University of California Press, 1963.

Smart, Charles Allen. *Viva Juárez*. New York: J. B. Lippincott Co., 1963.

Sobarzo, Horacio. *Crónica de la aventura de Raousset-Boulbon en Sonora*. México: Librería de Manuel Porrúa, S.A., 1954.

Sosa, Francisco. *Las estatutas de la Reforma: Noticias biográficas de los personajes en ellas representados*. Segunda edición. México: Oficina Tipografía de la Secretaría de Fomento, 1900.

Soulie, Maurice. *The Wolf Cub: The Great Adventure of Count Gaston de Raousset-Boulbon in California and Sonora, 1850-1854*. Translated by Farrel Symons. Indianapolis: The Bobbs-Merrill Co., 1927.

Spanish Culture in the United States. Madrid: Revista Geográfica Española, n.d.

Spicer, Edward H. *Cycles of Conquest: The Impact of Spain, Mexico and the United States on the Indians of the Southwest, 1533-1960.* Tucson: The University of Arizona Press, 1962.

──── , ed. *Perspectives in American Indian Culture Change.* Chicago: The University of Chicago Press, 1961.

Stevenson, Sara Yorke. *Maximilian in Mexico: A Woman's Reminiscences of the French Intervention, 1862-1867.* New York: The Century Co., 1899.

Tannenbaum, Frank. *Mexico: The Struggle for Peace and Bread.* New York: Alfred A. Knopf, 1954.

Troncoso, Francisco P. *Las guerras con las tribus Yaqui y Mayo del estado de Sonora.* México: Tipografía del Departamento del Estado Mayor, 1905.

Turner, John Kenneth. *Barbarous Mexico.* Chicago: Charles Kerr and Co., n.d.

Urchurtu, Manuel R. *Apuntes biográficos del señor D. Ramón Corral: Desde su nacimiento hasta encargarse del gobierno del distrito federal (1854 á 1900).* México: Eusebio Gómez de la Puente, 1910.

Villa, Eduardo W. *Galería de Sonorenses ilustres.* Hermosillo: Impulsora de Artes Graficos, 1948.

──── *Historia del estado de Sonora.* Segunda edición. Hermosillo: Editorial Sonora, 1951.

Vivo, Jorge A. *Geografía de México.* Segunda edición. México: Instituto Panamericano de Geografía e Historia, 1949.

Wells, William V. *Walker's Expedition to Nicaragua; A History of the Central American War; and the Sonora and Kinney Expeditions, Including Diplomatic Correspondence.* New York: Stringer and Townsend, 1856.

Williams, Mary. *The People and Politics of Latin America.* Boston: Ginn and Co., 1938.

Wristin, Henry Merrit. *Executive Agents in American Foreign Relations.* Baltimore: Johns Hopkins Press, 1929.

Wyllys, Rufus Kay. *Arizona: The History of a Frontier State.* Phoenix: Hobson and Herr, 1950.

──── *The French in Sonora, 1850-1854.* Berkeley: University of California Press, 1932.

──── *Pioneer Padre: The Life and Times of Eusebio Kino.* Dallas: The Southwest Press, 1935.

Zúñiga, Ignacio. *Rápida ojeada al estado de Sonora, territorio de California y Arizona.* Segunda serie. México: Ediciones Vargas Rea, 1948.

Periodical Articles

Alisky, Marvin. "Surging Sonora," *Arizona Highways.* XL (November, 1964), 17, 32-38.

Beals, Ralph L. "The Aboriginal Culture of the Cáhita Indians," *Ibero-Americana.* University of California, Berkeley, 1943.

Bolton, Herbert E. "The Mission as a Frontier Institution in the Spanish-American Colonies," *American Historical Review*, XXIII (October, 1917), 42-61.

Caywood, Louis R. "The Spanish Missions of Northwestern New Spain, Franciscan Period, 1768-1836," *The Kiva*, VI (January, 1941), 13-16.

―――"The Spanish Missions of Northwestern New Spain, Jesuit Period, 1687-1767," *The Kiva*, V (November, 1939), 8-12.

Coleman, Evans, Jr. "Senator Gwinn's Plan for the Colonization of Sonora," *The Overland Monthly*, XVII, Second Series (May, 1891), 497-519; XVII (June, 1891), 593-607; XVIII (August, 1891), 203-213.

Eaton, Clement. "Frontier Life in Southern Arizona, 1858-1861," *Southwestern Historical Quarterly*, XXXVI (January, 1933).

Eckhardt, George P. "Arispe, Sonora, a Pivot in History." George P. Eckhardt Collection in the Arizona Historical Society, Tucson, Arizona.

Ezell, Paul. "Indians Under the Law, Mexico, 1821-1847," *América Indígena*, XV (Julio, 1955), 199-213.

Gardiner, C. H. "Foreign Travelers Accounts of Mexico, 1810-1910," *Americas*, VIII (January, 1954), 321-351.

Garza, Ramiro de. "Don Ignacio Pesqueira ¿Es un Héroe?" *Revista Directorio Sonora*. Manuel Humberto Ramírez, editor. Navojoa, Sonora, 1957, pp. 19-30.

Hardy, Osgood. "El Ferrocarril Sud-Pacífico," *Pacific Historical Review*, XX (August, 1951), 261-269.

Haskett, Bert. "Early History of the Cattle Industry in Arizona," *Arizona Historical Review*, VI (October, 1935), 3-42.

―――"History of the Sheep Industry in Arizona," *Arizona Historical Review*, VII (July, 1936), 3-49.

Kelly, Tim. "Ambos Nogales," *Arizona Highways*, XL (November, 1964), 2-6, 46-47.

Mattison, Ray H. "Early Spanish and Mexican Settlements in Arizona," *New Mexico Historical Review*, XXI (October, 1946), 273-327.

Mecham, J. Lloyd. "The Origins of Federalism in Mexico," *Hispanic American Historical Review*, XVIII (May, 1938), 164-182.

Merriam, James F. "Report of James F. Merriam, on the Yaqui Land Grant," to Mr. Walter S. Lozan, President, Sonora and Sinaloa Irrigation Company, June 13, 1892.

Ogle, Ralph H. "Federal Control of Western Apaches, 1848-1886," *New Mexico Historical Review*, XIV (October, 1939), 309-365.

Park, Joseph F. "The Apaches in Mexican-American Relations, 1848-1861," *Arizona and the West*, III (Summer, 1961), 129-146.

Pesqueira, Hector. "Rectificando Datos de la Vida del Gral. Ignacio Pesqueira," *El Imparcial*, January 16, 1952.

Rippy, J. Fred. "Indians of the Southwest in the Diplomacy of the United States and Mexico, 1848-1853," *Hispanic American Historical Review*, II (August, 1919).

―――"A Ray of Light on the Gadsden Treaty," *Southwest Historical Quarterly*, XXIV (January, 1921).

Rippy, J. Fred. "Anglo-American Filibusters and the Gadsden Treaty," *Hispanic American Historical Review*, V (May, 1922), 155-180.

Rowland, Donald. "The Sonora Frontier of New Spain, 1735-1745," *New Spain and Anglo-America West*, I (1932), 147-164.

Smith, Ralph A. "Apache Plunder Trails Southward, 1831-1840," *New Mexico Historical Review*, XXXVII (January, 1962), 20-42.

Spicer, Edward H. "Potam, a Yaqui Village in Sonora," *American Anthropological Association, Memoir 77* (August, 1954).

Stevens, Robert C. "The Apache Menace in Sonora, 1831-1849," *Arizona and the West*, VI (Autumn, 1964), 211-222.

Stoner, Victor R. "The Spanish Missions of the Santa Cruz Valley," *The Kiva*, I (May, 1936), 1-4.

Wagoner, J. J. "History of the Cattle Industry in Southern Arizona, 1540-1940," *University of Arizona Social Science Bulletin*, XXIII (April, 1952).

Wyllys, Rufus Kay. "Henry A. Crabb – A Tragedy of the Sonora Frontier," reprinted for the *Pacific Historical Review*, IX (June, 1940), 183-194.

Newspapers

Alta California, San Francisco, 1856-1859.

Arizona Sentinel, Yuma, 1872-1878.

Arizona Weekly Citizen, Tucson, 1870-1880.

Boletín de Debates del Congreso del Estado, Ures, November 15, 1877 to March 29, 1878.

Boletín Oficial, Alamos, February 26-29, 1876.

Boletín Oficial, Ures, 1876-1879.

Boletín Oficial de la División de Sonora, Cienequito, May 9-13, 1865.

El Amigo del Pueblo, Ures, June 4, 1875 to February 28, 1876.

El Club de la Reforma, Hermosillo, April 29, 1877 to June 3, 1877.

El Convencional, Guaymas, June 4-13, 1875.

El Defensor del Pueblo, Guaymas, June 18, 1875.

El Demócrata, Alamos, May 5, 1877 to August 4, 1878.

El Eco de Occidente, Guaymas, May 2, 1878 to November 6, 1878.

El Eco de Sonora, Hermosillo, December 12, 1870 to April 17, 1871.

El Elector, Alamos, February 24,, 1875.

El Fantasma, Alamos, July 16-30, 1875.

El Golfo de Cortés, Guaymas, July 10, 1872 to March 5, 1874.

El Independiente, Hermosillo, May 13, 1875 to June 2, 1875.

El Látigo, Guaymas, July 11, 1873.

El Mochuelo, Ures, April 27, 1873 to October 30, 1873.

El Municipio, Guaymas, February 1, 1878 to October 17, 1878.

El Perico, Alamos, July 17, 1878.

El Plan de Tuxtepec, Guaymas, February 4, 1877 to July 23, 1877.

El Pueblo, Alamos, April 28, 1877 to October 22, 1878.

El Pueblo de Sonora, Ures, December 3, 1867 to February 25, 1868.

El Pueblo Independiente, Ures, June 4, 1875.

El Pueblo Sonorense, Ures, November 22, 1872 to January 3, 1873.

El Susurro, Guaymas, July 28, 1877 to September 28, 1877.

El Torito, Guaymas, May 18, 1878 to September 27, 1878.

El Trece de Julio, Guaymas, February 16, 1877 to March 16, 1877.

El Triumfo de Sonora, Guaymas, May 23, 1877 to June 9, 1877.

El Voto Libre, Ures,, March 31, 1871 to June 30, 1871.

Garantías Individuales, Guaymas, March 18, 1876 to May 15, 1876.

La Asociación del Pueblo, Guaymas, September 9, 1870 to February 17, 1871.

La Balanza Popular, Hermosillo, February 21, 1871.

La Balanza Popular, Ures, June 16, 1871.

La Calavera, Ures, April 27, 1863 to February 19, 1864.

La Constitución, Alamos, Hermosillo, Ures, 1879-1886.

La Crónica Judicial, Ures, May 15, 1862 to April 15, 1863.

La Era Nueva, Hermosillo, November 25, 1877 to July 28, 1878.

La Estrella de Occidente, Hermosillo, August 20, 1866.

La Estrella de Occidente, Ures, 1859-1876.

La Integridad Nacional, Ures, July 18, 1856 to August 1, 1856.

La Ley, Guaymas, November 2, 1878 to December 10, 1878.

La Opinión del Pueblo, Hermosillo, June 6, 1875.

La Opinión Pública, Hermosillo, July 18, 1878 to August 1, 1878.

La Paz, Guaymas, May 17, 1876.

La Prensa, Guaymas, July 24, 1876 to August 29, 1877.

La Reconstrucción, Hermosillo, March 27, 1877 to June 14, 1877.

La Regeneración, Hermosillo, June 14, 1876 to July 20, 1876.

La Sombra Tena, Ures, June 18, 1871.

La Verdad, Hermosillo, October 12, 1878 to November 2, 1878.

La Voz de Alamos, April 8, 1876 to August 29, 1878.

La Voz de Sonora, Ures, 1855-1859.

La Voz de Ures, April 13, 1877 to June 15, 1877.

Las Cinco Vocales, Guaymas, June 10, 1876 to December 10, 1876.

Periódico Oficial del Departamento de Sonora, Ures, August 25, 1865 to May 18, 1866.

San Francisco Daily Bulletin, 1856-1864.

The Southern Arizonian, November 16, 1867.

Unas de Tantas, Ures, March 26, 1863 to June 18, 1863.

Unión y Progreso, Guaymas, December 1, 1876 to May 23, 1877.

Weekly Arizonian, Tucson, 1859-1871.

Unpublished Materials

Bents, Doris W. "The History of Tubac, 1752-1948." Unpublished Master's thesis, University of Arizona, Tucson, 1949.

Brinckerhoff, Sidney B. "Spanish Control of the Arizona Apache, 1772-1821 — An Appraisal." In the possession of Dr. Manuel Servín, University of Southern California, Los Angeles.

Caldwell, June. "Filibustering in Sonora, 1841-1857." Caldwell Collection in the Arizona Historical Society, Tucson, Arizona.

Manson, Clara. "Indian Uprisings in Sonora, Mexico." Unpublished Master's thesis, University of Southern California, Los Angeles, 1936.

Morrisey, Richard John. "History of the Cattle Industry in Arizona." Unpublished Master's thesis, University of California, Berkeley, 1941.

Park, Joseph F. *The History of Mexican Labor in Arizona During the Territorial Period*. Tucson: University of Arizona Press, forthcoming.

Stevens, Robert Conway. "Mexico's Forgotten Frontier: A History of Sonora, 1821-1846." Unpublished Ph.D. dissertation, University of California, Berkeley, 1963.

Whitermore, W. V. "John Charles Handy, M. D. (Tucson, 1871-1892)." Found in John Charles Handy Collection, Arizona Historical Society, Tucson, Arizona.

Index